Intermediate

Phonics Intervention Centers

Vowel Digraphs

Writing: Camille Liscinsky
Content Editing: De Gibbs
Lisa Vitarisi Mathews
Copy Editing: Cathy Harber
Art Direction: Cheryl Puckett
Cover Design: Liliana Potigian
Illustrator: Matt Ward
Design/Production: Arynne Elfenbein
Kathy Kopp
Yuki Meyer
Marcia Smith

EMC 3527

Congratulations on your purchase of some of the finest teaching materials in the world.

For information about other Evan-Moor products, call 1-800-777-4362, fax 1-800-777-4332, or visit our Web site, www.evan-moor.com.

18 Lower Ragsdale Drive, Monterey, CA 93940-5746. Printed in USA.

Contents

How to Use This Book

The centers in this book are designed to be completed in a small-group setting. All materials are included for groups of up to 6 students. The activities have been carefully crafted to meet the needs of students receiving Tier 2 Response to Intervention instruction, as well as the needs of any other students who are learning foundational phonics skills. The target skills in *Vowel Digraphs* include recognizing digraphs that stand for long-vowel sounds, distinguishing the sounds of the ***oo***, ***au***, and ***aw*** digraphs, and applying those sounds to read words spelled with vowel digraphs.

For the Teacher

Lesson Plan

The skills in each unit are taught through teacher-led explicit instruction and are practiced through phonemic-awareness, hands-on, and written activities.

A fully scripted lesson plan cycles through auditory, oral, visual, and hands-on letter-sound activities that help students decode and read new words.

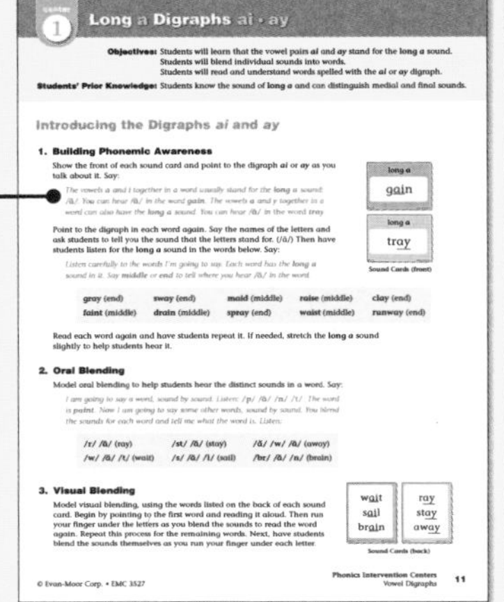

front

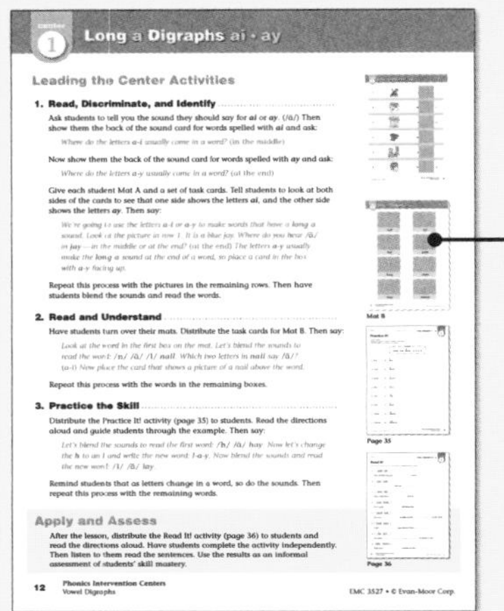

back

Scaffolded activities help guide students through the lesson.

Sound Cards

Vocabulary cards feature target sounds and aid students in blending sounds to read words.

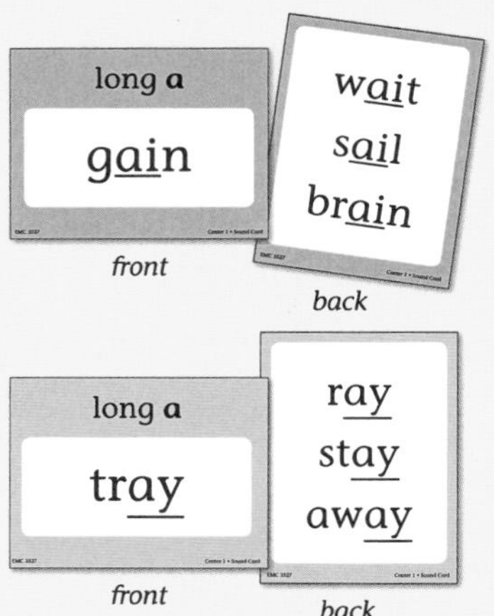

front back

front back

Answer Keys

Each center includes a two-sided page of answer keys, showing mat activities on one side and written application activities on the other side.

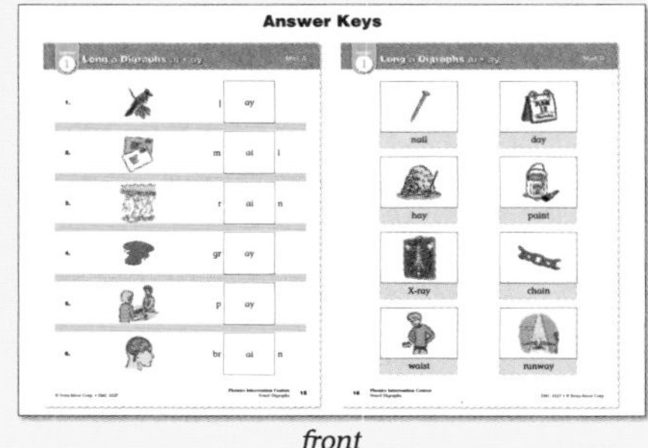

front

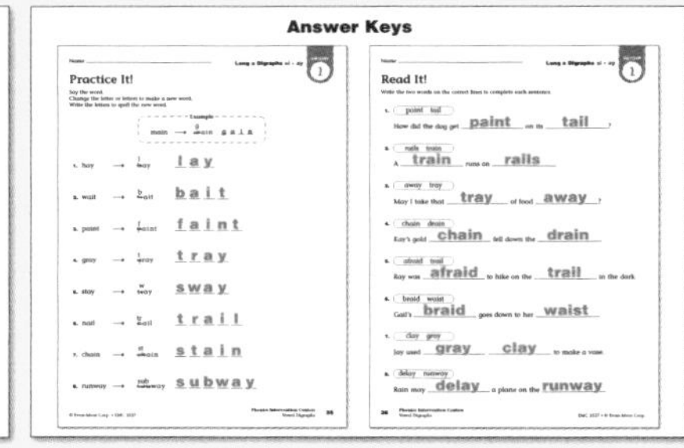

back

For the Student

Activity Mats and Task Cards

Each unit has six sets of activity mats and corresponding task cards, providing individual group members with their own materials for practicing the target skill.

Full-color illustrations provide context for word meaning and aid comprehension.

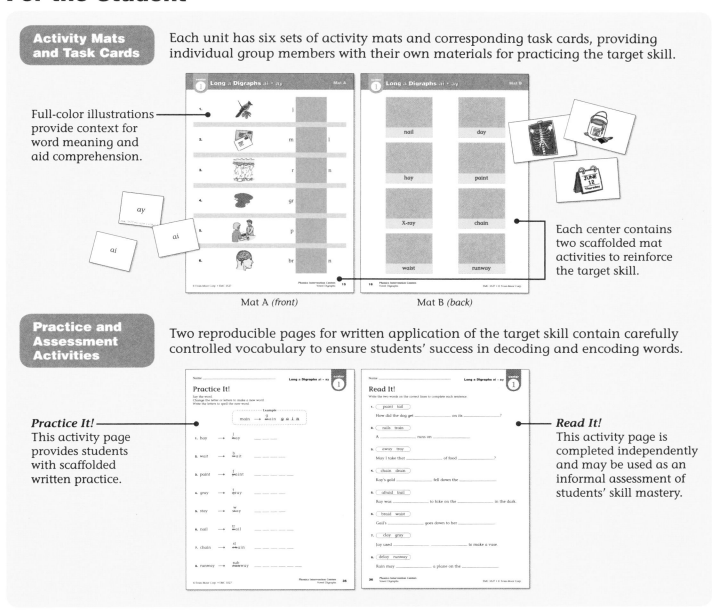

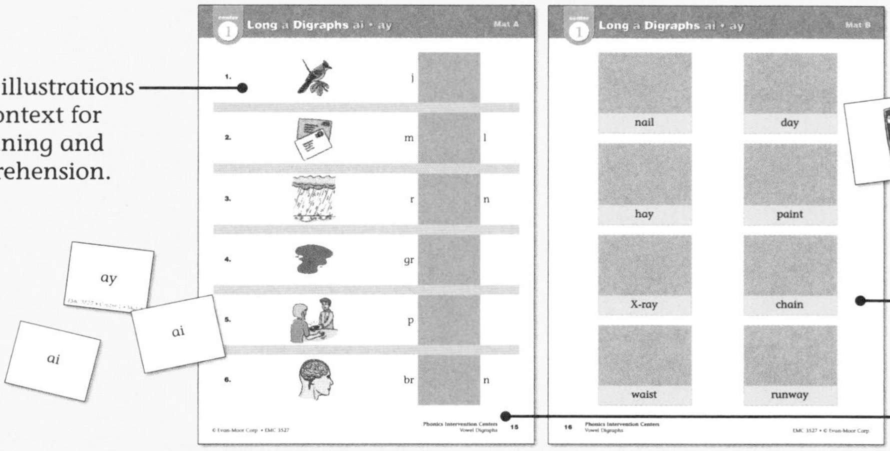

Each center contains two scaffolded mat activities to reinforce the target skill.

Mat A *(front)*

Mat B *(back)*

Practice and Assessment Activities

Two reproducible pages for written application of the target skill contain carefully controlled vocabulary to ensure students' success in decoding and encoding words.

Practice It!
This activity page provides students with scaffolded written practice.

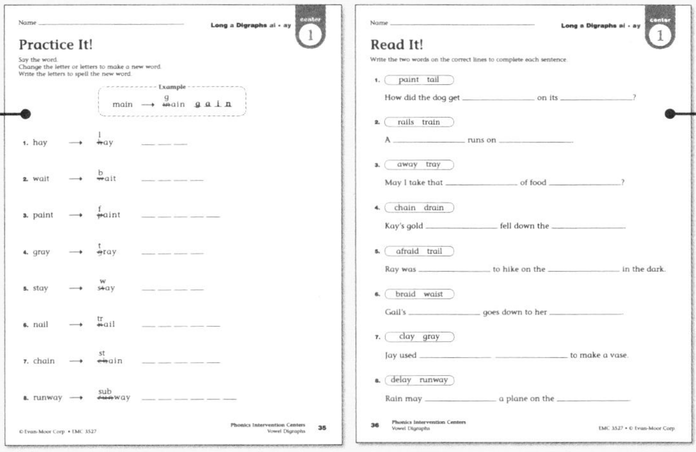

Read It!
This activity page is completed independently and may be used as an informal assessment of students' skill mastery.

Record Forms

Two reproducible record forms are included for tracking and assessing students' progress, individually or as a group. The *Group Progress Record* provides space for written comments and an assessment of skill mastery for each student in a particular group. The *Student Progress Record* includes a detailed breakdown of each center's objectives to informally assess an individual student's skill mastery.

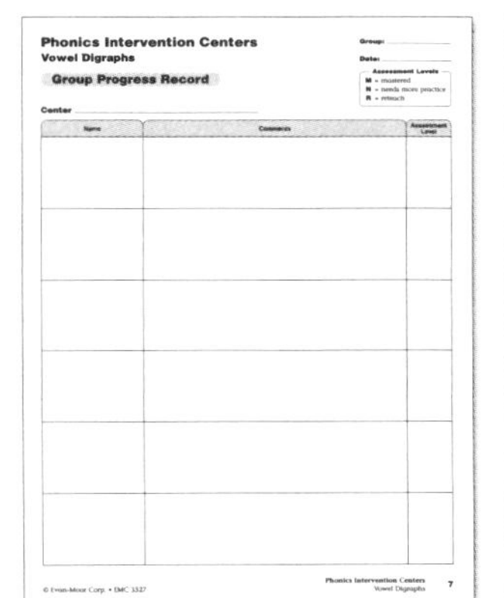
Phonics Intervention Centers
Vowel Digraphs
Group Progress Record

Phonics Intervention Centers
Vowel Digraphs
Student Progress Record

How to Make and Store the Centers

You Will Need

- pocket-style folders (1 per center)
- business-size envelopes or small, self-locking plastic bags (12 per center)
- scissors, tape, marking pen
- laminating materials and equipment

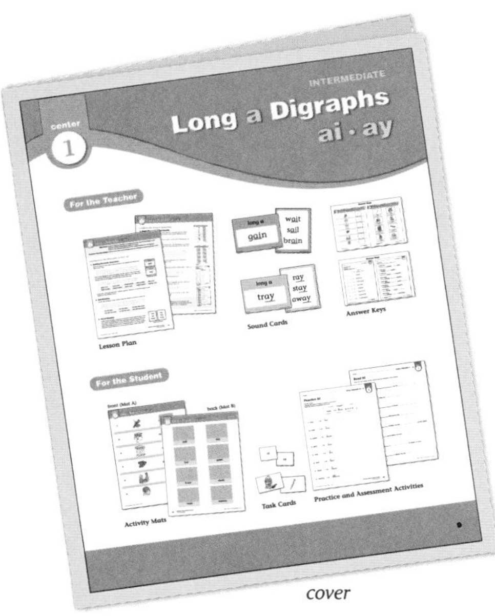

cover

Steps to Follow (for each center)

1. Remove the perforated pages and laminate all color pages. (Do not laminate the *Practice It!* and *Read It!* activities.)
2. Attach the cover page to the front of the folder.
3. Place the lesson plan in the left-hand pocket.
4. Cut apart the sound cards and the set of answer keys and place them with the lesson plan in the left-hand pocket of the folder.
5. Place all activity mats in the right-hand pocket.
6. Cut apart the task cards for Mat A and Mat B and sort them by student number (located on the back of most cards).
7. Keep each set of cards in a separate envelope or plastic bag and place them in the right-hand pocket of the folder.
8. Reproduce one copy of the *Practice It!* and *Read It!* activities for each student and place them in the right-hand pocket of the folder.

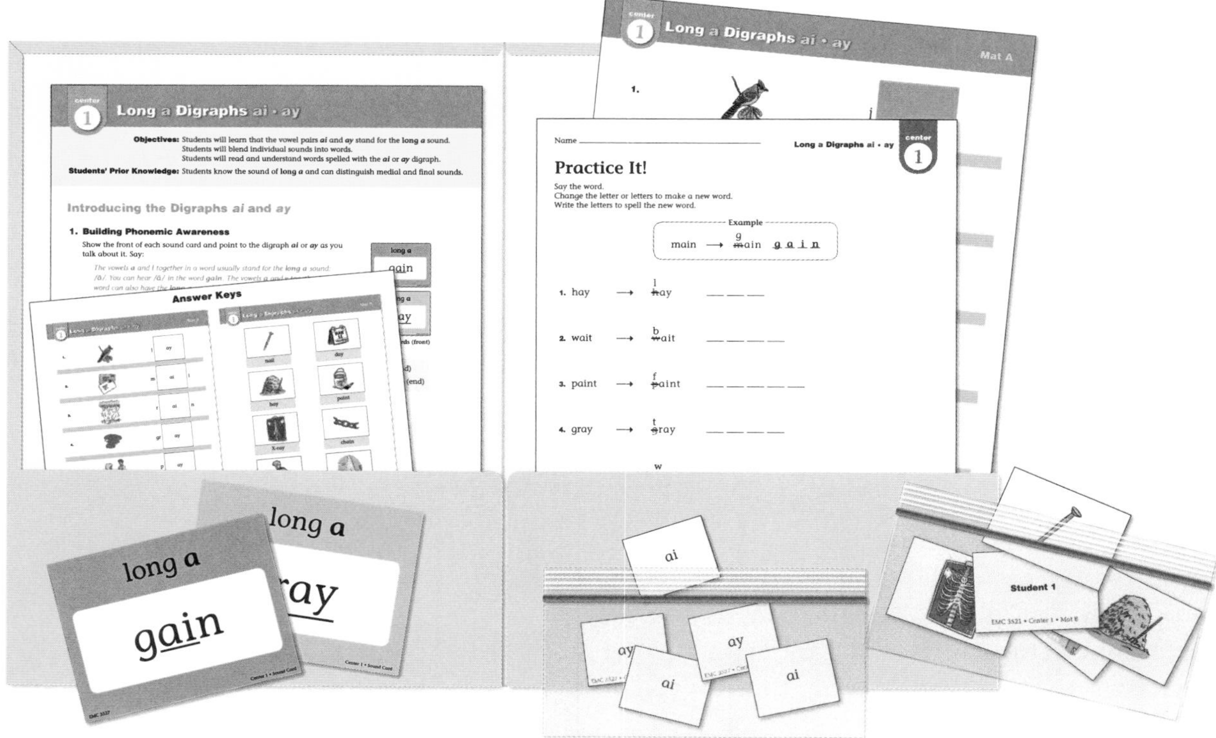

Phonics Intervention Centers
Vowel Digraphs

Group: ______________

Date: ______________

Assessment Levels
M = mastered
N = needs more practice
R = reteach

Group Progress Record

Center ______________________________

Name	Comments	Assessment Level

Name: ______________________

Phonics Intervention Centers
Vowel Digraphs

Student Progress Record

Assessment Levels
M = mastered
N = needs more practice
R = reteach

	Date / Assessment	Date / Assessment	Date / Assessment
1 Long *a* Digraphs *ai* • *ay*			
Distinguishes the **long *a*** sound of the ***ai*** and ***ay*** digraphs			
Blends individual sounds into words			
Reads and understands words with the ***ai*** or ***ay*** digraph			
2 Long *e* Digraphs *ea* • *ee*			
Distinguishes the **long *e*** sound of the ***ea*** and ***ee*** digraphs			
Blends individual sounds into words			
Reads and understands words with the ***ea*** or ***ee*** digraph			
3 Long *i* Digraphs *ie* • *igh*			
Distinguishes the **long *i*** sound of the ***ie*** and ***igh*** digraphs			
Blends individual sounds into words			
Reads and understands words with the ***ie*** or ***igh*** digraph			
4 Long *o* Digraphs *oa* • *ow*			
Distinguishes the **long *o*** sound of the ***oa*** and ***ow*** digraphs			
Blends individual sounds into words			
Reads and understands words with the ***oa*** or ***ow*** digraph			
5 Long *u* Digraphs *ew* • *ue*			
Distinguishes the **long *u*** sound of the ***ew*** and ***ue*** digraphs			
Blends individual sounds into words			
Reads and understands words with the ***ew*** or ***ue*** digraph			
6 The *oo* Digraph			
Distinguishes the /o͝o/ and /o͞o/ sounds of the ***oo*** digraph			
Blends individual sounds into words			
Reads and understands words with the ***oo*** digraph			
7 The *au* • *aw* Digraphs			
Distinguishes the /ô/ sound of the ***au*** and ***aw*** digraphs			
Blends individual sounds into words			
Reads and understands words with the ***au*** or ***aw*** digraph			
8 Vowel Digraphs Review			
Reads and understands words spelled with vowel digraphs			

center 1

INTERMEDIATE

Long a Digraphs ai • ay

For the Teacher

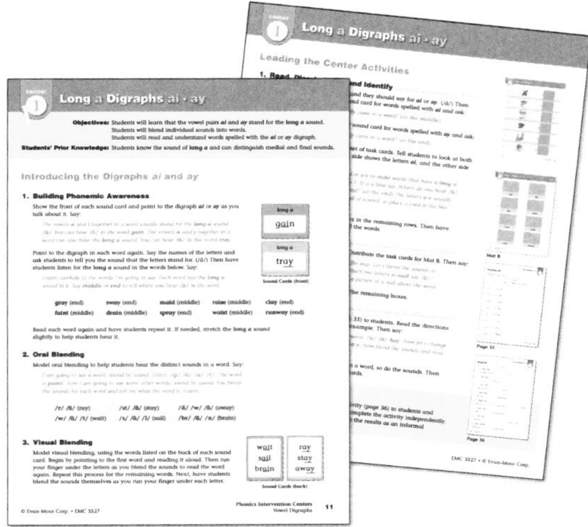

Lesson Plan

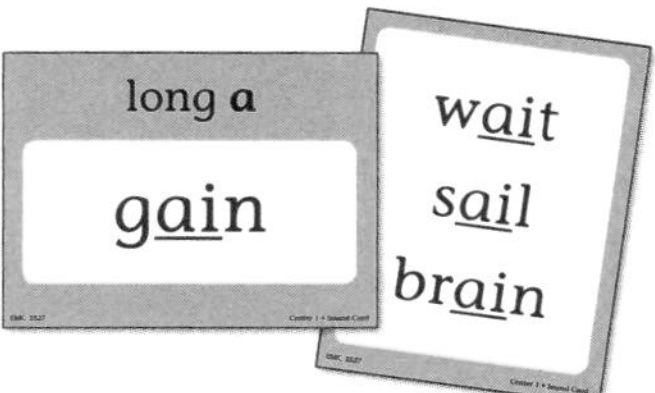

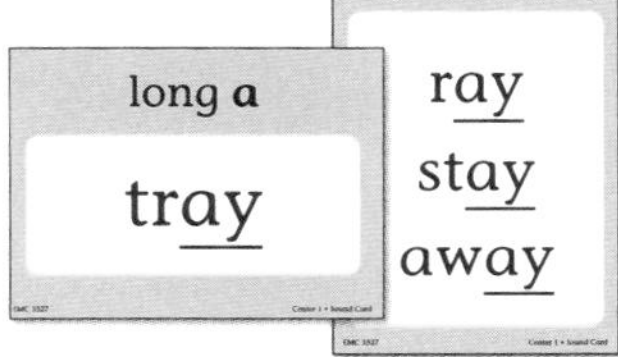

Sound Cards

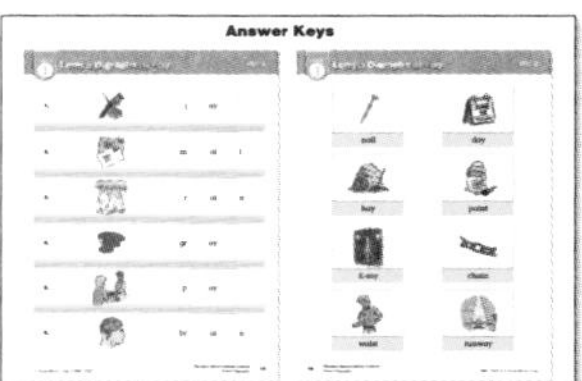

Answer Keys

For the Student

front (Mat A)

back (Mat B)

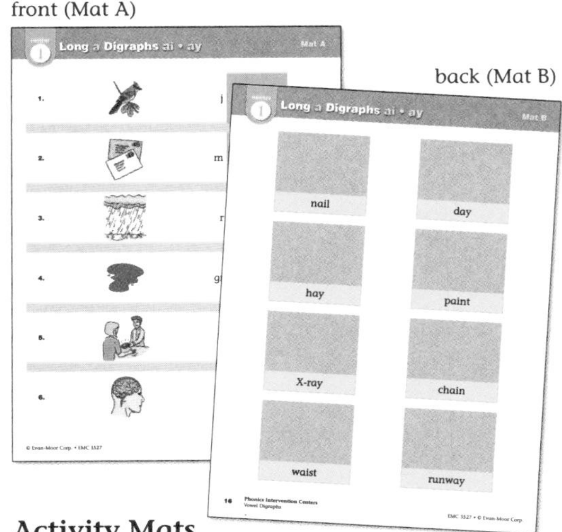

Activity Mats

Task Cards

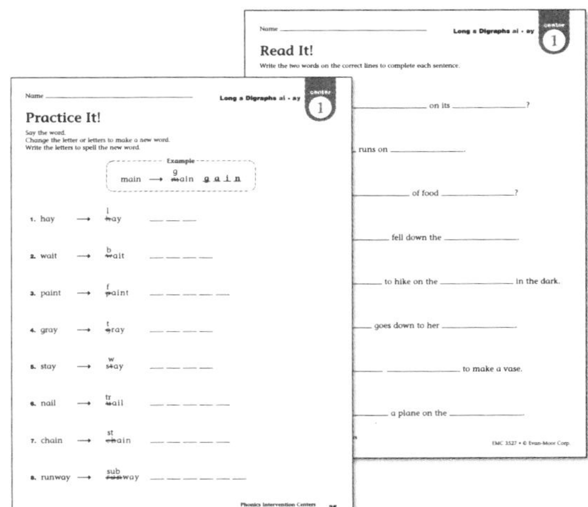

Practice and Assessment Activities

Long a Digraphs ai • ay

Objectives: Students will learn that the vowel pairs ***ai*** and ***ay*** stand for the **long *a*** sound.
Students will blend individual sounds into words.
Students will read and understand words spelled with the ***ai*** or ***ay*** digraph.

Students' Prior Knowledge: Students know the sound of **long *a*** and can distinguish medial and final sounds.

Introducing the Digraphs *ai* and *ay*

1. Building Phonemic Awareness

Show the front of each sound card and point to the digraph ***ai*** or ***ay*** as you talk about it. Say:

*The vowels **a** and **i** together in a word usually stand for the **long a** sound: /ā/. You can hear /ā/ in the word **gain**. The vowels **a** and **y** together in a word can also have the **long a** sound. You can hear /ā/ in the word **tray**.*

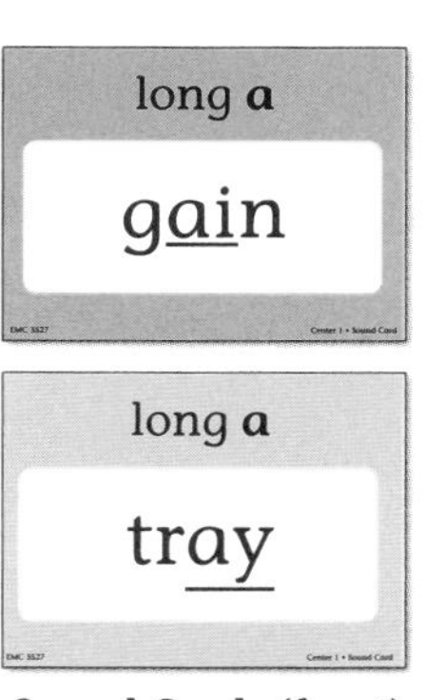

Sound Cards (front)

Point to the digraph in each word again. Say the names of the letters and ask students to tell you the sound that the letters stand for. (/ā/) Then have students listen for the **long *a*** sound in the words below. Say:

*Listen carefully to the words I'm going to say. Each word has the **long a** sound in it. Say **middle** or **end** to tell where you hear /ā/ in the word.*

gray (end)	**sway** (end)	**maid** (middle)	**raise** (middle)	**clay** (end)
faint (middle)	**drain** (middle)	**spray** (end)	**waist** (middle)	**runway** (end)

Read each word again and have students repeat it. If needed, stretch the **long *a*** sound slightly to help students hear it.

2. Oral Blending

Model oral blending to help students hear the distinct sounds in a word. Say:

*I am going to say a word, sound by sound. Listen: /p/ /ā/ /n/ /t/. The word is **paint**. Now I am going to say some other words, sound by sound. You blend the sounds for each word and tell me what the word is. Listen:*

/r/ /ā/ (ray)	**/st/ /ā/** (stay)	**/ă/ /w/ /ā/** (away)
/w/ /ā/ /t/ (wait)	**/s/ /ā/ /l/** (sail)	**/br/ /ā/ /n/** (brain)

3. Visual Blending

Model visual blending, using the words listed on the back of each sound card. Begin by pointing to the first word and reading it aloud. Then run your finger under the letters as you blend the sounds to read the word again. Repeat this process for the remaining words. Next, have students blend the sounds themselves as you run your finger under each letter.

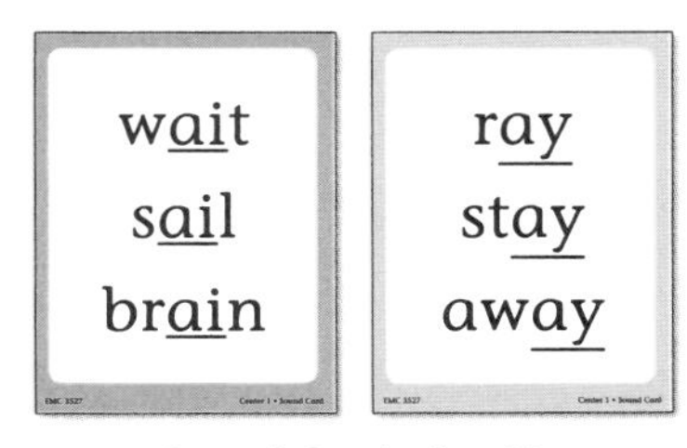

Sound Cards (back)

Leading the Center Activities

1. Read, Discriminate, and Identify

Ask students to tell you the sound they should say for ***ai*** or ***ay***. (/ā/) Then show them the back of the sound card for words spelled with ***ai*** and ask:

*Where do the letters **a-i** usually come in a word?* (in the middle)

Now show them the back of the sound card for words spelled with ***ay*** and ask:

*Where do the letters **a-y** usually come in a word?* (at the end)

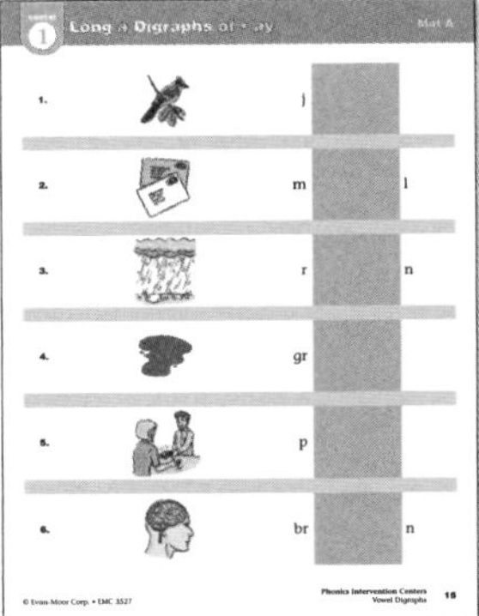

Mat A

Give each student Mat A and a set of task cards. Tell students to look at both sides of the cards to see that one side shows the letters ***ai***, and the other side shows the letters ***ay***. Then say:

*We're going to use the letters **a-i** or **a-y** to make words that have a **long a** sound. Look at the picture in row 1. It is a blue jay. Where do you hear /ā/ in **jay**—in the middle or at the end?* (at the end) *The letters **a-y** usually make the **long a** sound at the end of a word, so place a card in the box with **a-y** facing up.*

Repeat this process with the pictures in the remaining rows. Then have students blend the sounds and read the words.

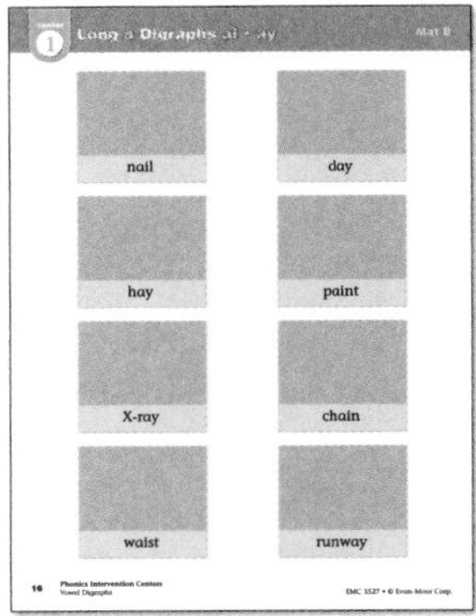

Mat B

2. Read and Understand

Have students turn over their mats. Distribute the task cards for Mat B. Then say:

*Look at the word in the first box on the mat. Let's blend the sounds to read the word: /n/ /ā/ /l/ **nail**. Which two letters in **nail** say /ā/?* (a-i) *Now place the card that shows a picture of a nail above the word.*

Repeat this process with the words in the remaining boxes.

Page 35

3. Practice the Skill

Distribute the Practice It! activity (page 35) to students. Read the directions aloud and guide students through the example. Then say:

*Let's blend the sounds to read the first word: /h/ /ā/ **hay**. Now let's change the **h** to an **l** and write the new word: **l-a-y**. Now blend the sounds and read the new word: /l/ /ā/ **lay**.*

Remind students that as letters change in a word, so do the sounds. Then repeat this process with the remaining words.

Apply and Assess

After the lesson, distribute the Read It! activity (page 36) to students and read the directions aloud. Have students complete the activity independently. Then listen to them read the sentences. Use the results as an informal assessment of students' skill mastery.

Page 36

long a

gain

Center 1 • Sound Card

EMC 3527

long a

tray

Center 1 • Sound Card

EMC 3527

Answer Keys

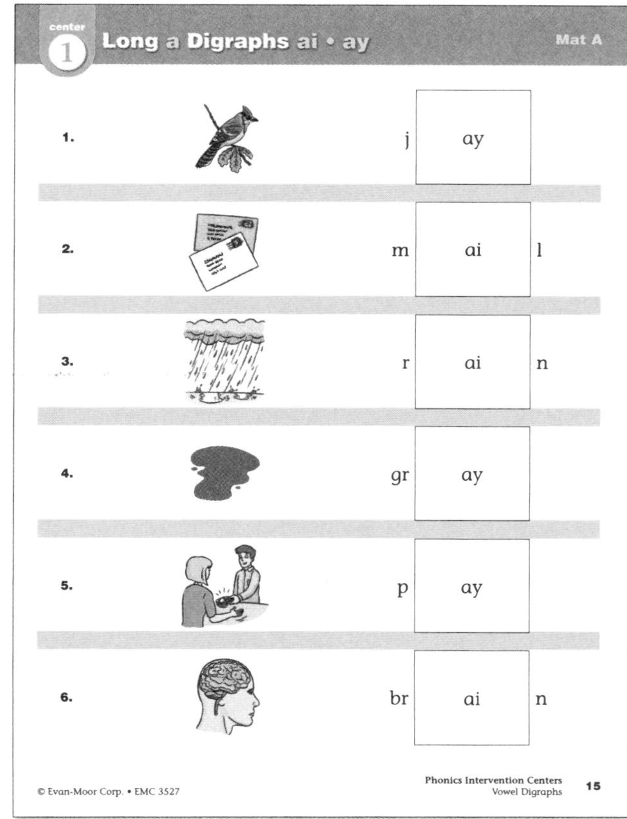
center 1 **Long a Digraphs ai • ay** Mat A

1.		j	ay	
2.		m	ai	l
3.		r	ai	n
4.		gr	ay	
5.		p	ay	
6.		br	ai	n

© Evan-Moor Corp. • EMC 3527 Phonics Intervention Centers Vowel Digraphs 15

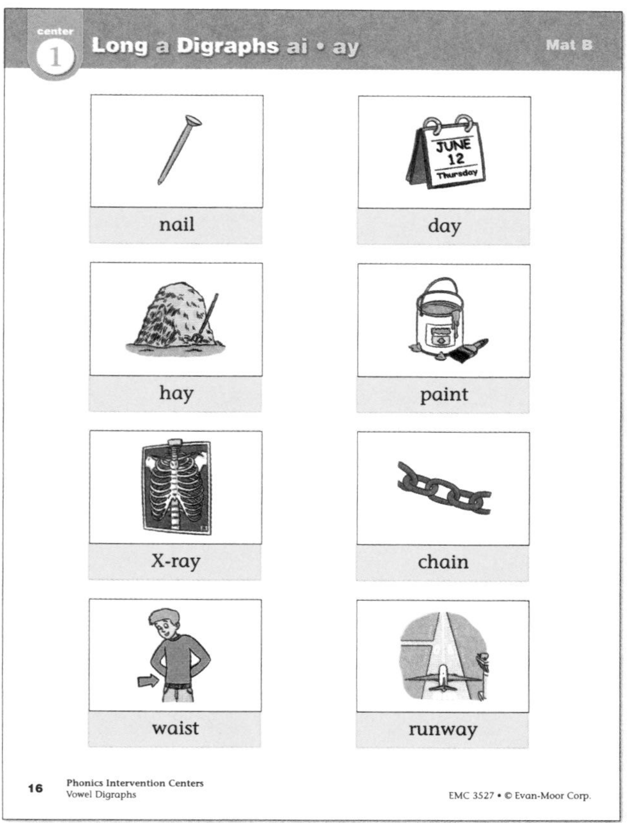
center 1 **Long a Digraphs ai • ay** Mat B

nail	day
hay	paint
X-ray	chain
waist	runway

16 Phonics Intervention Centers Vowel Digraphs EMC 3527 • © Evan-Moor Corp.

ray

stay

away

EMC 3527 Center 1 • Sound Card

wait

sail

brain

EMC 3527 Center 1 • Sound Card

Answer Keys

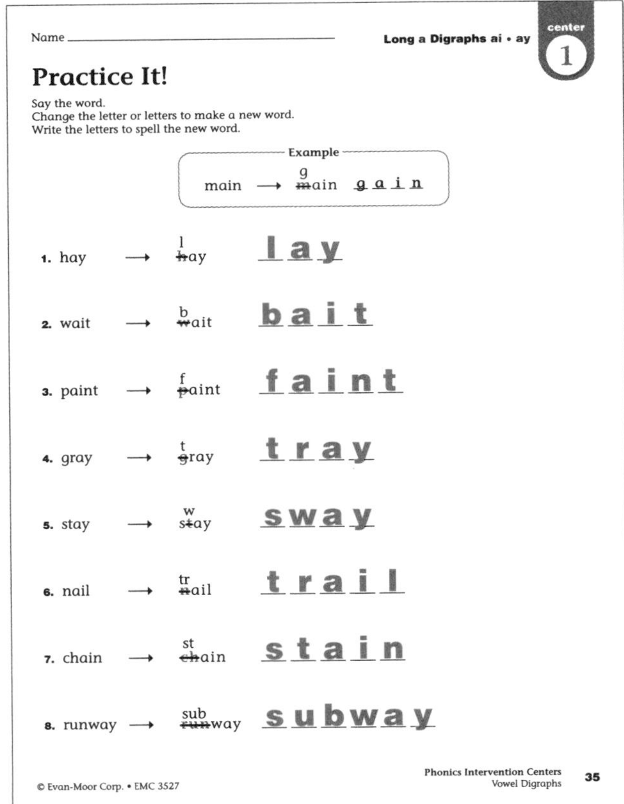
Name ______________________ **Long a Digraphs ai • ay** center 1

Practice It!

Say the word.
Change the letter or letters to make a new word.
Write the letters to spell the new word.

Example: main → ~~m~~ (g) ain → g a i n

1. hay → ~~h~~ (l) ay → l a y
2. wait → ~~w~~ (b) ait → b a i t
3. paint → ~~p~~ (f) aint → f a i n t
4. gray → ~~g~~ (t) ray → t r a y
5. stay → s~~t~~ (w) ay → s w a y
6. nail → ~~n~~ (tr) ail → t r a i l
7. chain → ~~ch~~ (st) ain → s t a i n
8. runway → ~~run~~ (sub) way → s u b w a y

© Evan-Moor Corp. • EMC 3527 Phonics Intervention Centers Vowel Digraphs 35

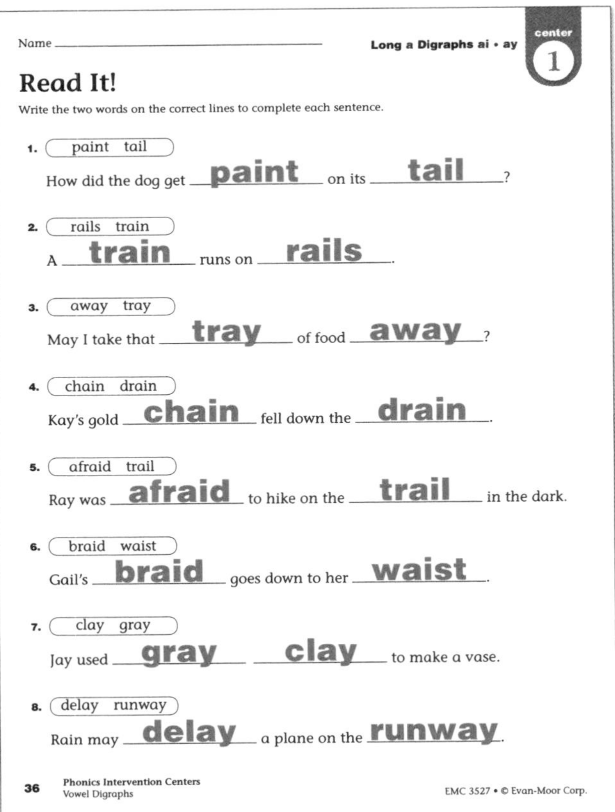
Name ______________________ **Long a Digraphs ai • ay** center 1

Read It!

Write the two words on the correct lines to complete each sentence.

1. (paint tail) How did the dog get **paint** on its **tail**?
2. (rails train) A **train** runs on **rails**.
3. (away tray) May I take that **tray** of food **away**?
4. (chain drain) Kay's gold **chain** fell down the **drain**.
5. (afraid trail) Ray was **afraid** to hike on the **trail** in the dark.
6. (braid waist) Gail's **braid** goes down to her **waist**.
7. (clay gray) Jay used **gray** **clay** to make a vase.
8. (delay runway) Rain may **delay** a plane on the **runway**.

36 Phonics Intervention Centers Vowel Digraphs EMC 3527 • © Evan-Moor Corp.

Long a Digraphs ai • ay

1.  j

2.  m l

3.  r n

4.  gr

5.  p

6. 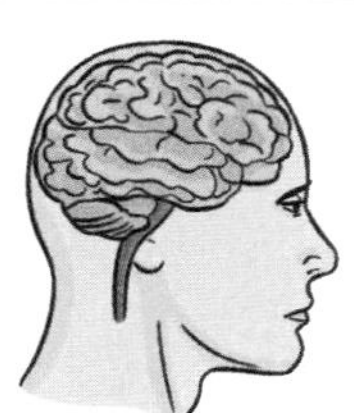 br n

Long a Digraphs ai • ay

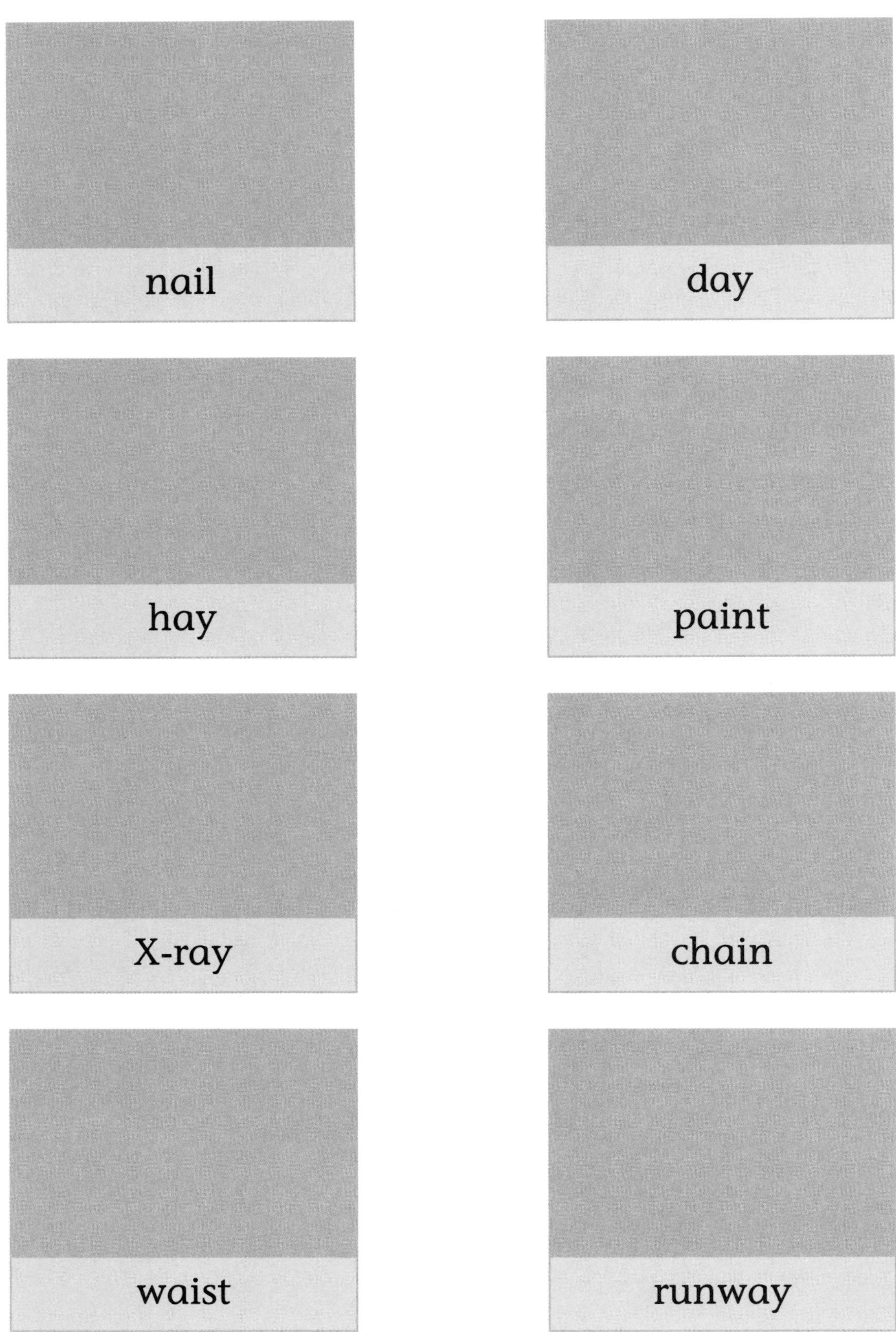

Long a Digraphs ai • ay

1.  j

2.  m l

3.  r n

4.  gr

5.  p

6. 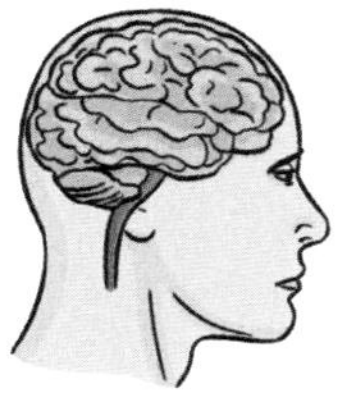 br n

Long a Digraphs ai • ay

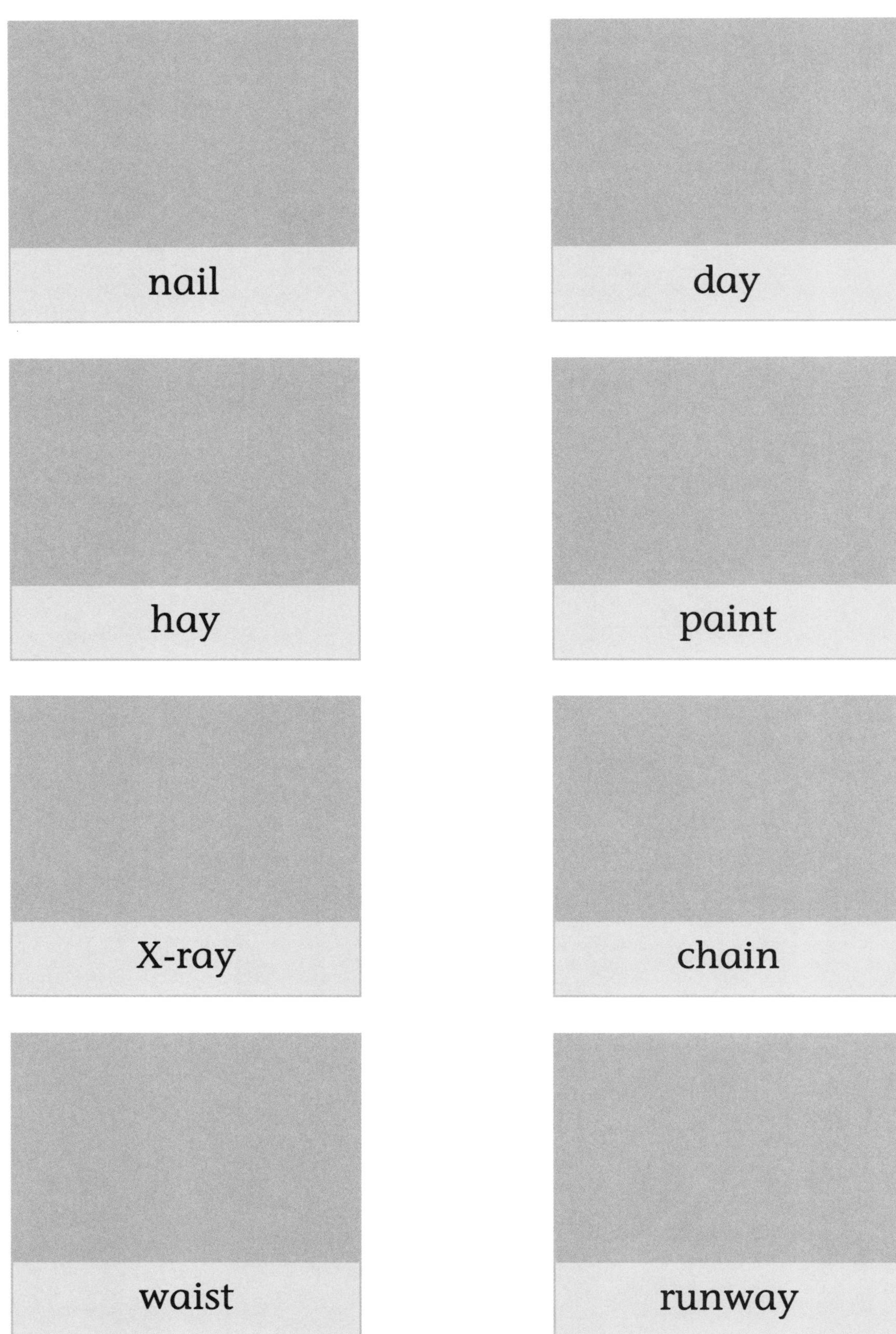

Long a Digraphs ai • ay

Mat A

1.		j		
2.		m		l
3.		r		n
4.		gr		
5.		p		
6.	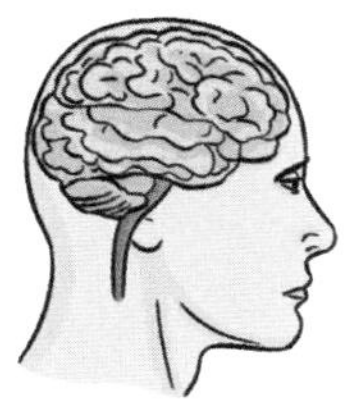	br		n

Long a Digraphs ai • ay

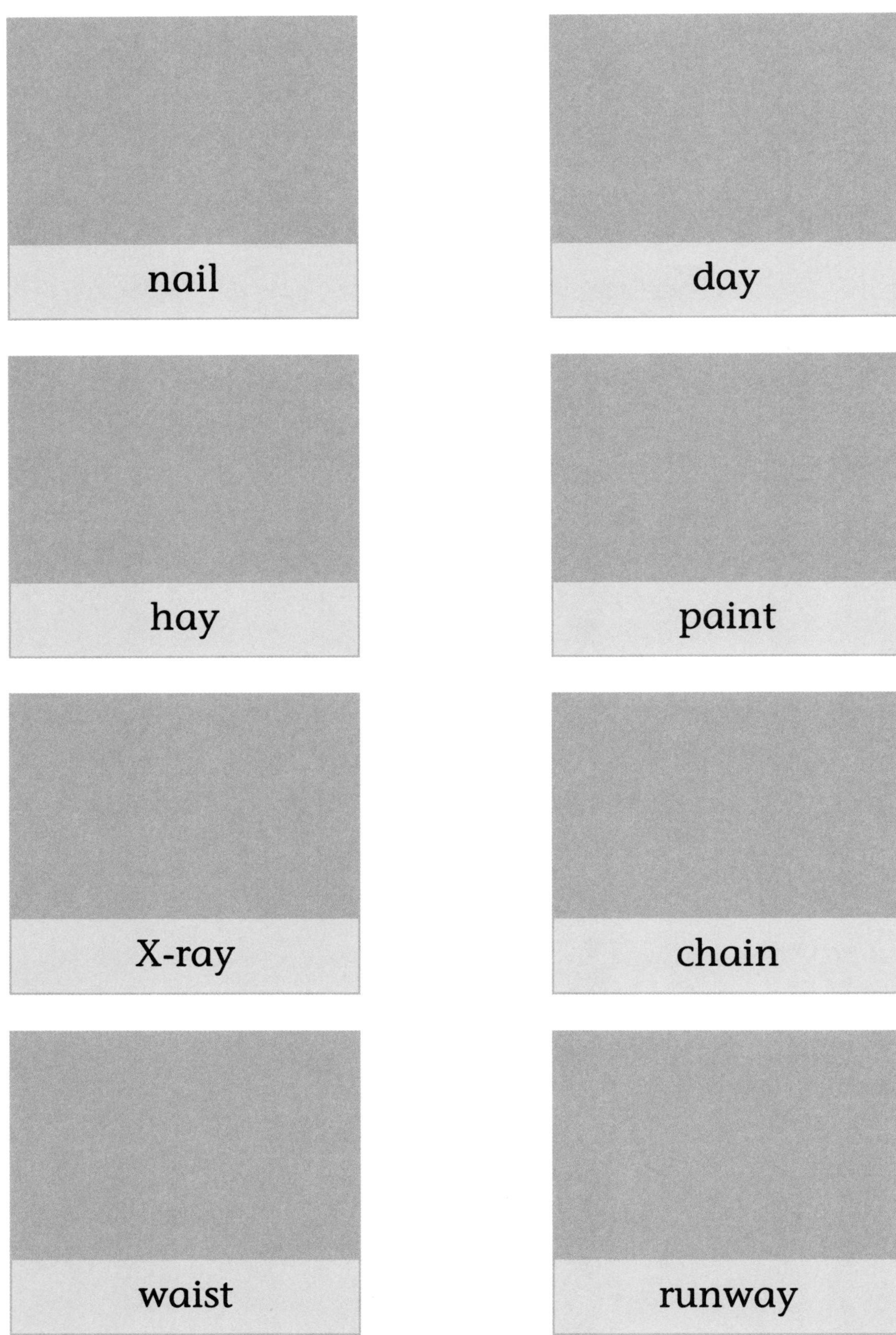

Long a Digraphs ai • ay

1.  j

2.  m l

3.  r n

4.  gr

5.  p

6. 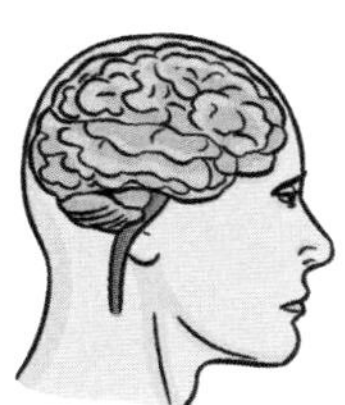 br n

Long a Digraphs ai • ay

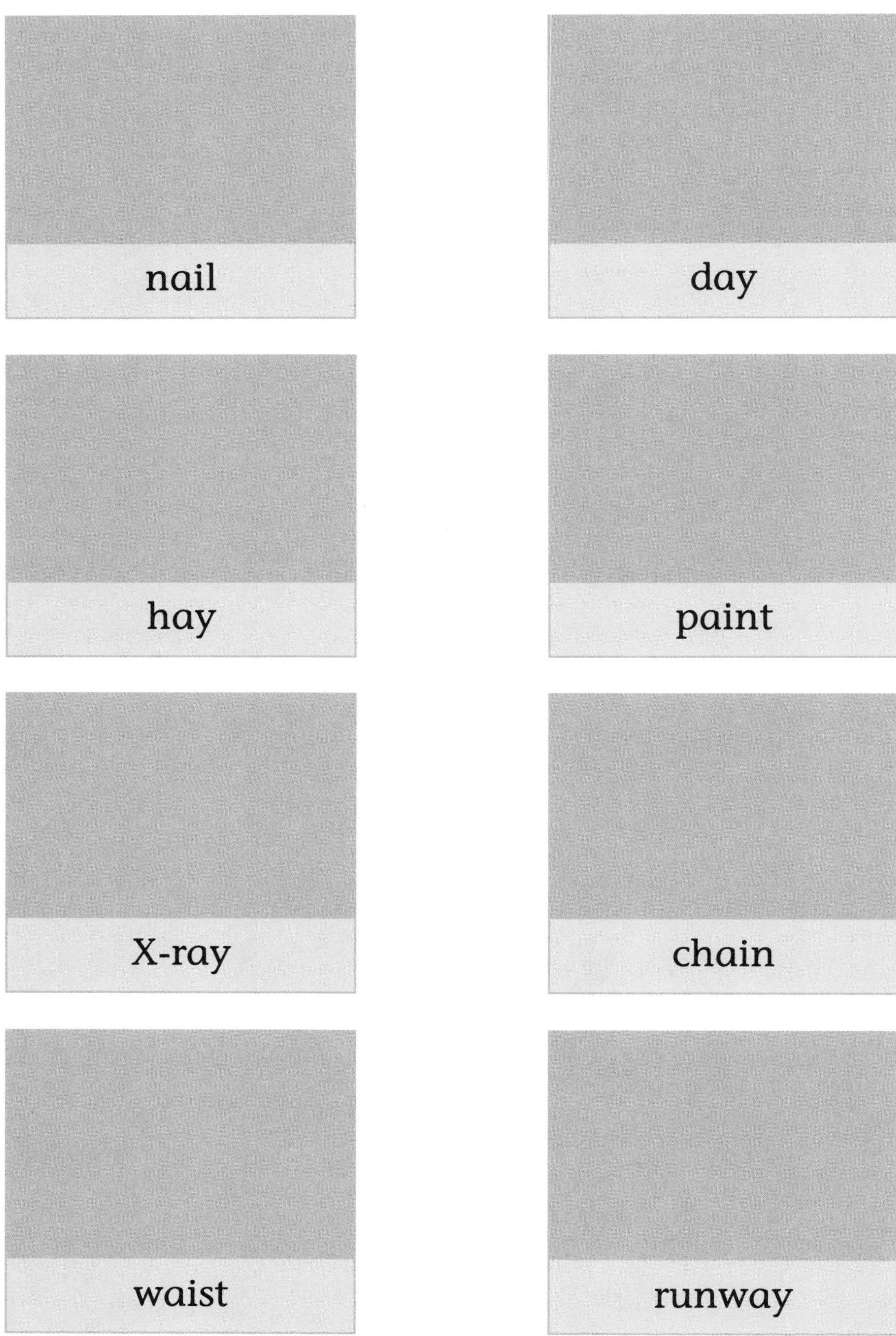

center 1

Long a Digraphs ai • ay

Mat A

1.	j		
2.	m		l
3.	r		n
4.	gr		
5.	p		
6.	br		n

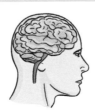

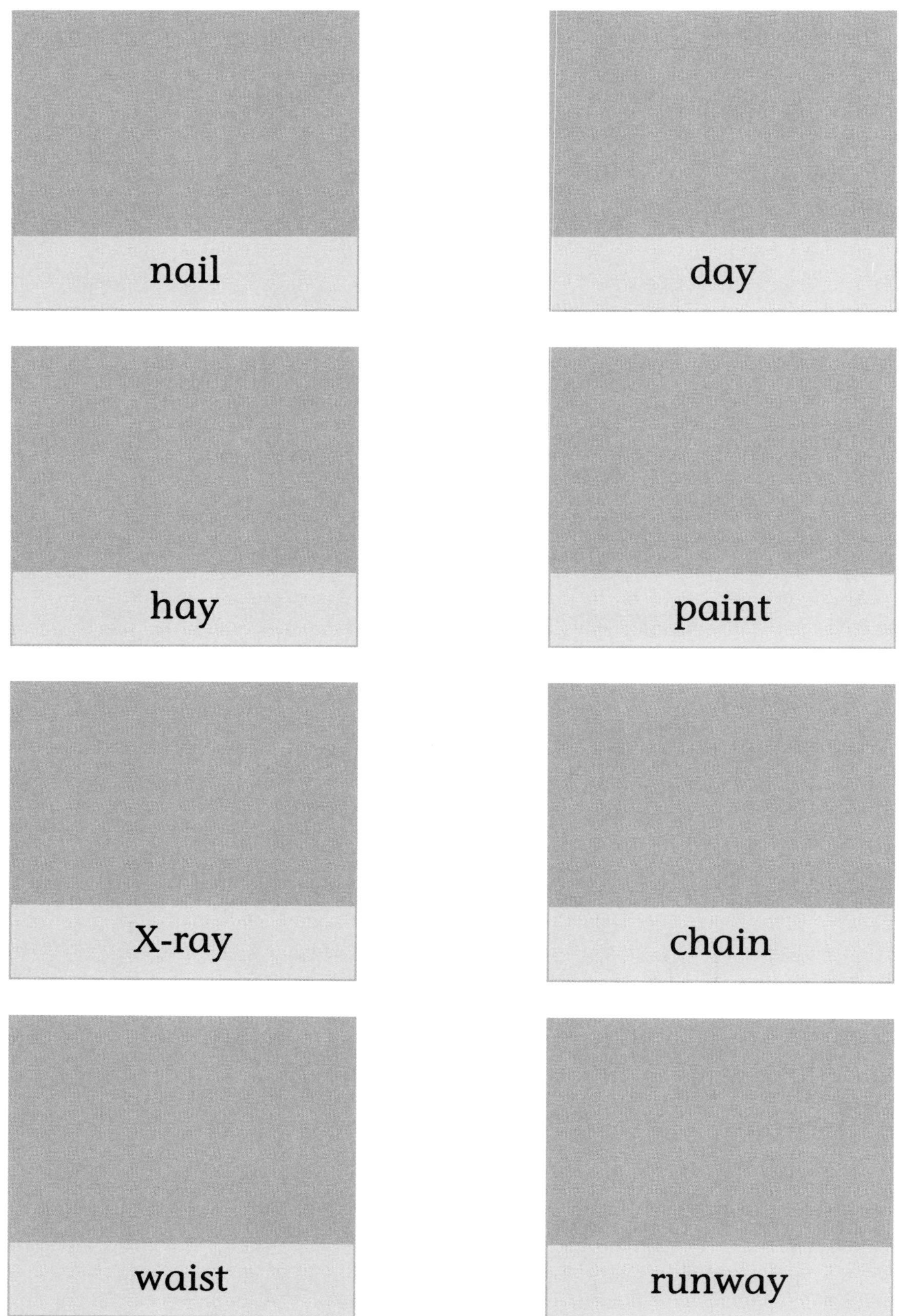
nail
day
hay
paint
X-ray
chain
waist
runway

Long a Digraphs ai • ay

1.		j	
2.		m	l
3.		r	n
4.		gr	
5.		p	
6.	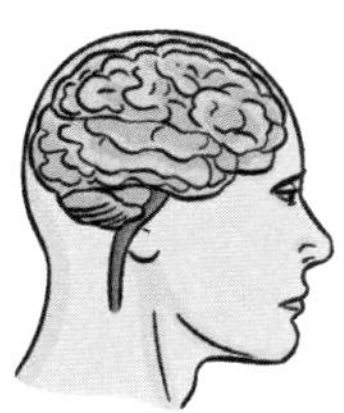	br	n

Long a Digraphs ai • ay

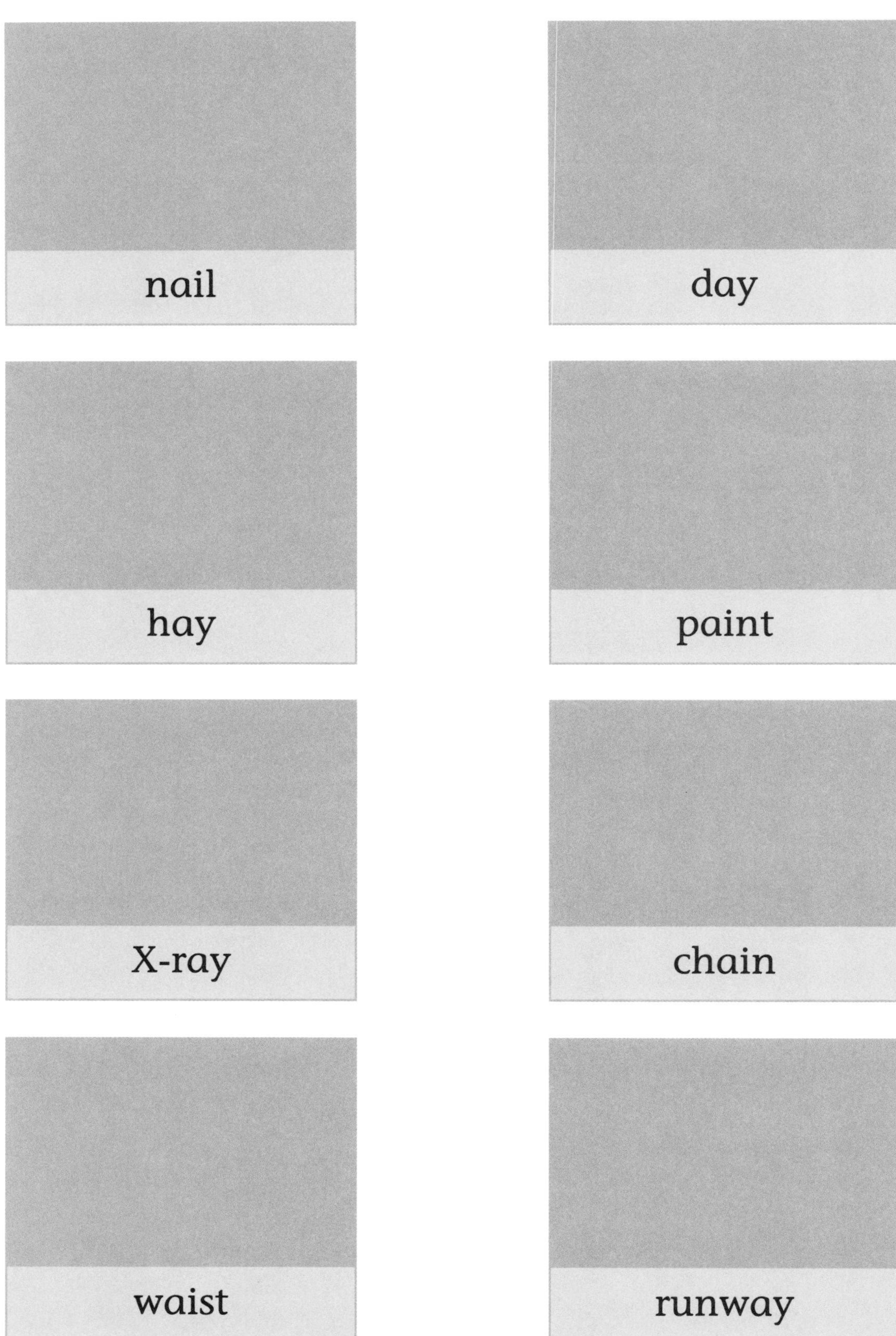

Task Cards

Student 6	ai	ai	ai	ai	ai	ai
Student 5	ai	ai	ai	ai	ai	ai
Student 4	ai	ai	ai	ai	ai	ai
Student 3	ai	ai	ai	ai	ai	ai
Student 2	ai	ai	ai	ai	ai	ai
Student 1	ai	ai	ai	ai	ai	ai

Task Cards

ay
EMC 3527 • Center 1 • Mat A

ay
EMC 3527 • Center 1 • Mat A

ay
EMC 3527 • Center 1 • Mat A

ay
EMC 3527 • Center 1 • Mat A

ay
EMC 3527 • Center 1 • Mat A

ay
EMC 3527 • Center 1 • Mat A

ay
EMC 3527 • Center 1 • Mat A

ay
EMC 3527 • Center 1 • Mat A

ay
EMC 3527 • Center 1 • Mat A

ay
EMC 3527 • Center 1 • Mat A

ay
EMC 3527 • Center 1 • Mat A

ay
EMC 3527 • Center 1 • Mat A

ay
EMC 3527 • Center 1 • Mat A

ay
EMC 3527 • Center 1 • Mat A

ay
EMC 3527 • Center 1 • Mat A

ay
EMC 3527 • Center 1 • Mat A

ay
EMC 3527 • Center 1 • Mat A

ay
EMC 3527 • Center 1 • Mat A

ay
EMC 3527 • Center 1 • Mat A

ay
EMC 3527 • Center 1 • Mat A

ay
EMC 3527 • Center 1 • Mat A

ay
EMC 3527 • Center 1 • Mat A

ay
EMC 3527 • Center 1 • Mat A

ay
EMC 3527 • Center 1 • Mat A

ay
EMC 3527 • Center 1 • Mat A

ay
EMC 3527 • Center 1 • Mat A

ay
EMC 3527 • Center 1 • Mat A

ay
EMC 3527 • Center 1 • Mat A

ay
EMC 3527 • Center 1 • Mat A

ay
EMC 3527 • Center 1 • Mat A

ay
EMC 3527 • Center 1 • Mat A

ay
EMC 3527 • Center 1 • Mat A

ay
EMC 3527 • Center 1 • Mat A

ay
EMC 3527 • Center 1 • Mat A

ay
EMC 3527 • Center 1 • Mat A

ay
EMC 3527 • Center 1 • Mat A

center 1

Task Cards

Mat B

Student 2

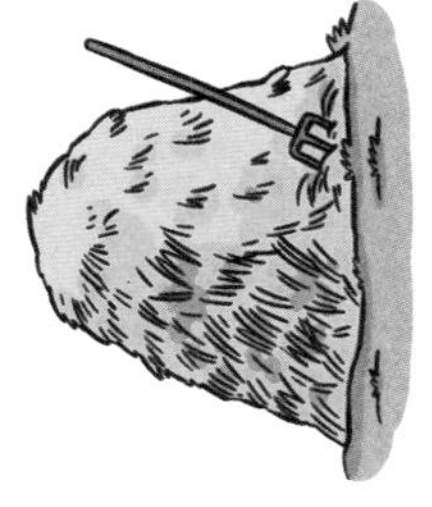

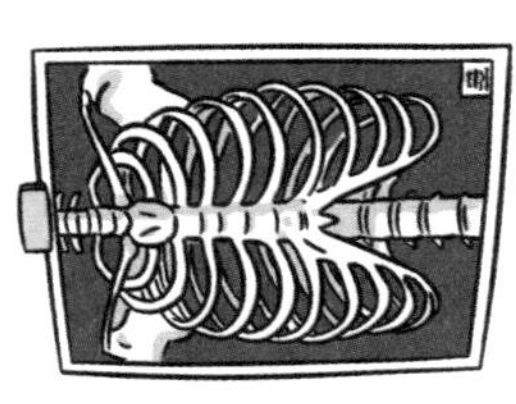

Student 1

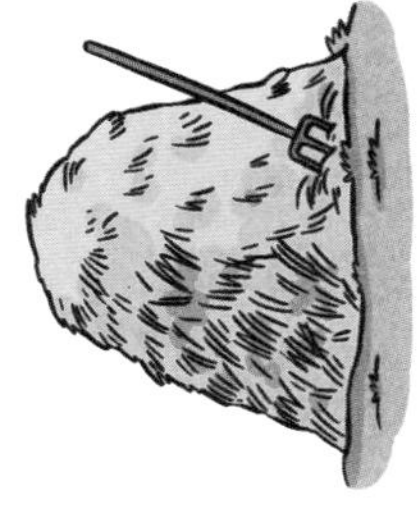

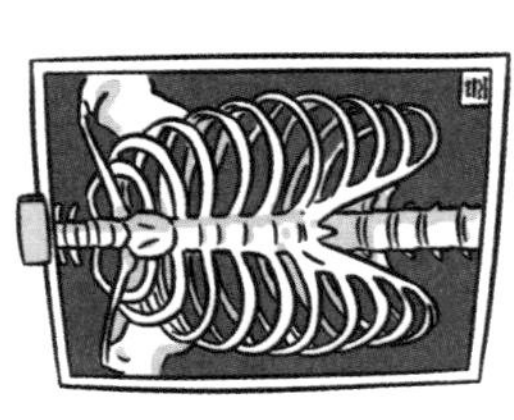

center 1

Task Cards

Mat B

Student 2
EMC 3527 • Center 1 • Mat B

Student 2
EMC 3527 • Center 1 • Mat B

Student 2
EMC 3527 • Center 1 • Mat B

Student 2
EMC 3527 • Center 1 • Mat B

Student 2
EMC 3527 • Center 1 • Mat B

Student 2
EMC 3527 • Center 1 • Mat B

Student 2
EMC 3527 • Center 1 • Mat B

Student 2
EMC 3527 • Center 1 • Mat B

Student 1
EMC 3527 • Center 1 • Mat B

Student 1
EMC 3527 • Center 1 • Mat B

Student 1
EMC 3527 • Center 1 • Mat B

Student 1
EMC 3527 • Center 1 • Mat B

Student 1
EMC 3527 • Center 1 • Mat B

Student 1
EMC 3527 • Center 1 • Mat B

Student 1
EMC 3527 • Center 1 • Mat B

Student 1
EMC 3527 • Center 1 • Mat B

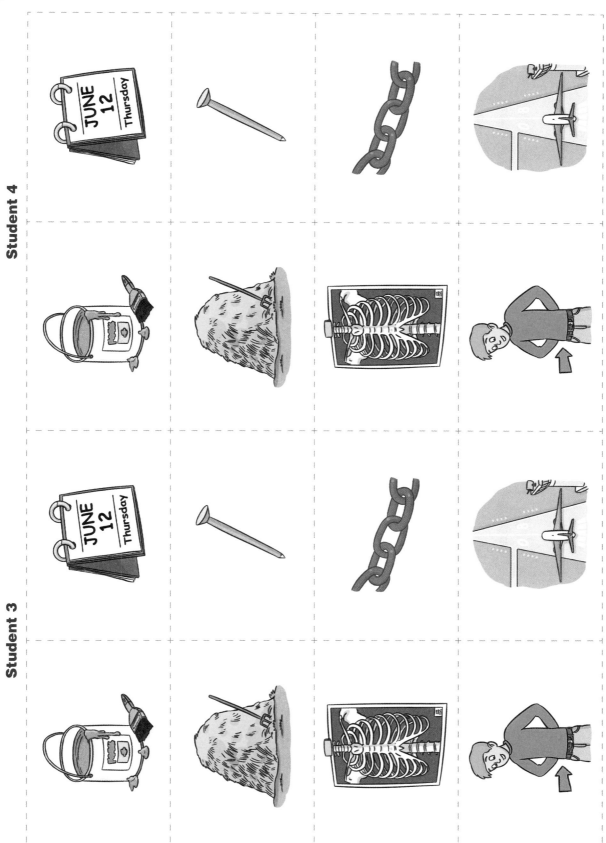

Student 4

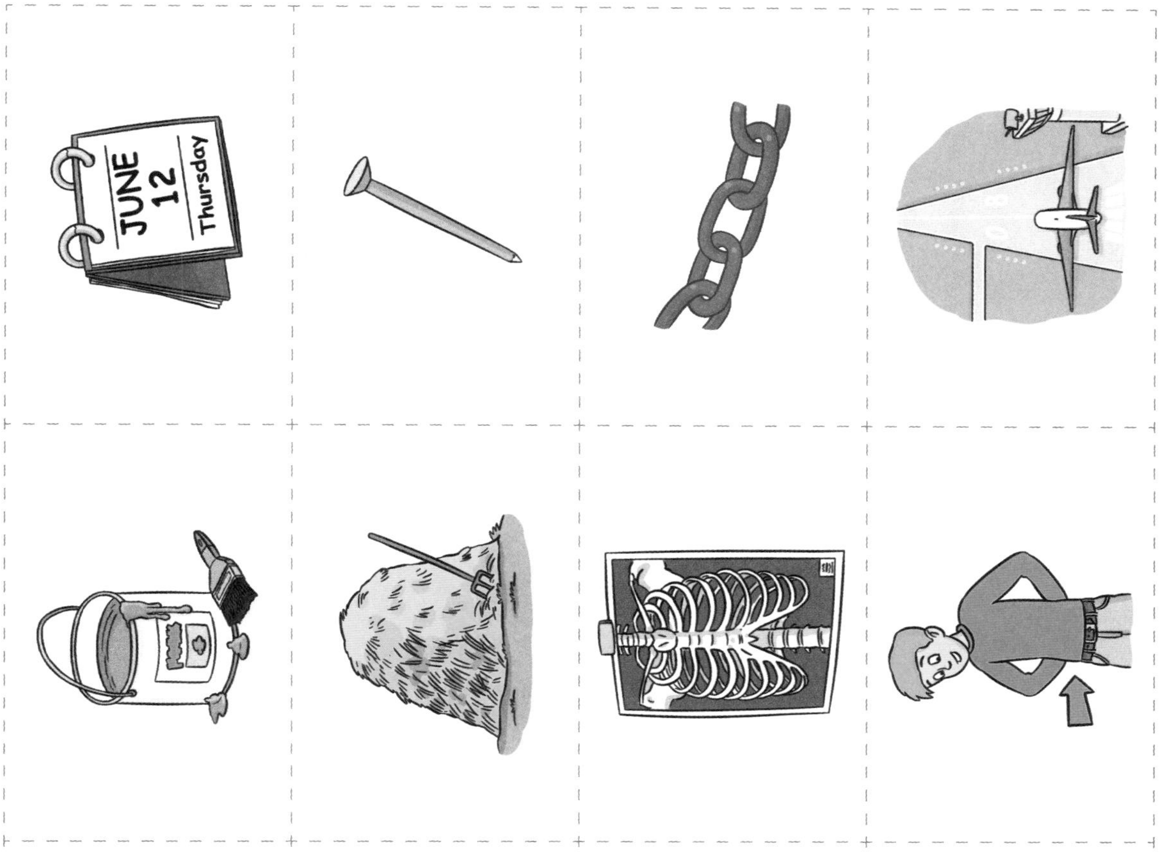

Student 3

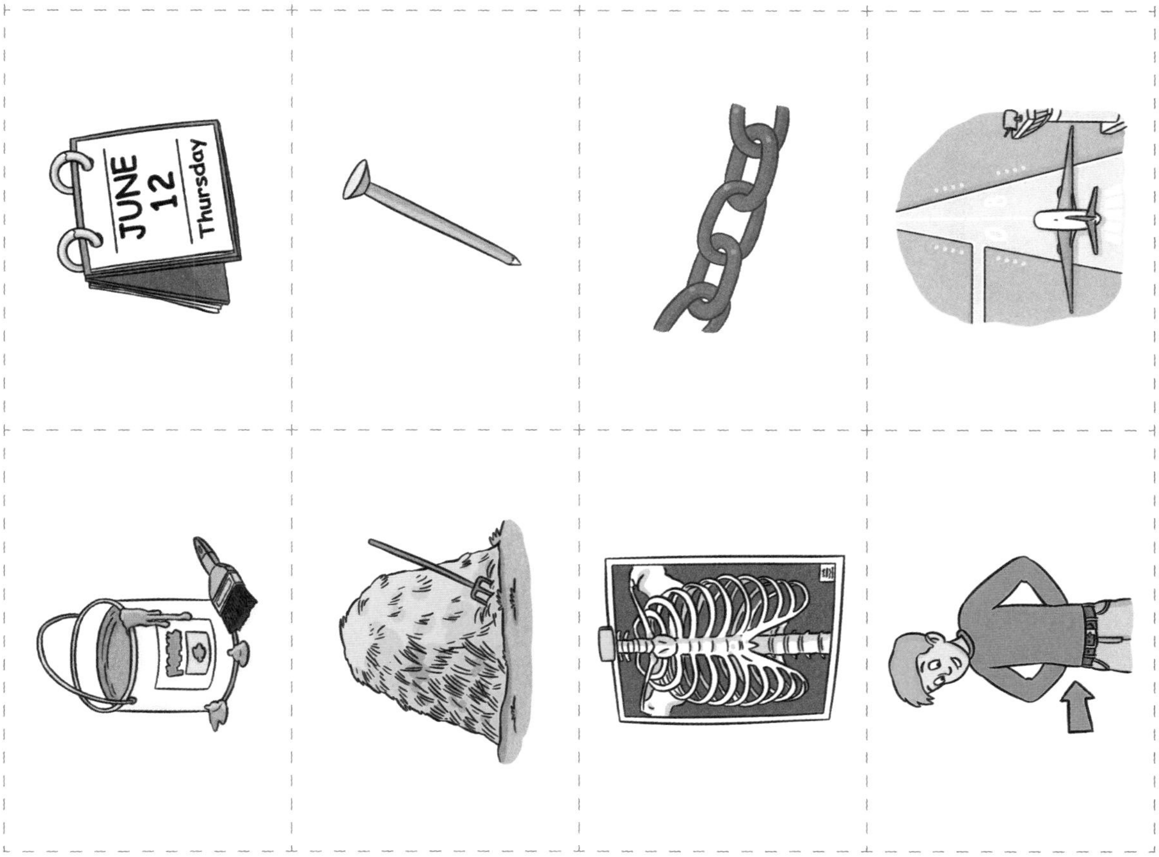

Student 4
EMC 3527 • Center 1 • Mat B

Student 4
EMC 3527 • Center 1 • Mat B

Student 4
EMC 3527 • Center 1 • Mat B

Student 4
EMC 3527 • Center 1 • Mat B

Student 4
EMC 3527 • Center 1 • Mat B

Student 4
EMC 3527 • Center 1 • Mat B

Student 4
EMC 3527 • Center 1 • Mat B

Student 4
EMC 3527 • Center 1 • Mat B

Student 3
EMC 3527 • Center 1 • Mat B

Student 3
EMC 3527 • Center 1 • Mat B

Student 3
EMC 3527 • Center 1 • Mat B

Student 3
EMC 3527 • Center 1 • Mat B

Student 3
EMC 3527 • Center 1 • Mat B

Student 3
EMC 3527 • Center 1 • Mat B

Student 3
EMC 3527 • Center 1 • Mat B

Student 3
EMC 3527 • Center 1 • Mat B

Task Cards

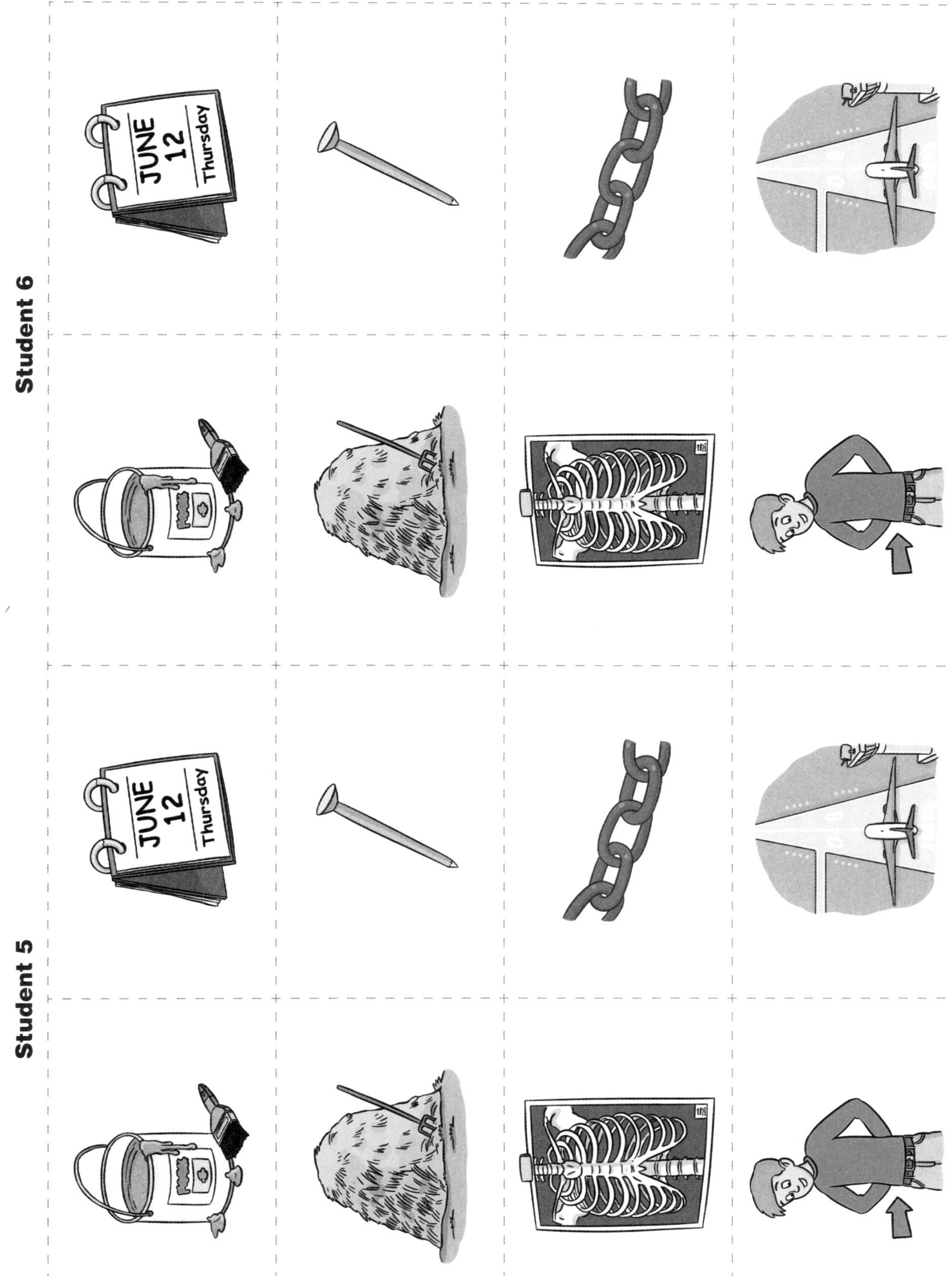

Student 6
EMC 3527 • Center 1 • Mat B

Student 6
EMC 3527 • Center 1 • Mat B

Student 6
EMC 3527 • Center 1 • Mat B

Student 6
EMC 3527 • Center 1 • Mat B

Student 6
EMC 3527 • Center 1 • Mat B

Student 6
EMC 3527 • Center 1 • Mat B

Student 6
EMC 3527 • Center 1 • Mat B

Student 6
EMC 3527 • Center 1 • Mat B

Student 5
EMC 3527 • Center 1 • Mat B

Student 5
EMC 3527 • Center 1 • Mat B

Student 5
EMC 3527 • Center 1 • Mat B

Student 5
EMC 3527 • Center 1 • Mat B

Student 5
EMC 3527 • Center 1 • Mat B

Student 5
EMC 3527 • Center 1 • Mat B

Student 5
EMC 3527 • Center 1 • Mat B

Student 5
EMC 3527 • Center 1 • Mat B

Name ____________________________________

Practice It!

Say the word.
Change the letter or letters to make a new word.
Write the letters to spell the new word.

Example

main → ~~m~~ain (g) g a i n

1. hay → ~~h~~ay (l) ___ ___ ___
2. wait → ~~w~~ait (b) ___ ___ ___ ___
3. paint → ~~p~~aint (f) ___ ___ ___ ___ ___
4. gray → ~~g~~ray (t) ___ ___ ___ ___
5. stay → s~~t~~ay (w) ___ ___ ___ ___
6. nail → ~~n~~ail (tr) ___ ___ ___ ___ ___
7. chain → ~~ch~~ain (st) ___ ___ ___ ___ ___
8. runway → ~~run~~way (sub) ___ ___ ___ ___ ___ ___

Read It!

Write the two words on the correct lines to complete each sentence.

1. paint tail

How did the dog get ____________ on its ____________?

2. rails train

A ____________ runs on ____________.

3. away tray

May I take that ____________ of food ____________?

4. chain drain

Kay's gold ____________ fell down the ____________.

5. afraid trail

Ray was ____________ to hike on the ____________ in the dark.

6. braid waist

Gail's ____________ goes down to her ____________.

7. clay gray

Jay used ____________ ____________ to make a vase.

8. delay runway

Rain may ____________ a plane on the ____________.

center 2

INTERMEDIATE

Long e Digraphs ea • ee

For the Teacher

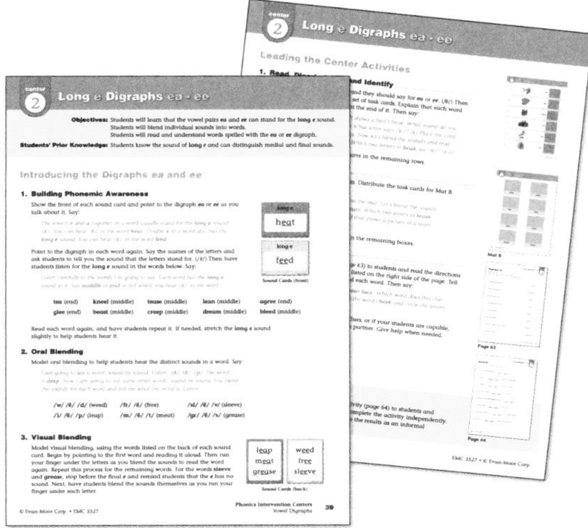
Lesson Plan

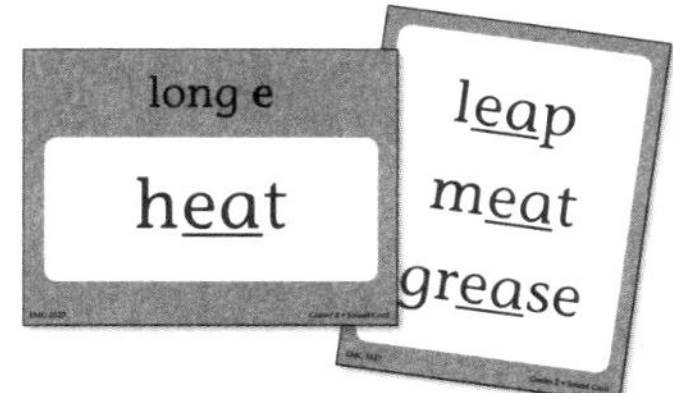

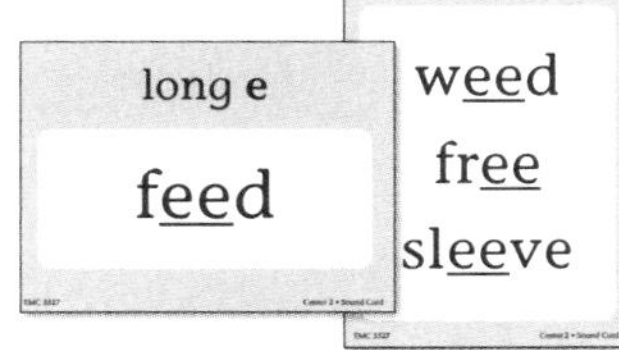

Sound Cards

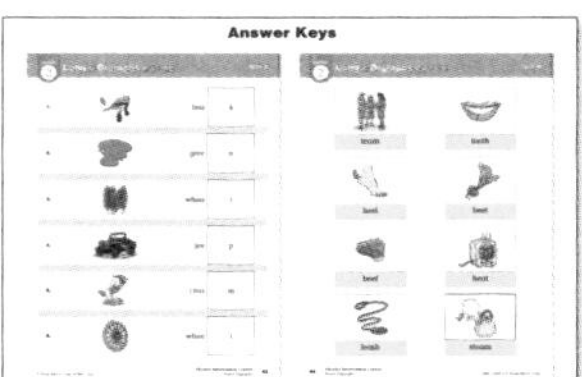

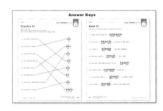

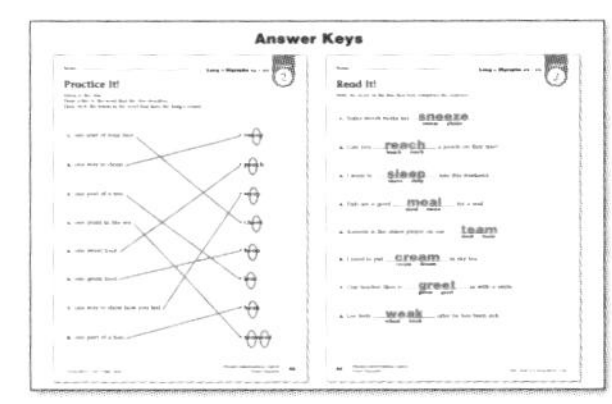
Answer Keys

For the Student

front (Mat A)

back (Mat B)

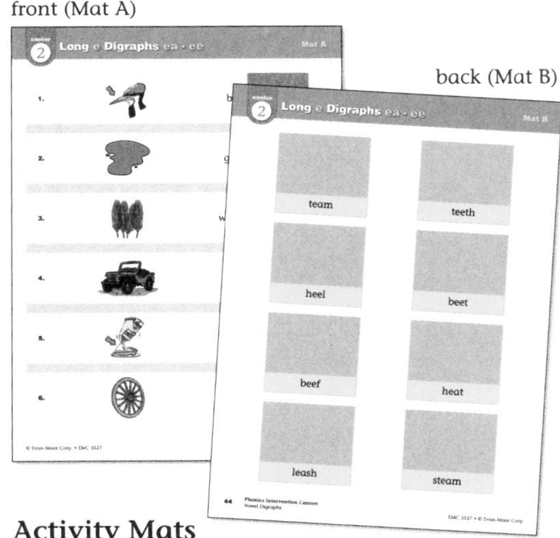

Activity Mats

Task Cards

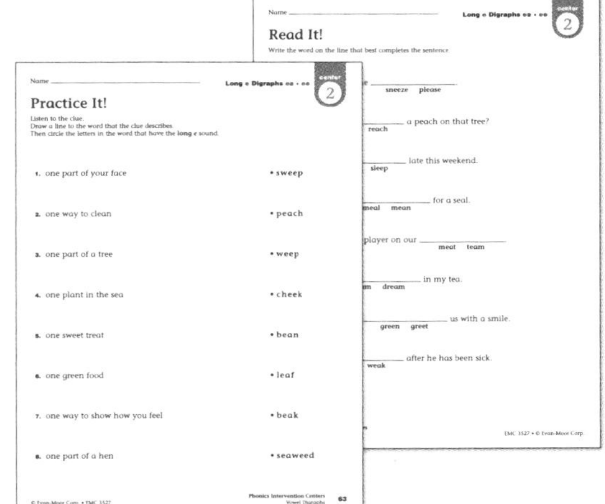

Read It!
Practice It!
1. one part of your face
2. one way to clean
3. one part of a tree
4. one plant in the sea
5. one sweet treat
6. one green food
7. one way to show how you feel
8. one part of a hen
• sweep
• peach
• weep
• cheek
• bean
• leaf
• beak
• seaweed

Practice and Assessment Activities

Long e Digraphs ea • ee

Objectives: Students will learn that the vowel pairs ***ea*** and ***ee*** can stand for the **long *e*** sound. Students will blend individual sounds into words. Students will read and understand words spelled with the ***ea*** or ***ee*** digraph.

Students' Prior Knowledge: Students know the sound of **long *e*** and can distinguish medial and final sounds.

Introducing the Digraphs *ea* and *ee*

1. Building Phonemic Awareness

Show the front of each sound card and point to the digraph ***ea*** or ***ee*** as you talk about it. Say:

*The vowels **e** and **a** together in a word usually stand for the **long e** sound: /ē/. You can hear /ē/ in the word **heat**. Double **e** in a word also has the **long e** sound. You can hear /ē/ in the word **feed**.*

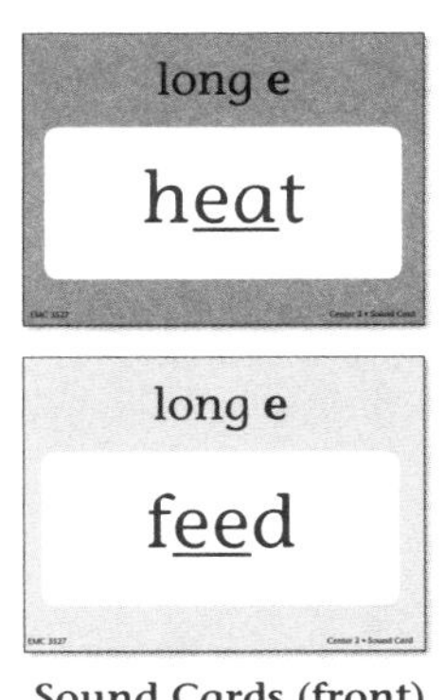

Sound Cards (front)

Point to the digraph in each word again. Say the names of the letters and ask students to tell you the sound that the letters stand for. (/ē/) Then have students listen for the **long *e*** sound in the words below. Say:

*Listen carefully to the words I'm going to say. Each word has the **long e** sound in it. Say **middle** or **end** to tell where you hear /ē/ in the word.*

tea (end)	**kneel** (middle)	**tease** (middle)	**lean** (middle)	**agree** (end)
glee (end)	**beast** (middle)	**creep** (middle)	**dream** (middle)	**bleed** (middle)

Read each word again, and have students repeat it. If needed, stretch the **long *e*** sound slightly to help students hear it.

2. Oral Blending

Model oral blending to help students hear the distinct sounds in a word. Say:

*I am going to say a word, sound by sound. Listen: /**d**/ /ē/ /**p**/. The word is **deep**. Now I am going to say some other words, sound by sound. You blend the sounds for each word and tell me what the word is. Listen:*

/**w**/ /ē/ /**d**/ (weed)	/**fr**/ /ē/ (free)	/**sl**/ /ē/ /**v**/ (sleeve)
/**l**/ /ē/ /**p**/ (leap)	/**m**/ /ē/ /**t**/ (meat)	/**gr**/ /ē/ /**s**/ (grease)

3. Visual Blending

Model visual blending, using the words listed on the back of each sound card. Begin by pointing to the first word and reading it aloud. Then run your finger under the letters as you blend the sounds to read the word again. Repeat this process for the remaining words. For the words **sleeve** and **grease**, stop before the final ***e*** and remind students that the ***e*** has no sound. Next, have students blend the sounds themselves as you run your finger under each letter.

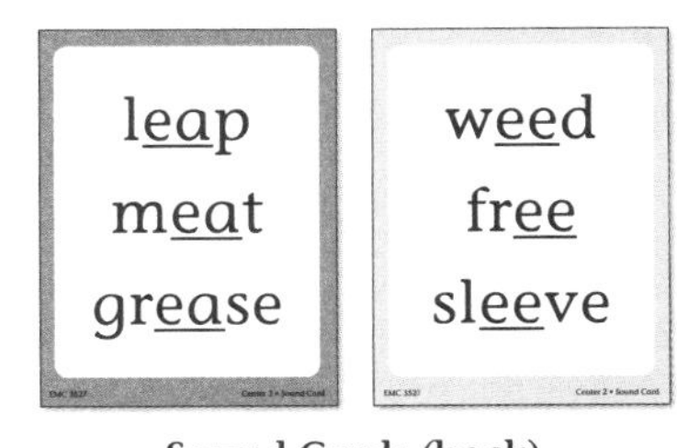

Sound Cards (back)

Leading the Center Activities

1. Read, Discriminate, and Identify

Ask students to tell you the sound they should say for ***ea*** or ***ee***. (/ē/) Then give each student Mat A and a set of task cards. Explain that each word on the mat is missing a letter at the end of it. Then say:

> *Look at the picture in row 1. It shows a bird's beak. What sound do you hear at the end of* ***beak****?* (/k/) *What letter says* **/k/***?* (k) *Place the card with the letter* **k** *on it in the box. Now let's blend the sounds and read the word:* **/b/ /ē/ /k/ beak***. Which two letters in* ***beak*** *say /ē/?* (e-a)

Repeat this process with the pictures in the remaining rows.

2. Read and Understand

Have students turn over their mats. Distribute the task cards for Mat B. Then say:

> *Look at the word in the first box on the mat. Let's blend the sounds to read the word:* **/t/ /ē/ /m/** ***team****. Which two letters in* ***team*** *say /ē/?* (e-a) *Now place the card that shows a picture of a team above the word.*

Repeat this process with the words in the remaining boxes.

3. Practice the Skill

Distribute the Practice It! activity (page 63) to students and read the directions aloud. Have students read the words listed on the right side of the page. Tell them to blend the sounds as they read each word. Then say:

> *Listen to the first clue:* ***one part of your face****. Which word does this clue describe?* (cheek) *Now draw a line to the word* ***cheek*** *and circle the letters in* ***cheek*** *that say /ē/.* (ee)

Repeat this process for the remaining clues, or if your students are capable, have them complete the activity with a partner. Give help when needed. Then go over the answers as a group.

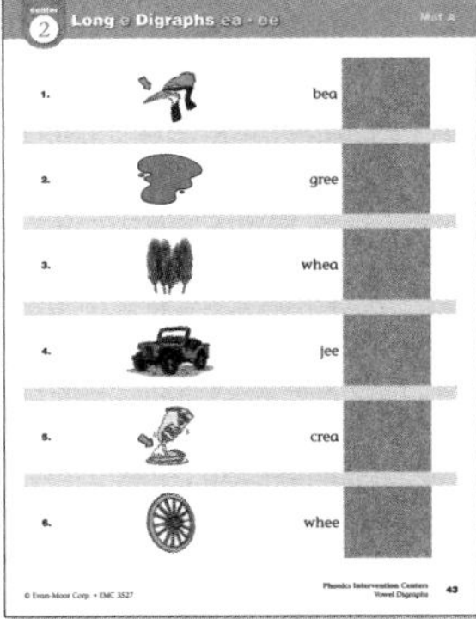

Mat A

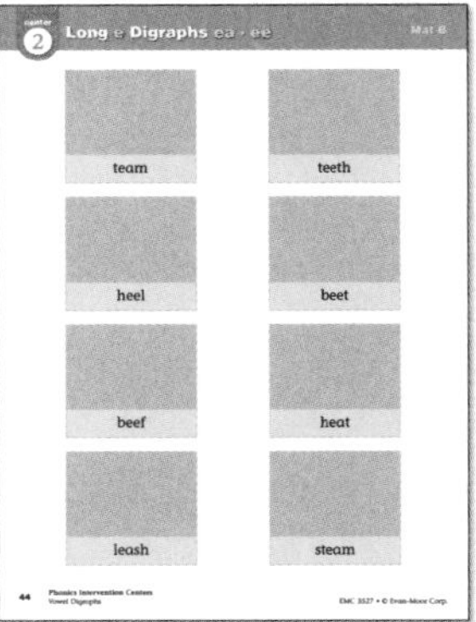

Mat B

Name ______ Long e Digraphs ea • ee

Practice It!

Listen to the clue.
Draw a line to the word that the clue describes.
Then circle the letters in the word that have the **long e** sound.

1. one part of your face • **sweep**
2. one way to clean • **peach**
3. one part of a tree • **weep**
4. one plant in the sea • **cheek**
5. one sweet treat • **bean**
6. one green food • **leaf**
7. one way to show how you feel • **beak**
8. one part of a hen • **seaweed**

© Evan-Moor Corp. • EMC 3527 Phonics Intervention Centers Vowel Digraphs 63

Page 63

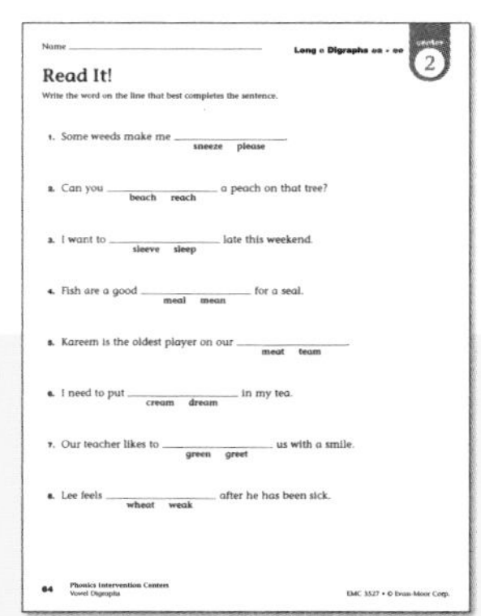

Name ______ Long e Digraphs ea • ee

Read It!

Write the word on the line that best completes the sentence.

1. Some weeds make me ______. **sneeze please**
2. Can you ______ a peach on that tree? **beach reach**
3. I want to ______ late this weekend. **sleeve sleep**
4. Fish are a good ______ for a seal. **meal mean**
5. Kareem is the oldest player on our ______. **meat team**
6. I need to put ______ in my tea. **cream dream**
7. Our teacher likes to ______ us with a smile. **green greet**
8. Lee feels ______ after he has been sick. **wheat weak**

64 Phonics Intervention Centers Vowel Digraphs EMC 3527 • © Evan-Moor Corp.

Page 64

Apply and Assess

After the lesson, distribute the Read It! activity (page 64) to students and read the directions aloud. Have students complete the activity independently. Then listen to them read the sentences. Use the results as an informal assessment of students' skill mastery.

long e

heat

Center 2 • Sound Card

EMC 3527

long e

feed

Center 2 • Sound Card

EMC 3527

Answer Keys

center 2 **Long e Digraphs ea • ee** Mat A

1.		bea	k
2.		gree	n
3.		whea	t
4.		jee	p
5.		crea	m
6.		whee	l

© Evan-Moor Corp. • EMC 3527 Phonics Intervention Centers Vowel Digraphs 43

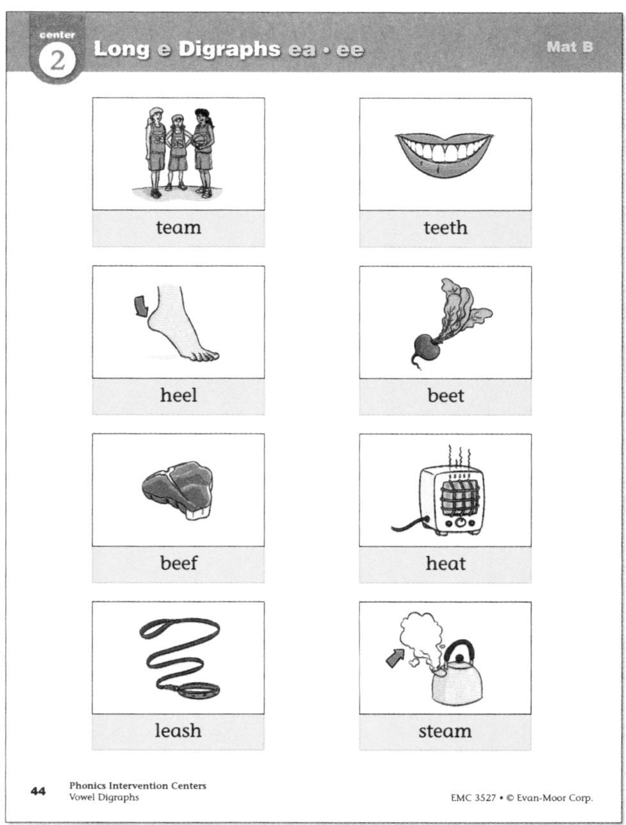
center 2 **Long e Digraphs ea • ee** Mat B

team	teeth
heel	beet
beef	heat
leash	steam

44 Phonics Intervention Centers Vowel Digraphs EMC 3527 • © Evan-Moor Corp.

weed

free

sleeve

EMC 3527 Center 2 • Sound Card

leap

meat

grease

EMC 3527 Center 2 • Sound Card

Answer Keys

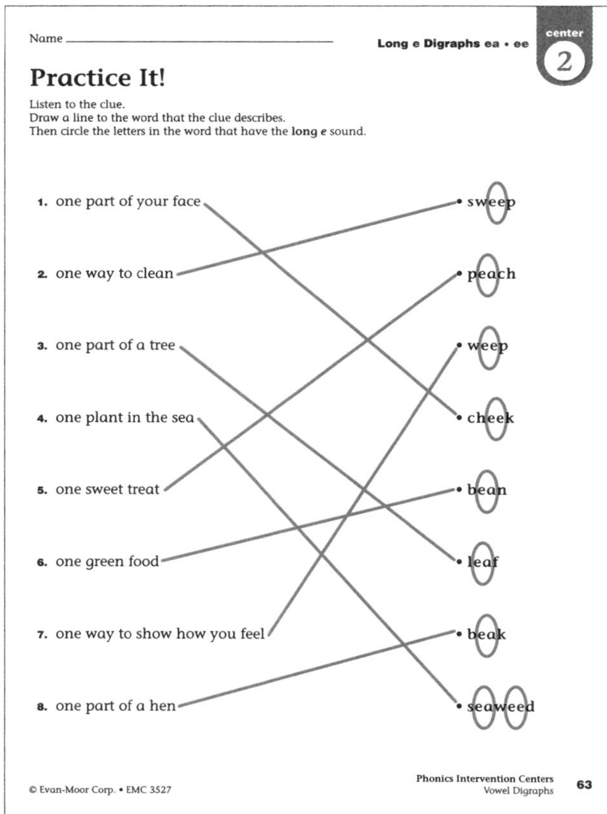

Name ______________________ Long e Digraphs ea • ee center 2

Practice It!

Listen to the clue.
Draw a line to the word that the clue describes.
Then circle the letters in the word that have the **long *e*** sound.

1. one part of your face
2. one way to clean
3. one part of a tree
4. one plant in the sea
5. one sweet treat
6. one green food
7. one way to show how you feel
8. one part of a hen

- sweep
- peach
- weep
- cheek
- bean
- leaf
- beak
- seaweed

© Evan-Moor Corp. • EMC 3527 Phonics Intervention Centers Vowel Digraphs 63

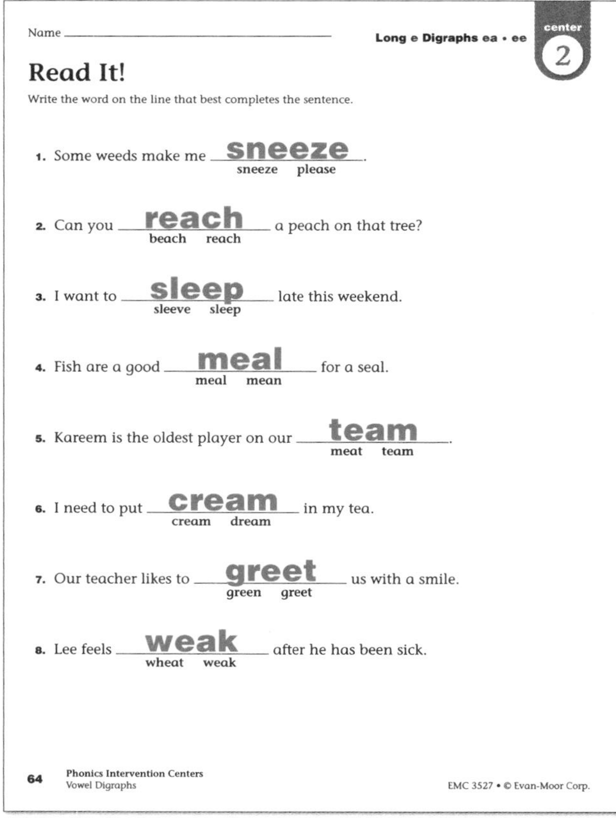

Name ______________________ Long e Digraphs ea • ee center 2

Read It!

Write the word on the line that best completes the sentence.

1. Some weeds make me **sneeze**. (sneeze please)
2. Can you **reach** a peach on that tree? (beach reach)
3. I want to **sleep** late this weekend. (sleeve sleep)
4. Fish are a good **meal** for a seal. (meal mean)
5. Kareem is the oldest player on our **team**. (meat team)
6. I need to put **cream** in my tea. (cream dream)
7. Our teacher likes to **greet** us with a smile. (green greet)
8. Lee feels **weak** after he has been sick. (wheat weak)

64 Phonics Intervention Centers Vowel Digraphs EMC 3527 • © Evan-Moor Corp.

Long e Digraphs ea • ee

Mat A

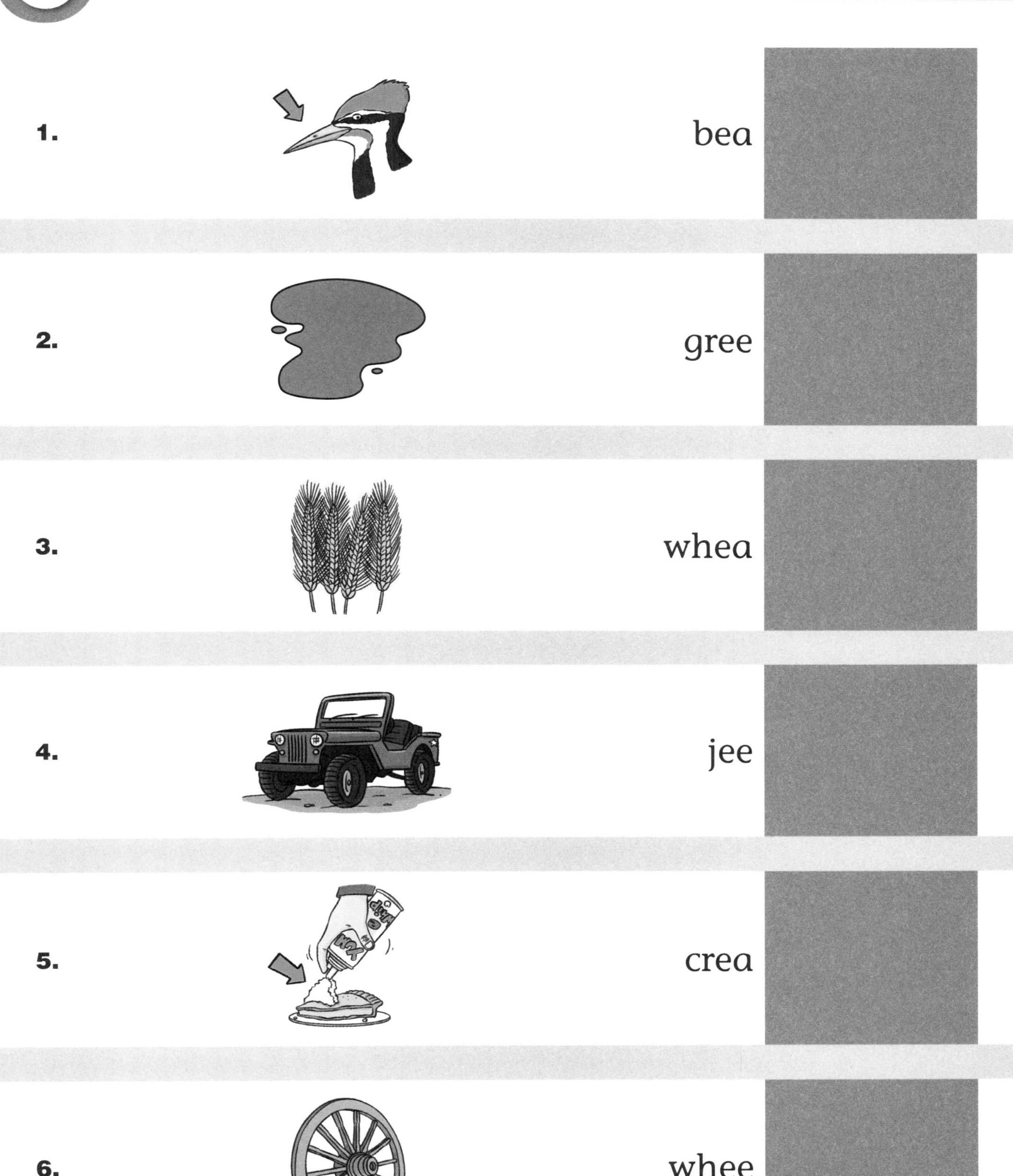

Long e Digraphs ea • ee

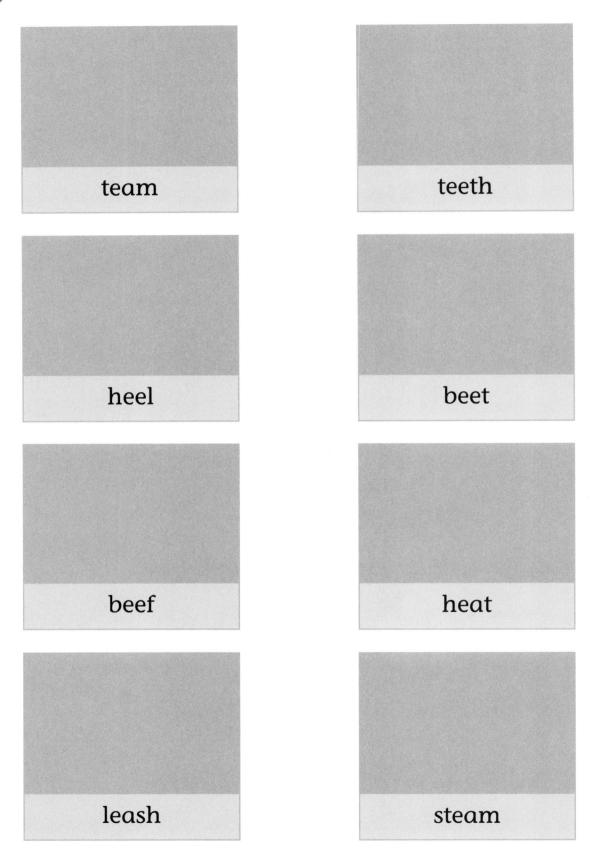

team

teeth

heel

beet

beef

heat

leash

steam

Long e Digraphs ea • ee

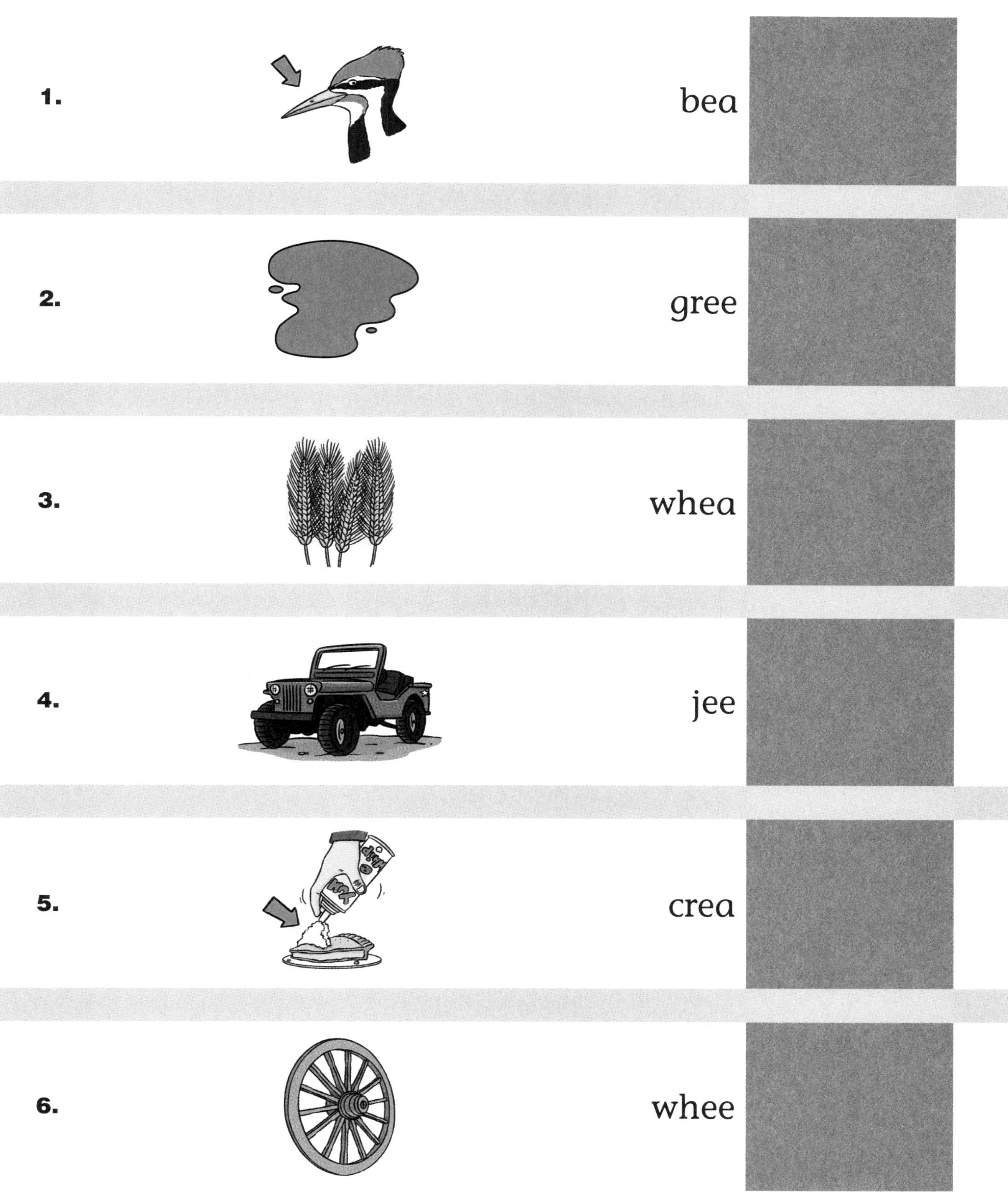

Long e Digraphs ea • ee

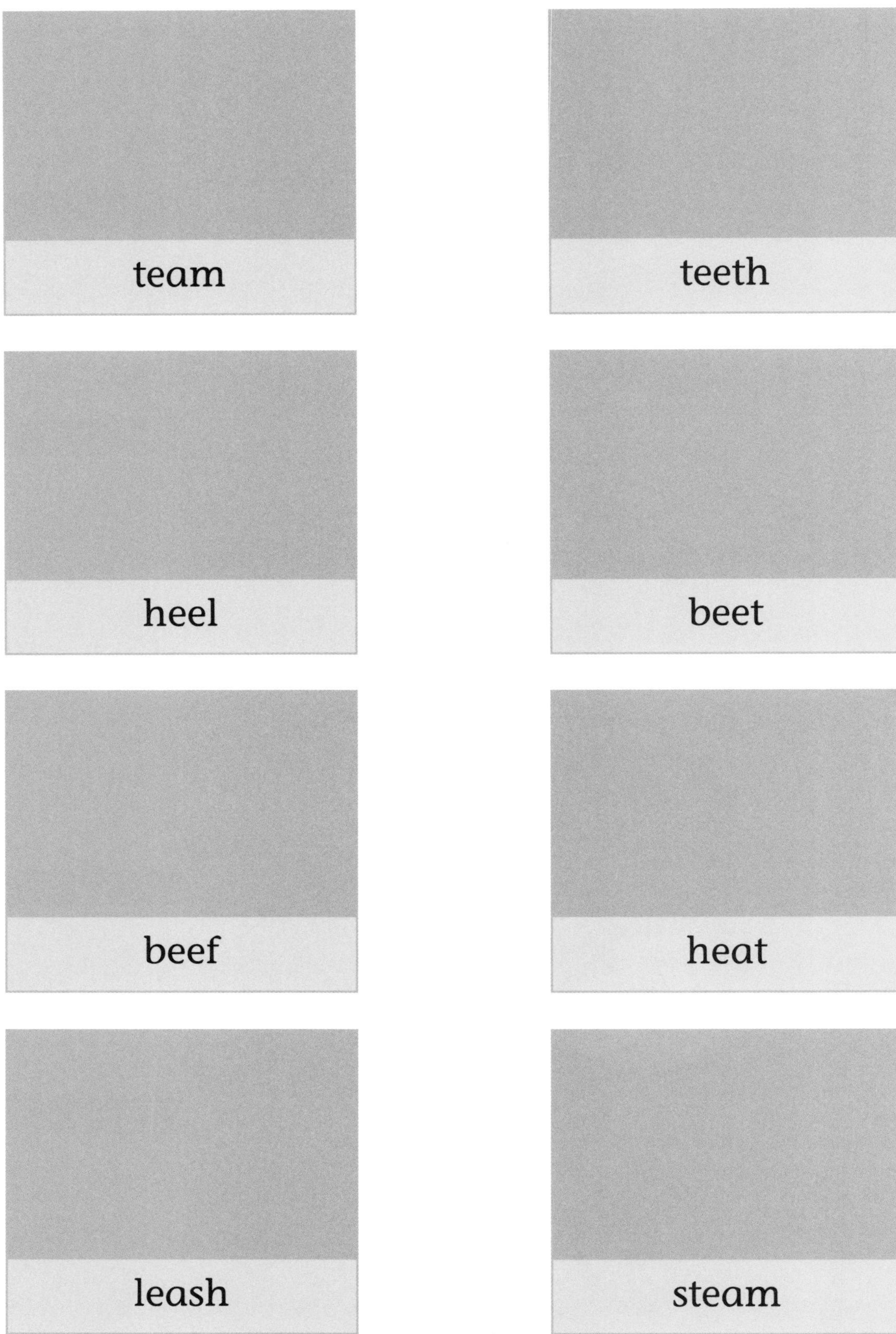

Long e Digraphs ea • ee

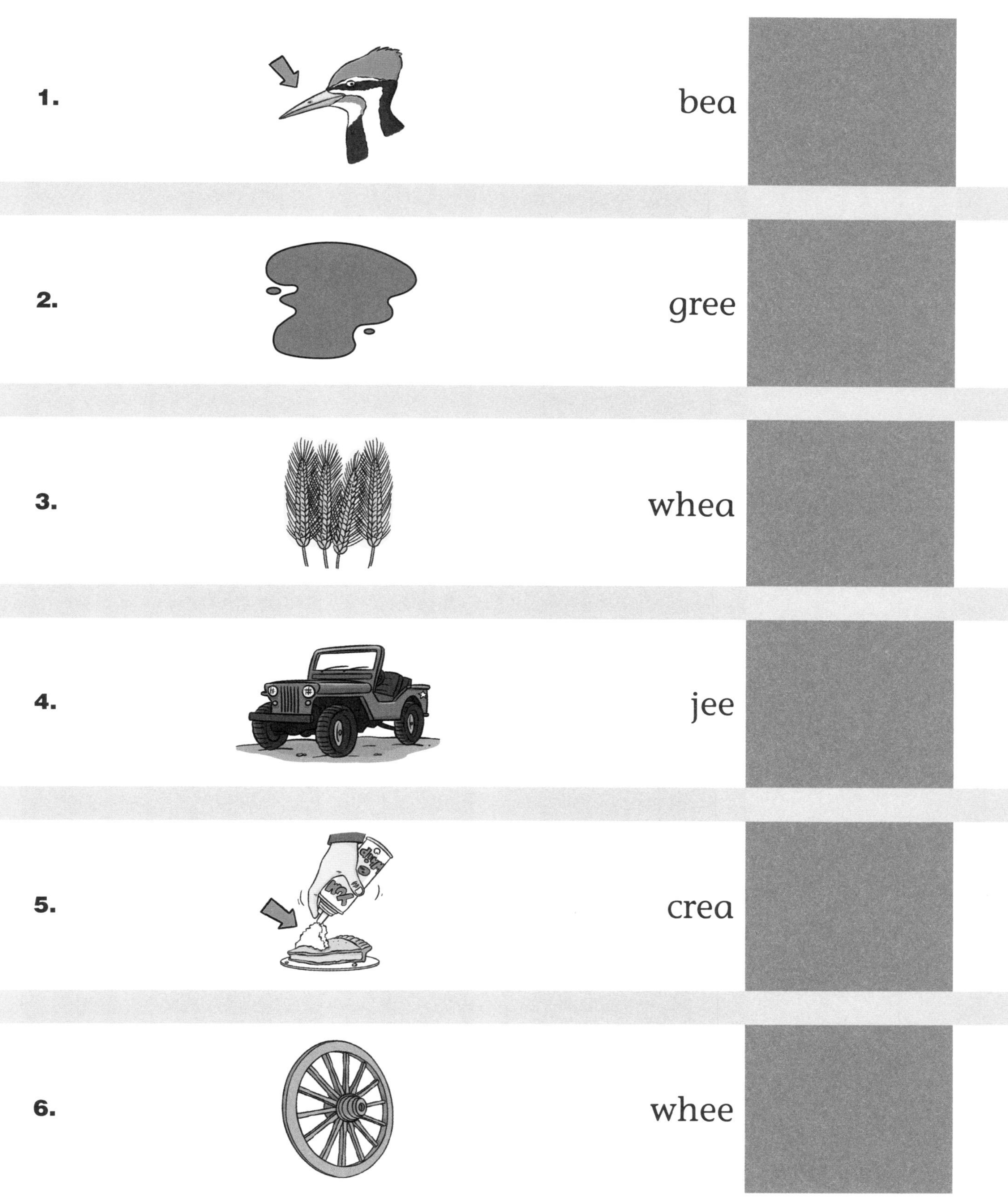

Long e Digraphs ea • ee

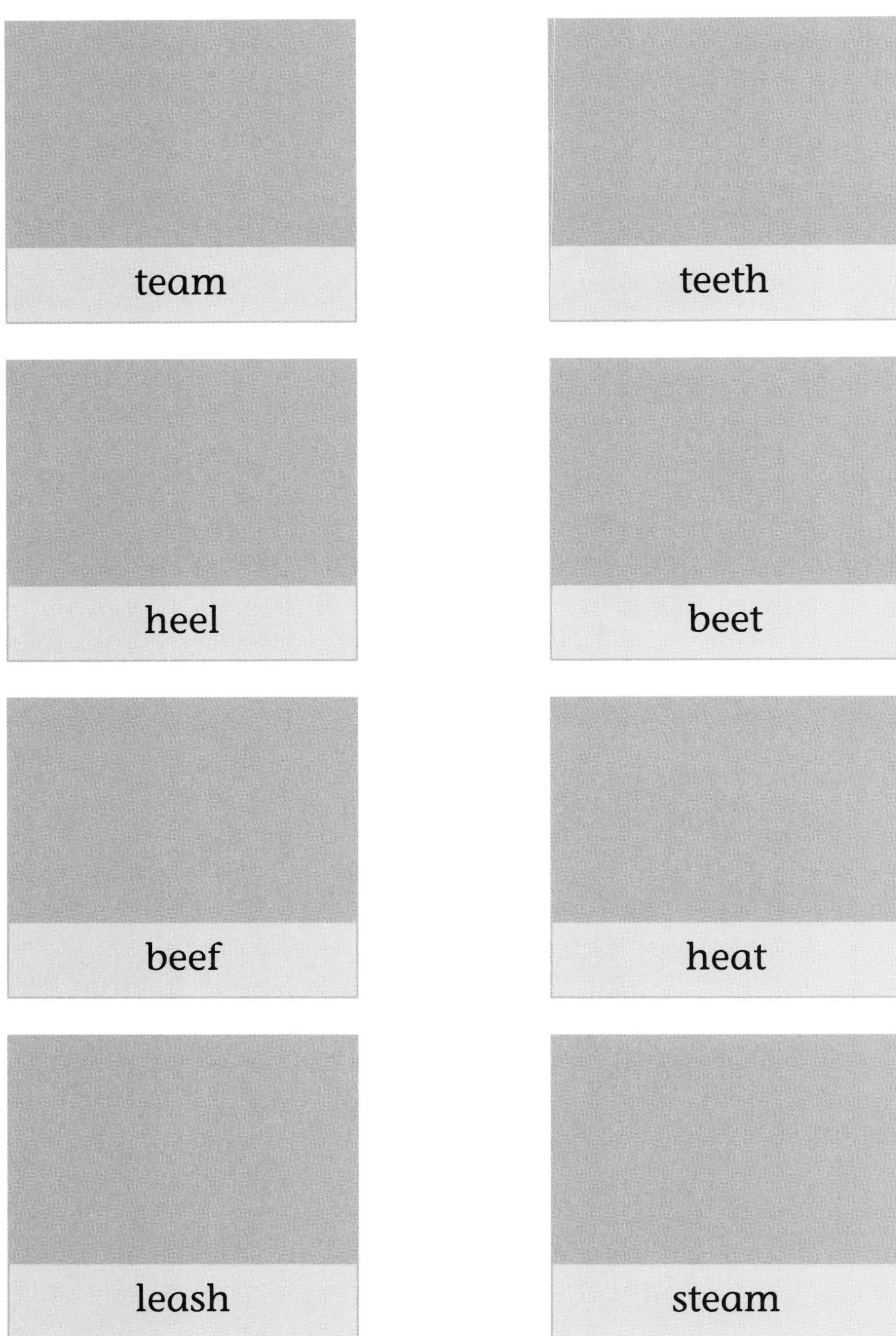

Long e Digraphs ea • ee

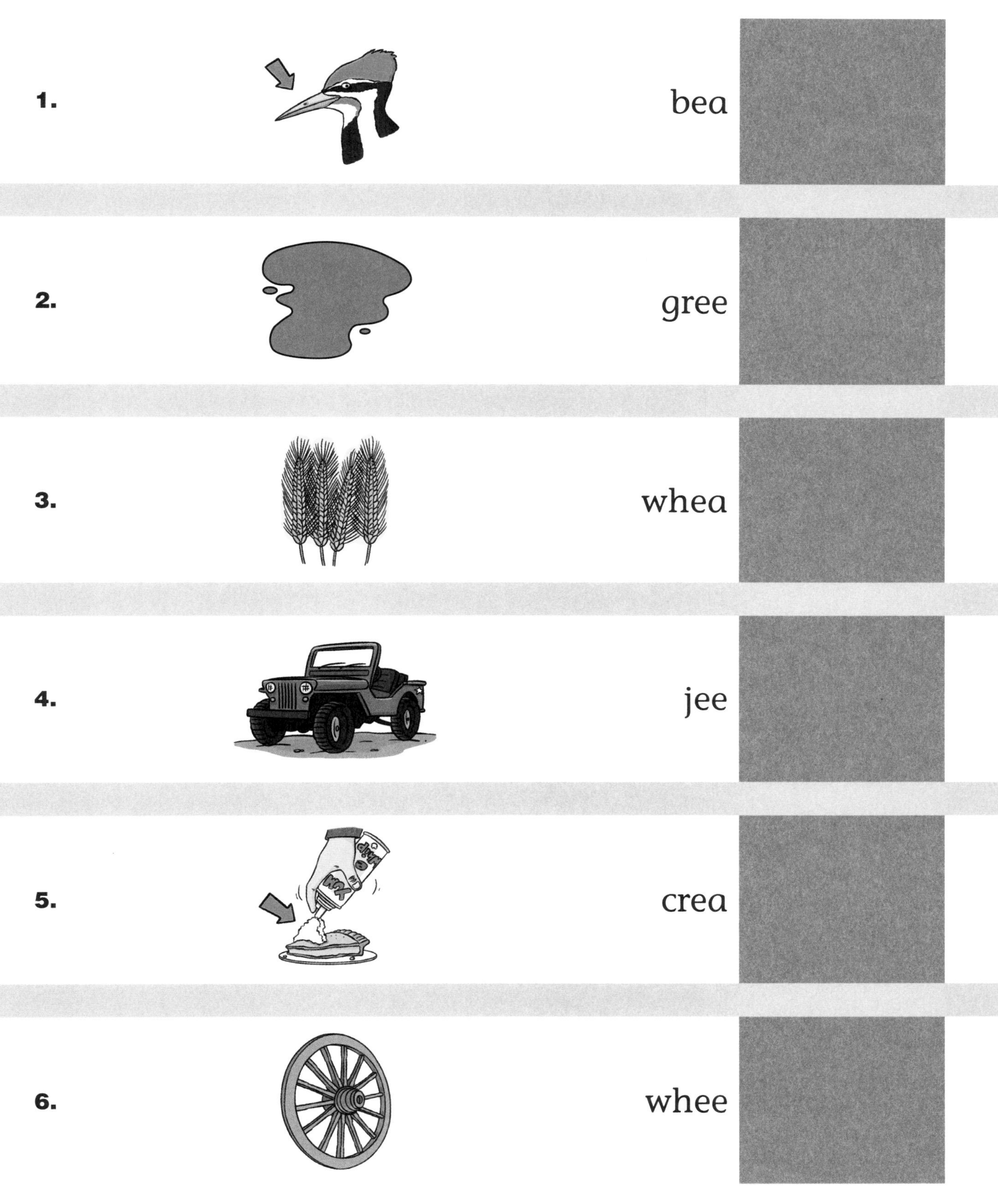

Long e Digraphs ea • ee

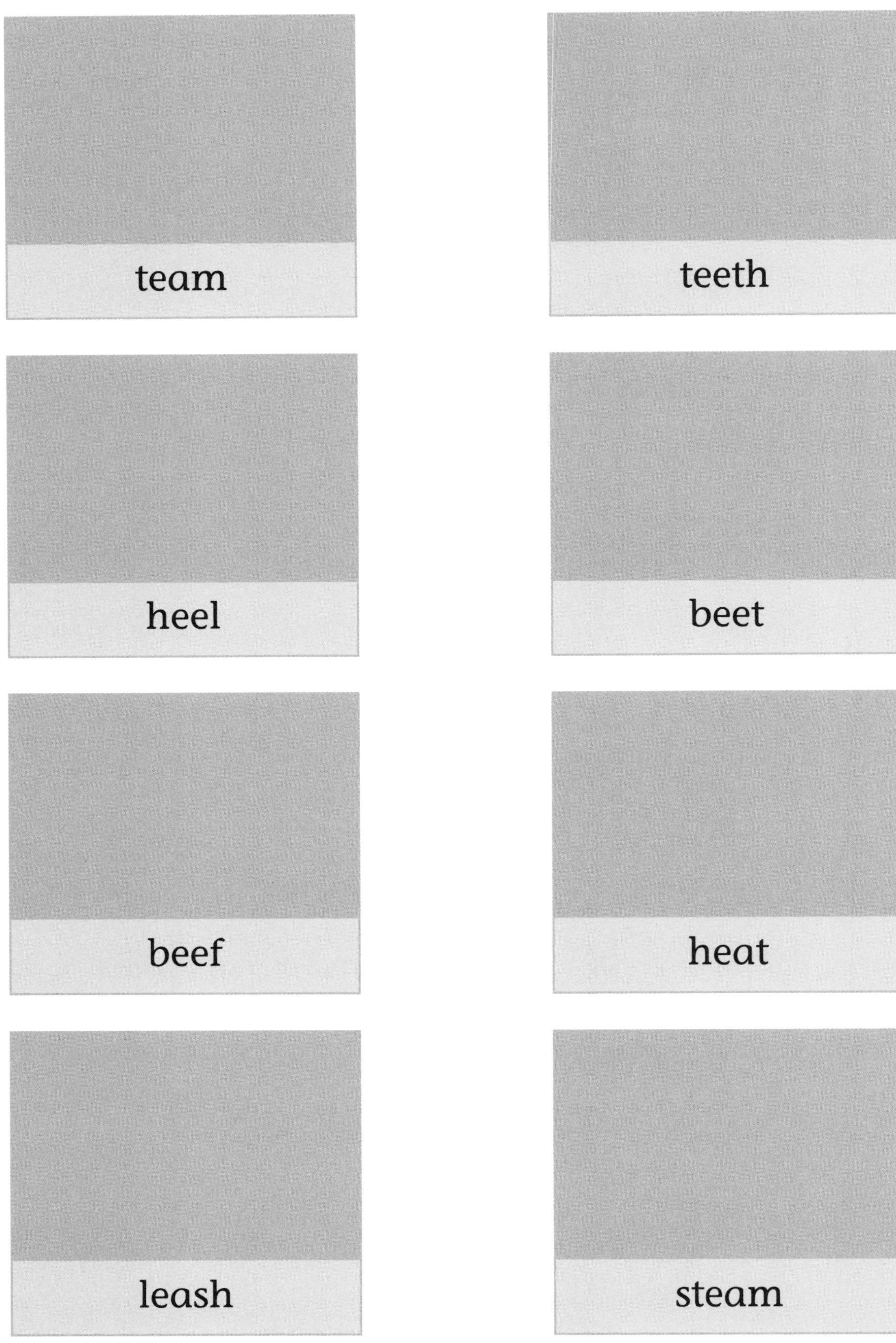

Long e Digraphs ea • ee

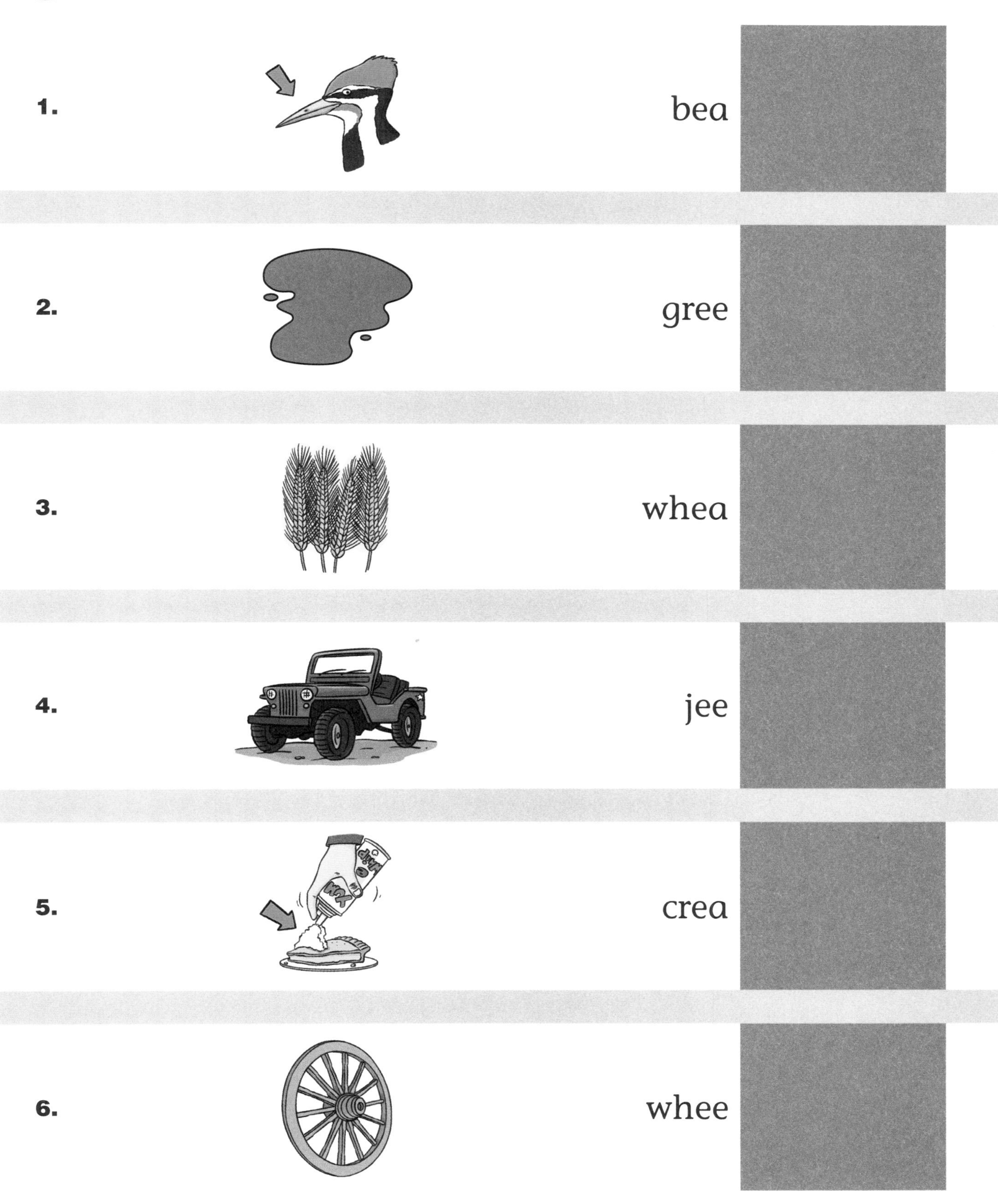

Long e Digraphs ea • ee

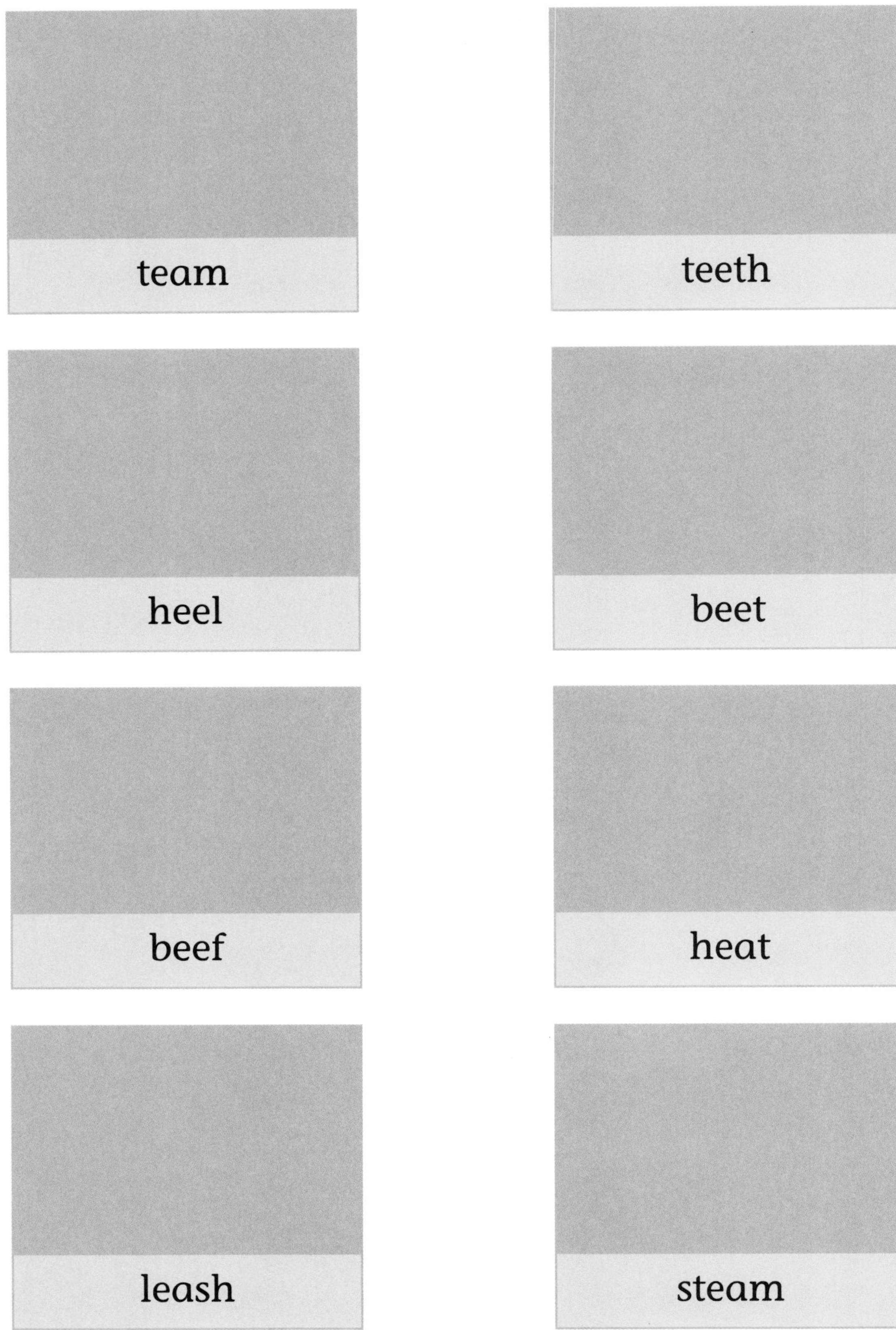

center 2

Long e Digraphs ea • ee

Mat A

1. 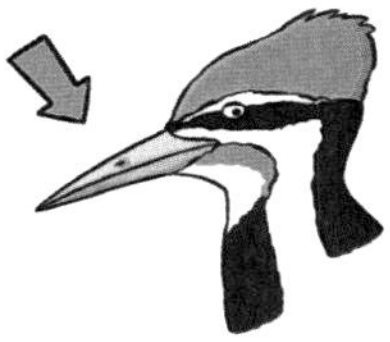 bea

2. 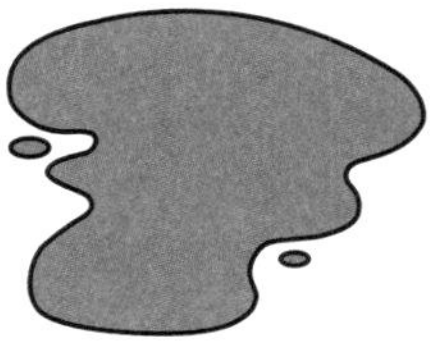 gree

3. 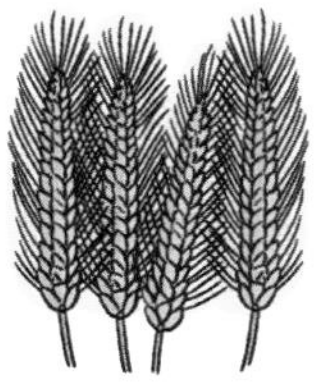 whea

4. 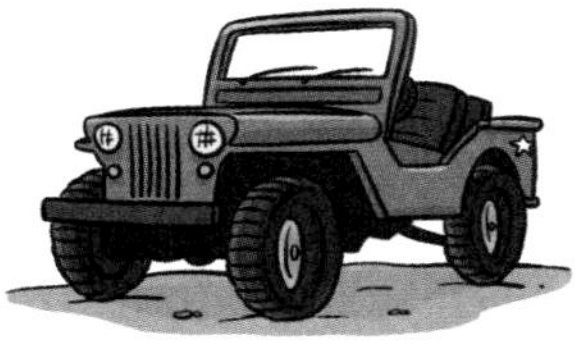 jee

5. 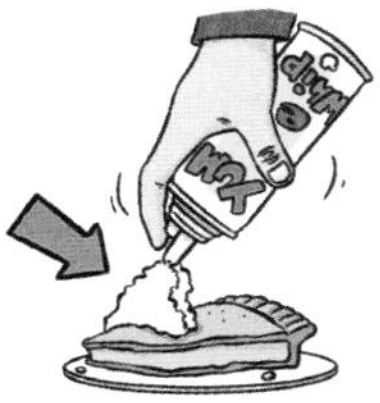 crea

6. 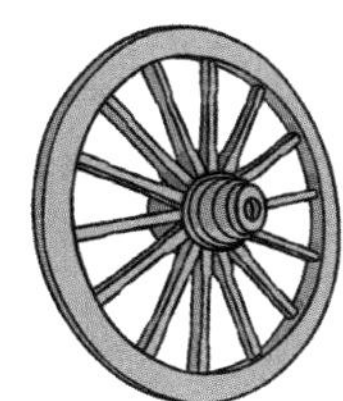 whee 

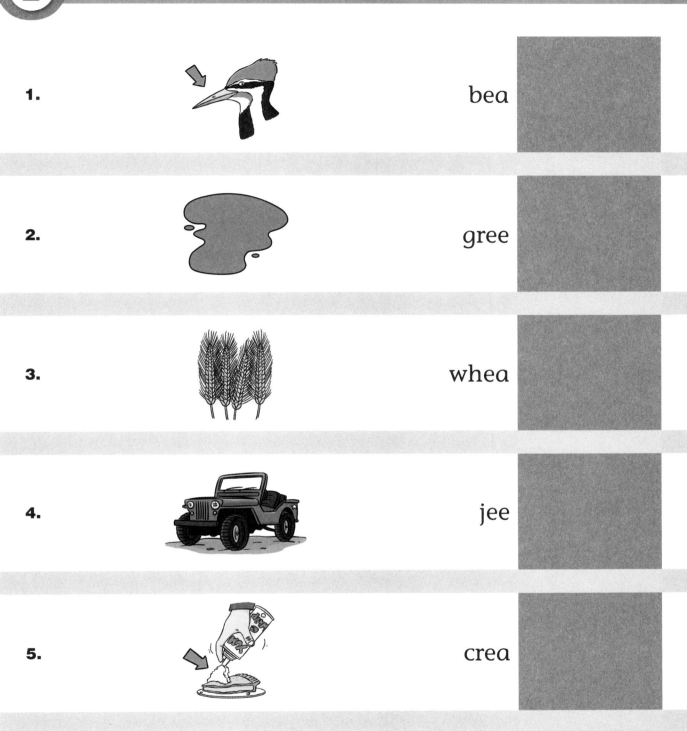

Long e Digraphs ea • ee

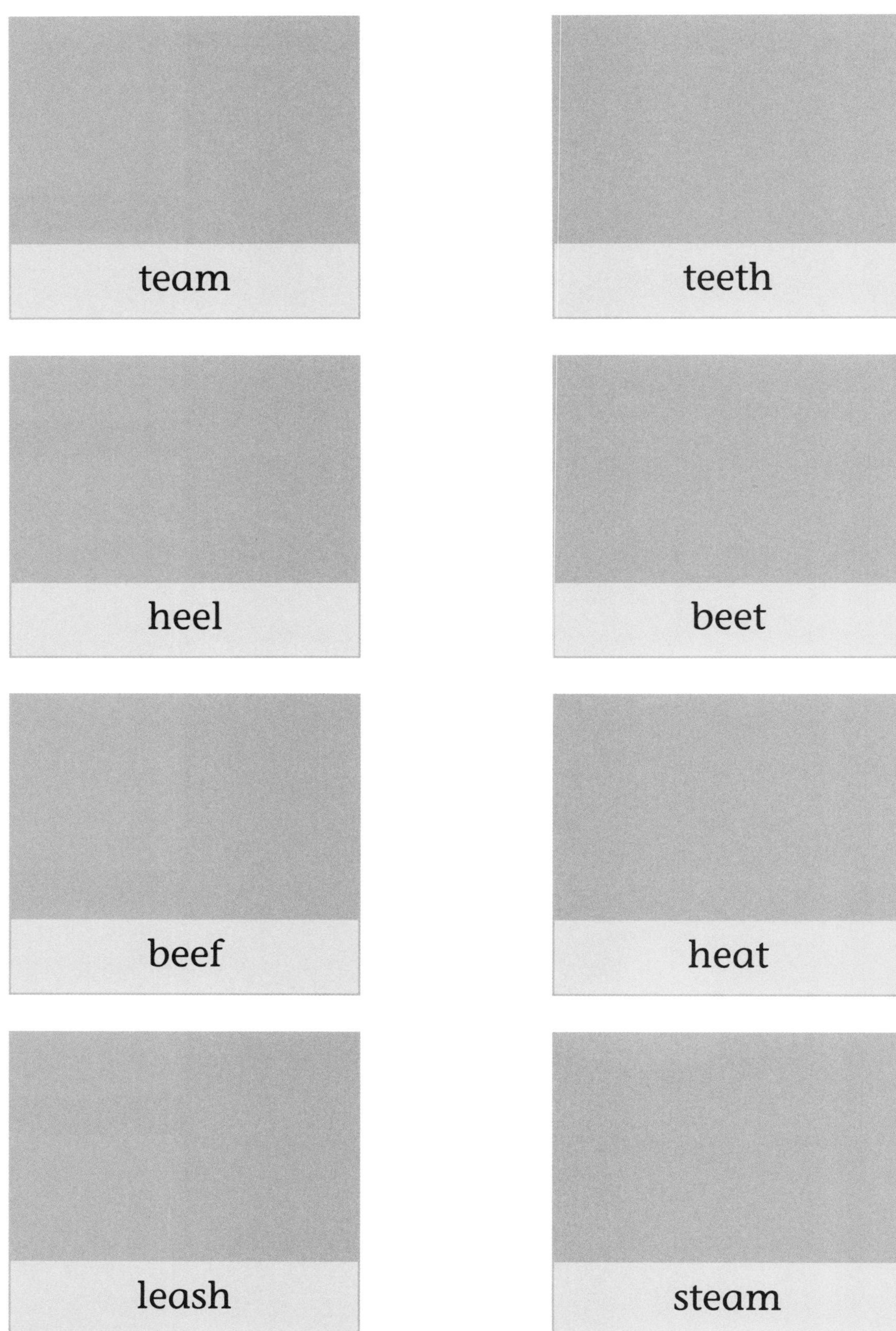

Task Cards

Mat A

Student 6	k	l	m	n	p	t
Student 5	k	l	m	n	p	t
Student 4	k	l	m	n	p	t
Student 3	k	l	m	n	p	t
Student 2	k	l	m	n	p	t
Student 1	k	l	m	n	p	t

Task Cards

Student 6
EMC 3527
Center 2 • Mat A

Student 5
EMC 3527
Center 2 • Mat A

Student 4
EMC 3527
Center 2 • Mat A

Student 3
EMC 3527
Center 2 • Mat A

Student 2
EMC 3527
Center 2 • Mat A

Student 1
EMC 3527
Center 2 • Mat A

Student 6
EMC 3527
Center 2 • Mat A

Student 5
EMC 3527
Center 2 • Mat A

Student 4
EMC 3527
Center 2 • Mat A

Student 3
EMC 3527
Center 2 • Mat A

Student 2
EMC 3527
Center 2 • Mat A

Student 1
EMC 3527
Center 2 • Mat A

Student 6
EMC 3527
Center 2 • Mat A

Student 5
EMC 3527
Center 2 • Mat A

Student 4
EMC 3527
Center 2 • Mat A

Student 3
EMC 3527
Center 2 • Mat A

Student 2
EMC 3527
Center 2 • Mat A

Student 1
EMC 3527
Center 2 • Mat A

Student 6
EMC 3527
Center 2 • Mat A

Student 5
EMC 3527
Center 2 • Mat A

Student 4
EMC 3527
Center 2 • Mat A

Student 3
EMC 3527
Center 2 • Mat A

Student 2
EMC 3527
Center 2 • Mat A

Student 1
EMC 3527
Center 2 • Mat A

Student 6
EMC 3527
Center 2 • Mat A

Student 5
EMC 3527
Center 2 • Mat A

Student 4
EMC 3527
Center 2 • Mat A

Student 3
EMC 3527
Center 2 • Mat A

Student 2
EMC 3527
Center 2 • Mat A

Student 1
EMC 3527
Center 2 • Mat A

Student 6
EMC 3527
Center 2 • Mat A

Student 5
EMC 3527
Center 2 • Mat A

Student 4
EMC 3527
Center 2 • Mat A

Student 3
EMC 3527
Center 2 • Mat A

Student 2
EMC 3527
Center 2 • Mat A

Student 1
EMC 3527
Center 2 • Mat A

Student 2

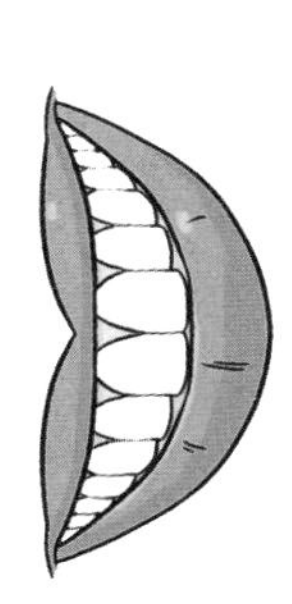

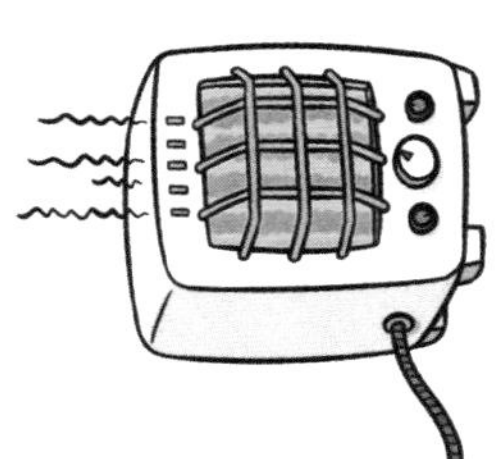

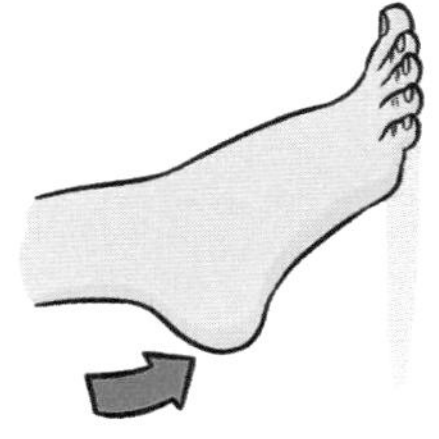
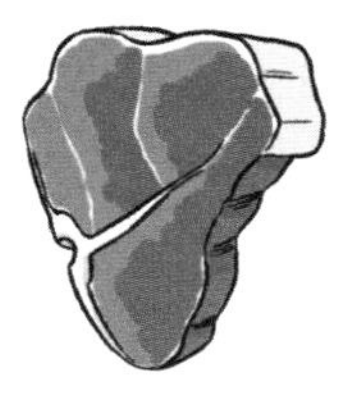

Student 1

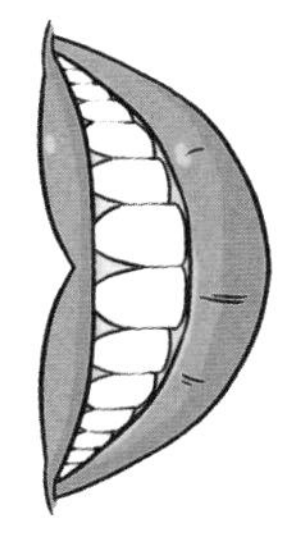

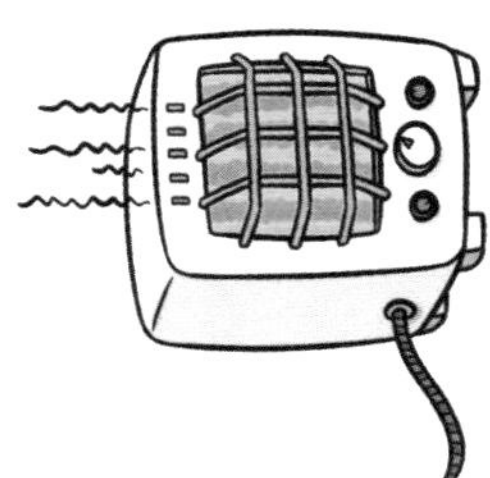

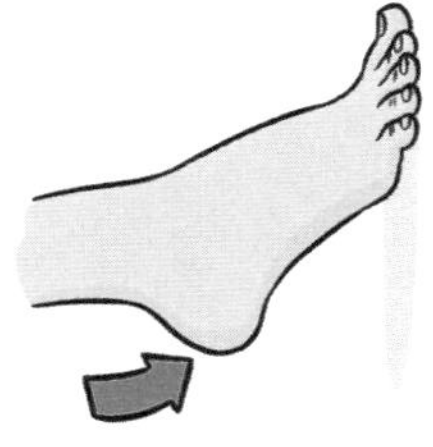
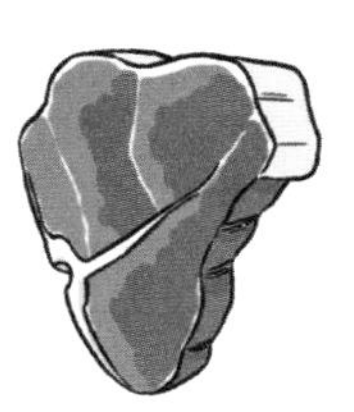

Task Cards

Mat B

Student 2

EMC 3527 • Center 2 • Mat B

Student 2

EMC 3527 • Center 2 • Mat B

Student 2

EMC 3527 • Center 2 • Mat B

Student 2

EMC 3527 • Center 2 • Mat B

Student 2

EMC 3527 • Center 2 • Mat B

Student 2

EMC 3527 • Center 2 • Mat B

Student 2

EMC 3527 • Center 2 • Mat B

Student 2

EMC 3527 • Center 2 • Mat B

Student 1

EMC 3527 • Center 2 • Mat B

Student 1

EMC 3527 • Center 2 • Mat B

Student 1

EMC 3527 • Center 2 • Mat B

Student 1

EMC 3527 • Center 2 • Mat B

Student 1

EMC 3527 • Center 2 • Mat B

Student 1

EMC 3527 • Center 2 • Mat B

Student 1

EMC 3527 • Center 2 • Mat B

Student 1

EMC 3527 • Center 2 • Mat B

Task Cards

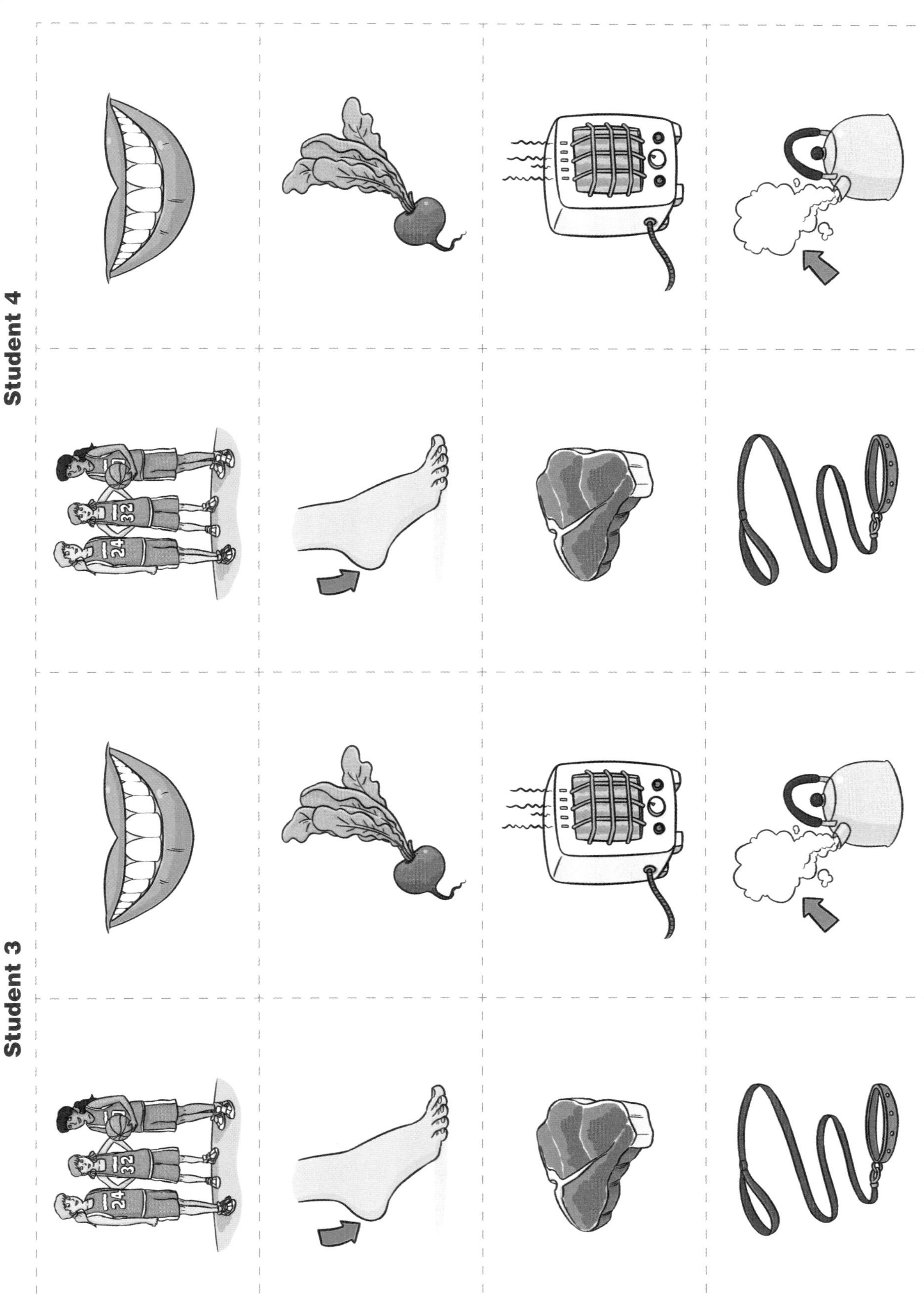

Task Cards

Student 4
EMC 3527 • Center 2 • Mat B

Student 4
EMC 3527 • Center 2 • Mat B

Student 4
EMC 3527 • Center 2 • Mat B

Student 4
EMC 3527 • Center 2 • Mat B

Student 4
EMC 3527 • Center 2 • Mat B

Student 4
EMC 3527 • Center 2 • Mat B

Student 4
EMC 3527 • Center 2 • Mat B

Student 4
EMC 3527 • Center 2 • Mat B

Student 3
EMC 3527 • Center 2 • Mat B

Student 3
EMC 3527 • Center 2 • Mat B

Student 3
EMC 3527 • Center 2 • Mat B

Student 3
EMC 3527 • Center 2 • Mat B

Student 3
EMC 3527 • Center 2 • Mat B

Student 3
EMC 3527 • Center 2 • Mat B

Student 3
EMC 3527 • Center 2 • Mat B

Student 3
EMC 3527 • Center 2 • Mat B

Task Cards

Mat B

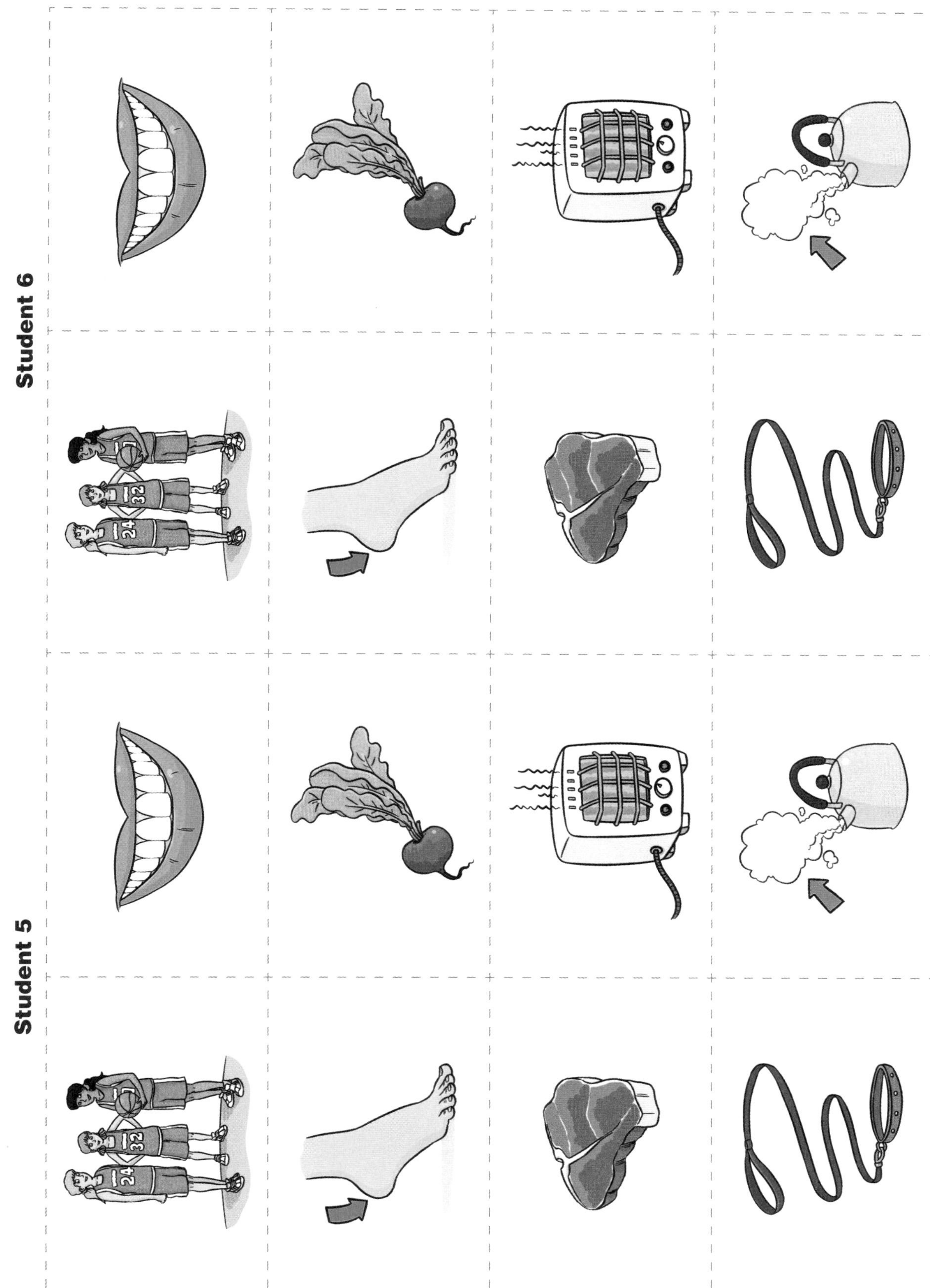

Task Cards

Student 6
EMC 3527 • Center 2 • Mat B

Student 6
EMC 3527 • Center 2 • Mat B

Student 6
EMC 3527 • Center 2 • Mat B

Student 6
EMC 3527 • Center 2 • Mat B

Student 6
EMC 3527 • Center 2 • Mat B

Student 6
EMC 3527 • Center 2 • Mat B

Student 6
EMC 3527 • Center 2 • Mat B

Student 6
EMC 3527 • Center 2 • Mat B

Student 5
EMC 3527 • Center 2 • Mat B

Student 5
EMC 3527 • Center 2 • Mat B

Student 5
EMC 3527 • Center 2 • Mat B

Student 5
EMC 3527 • Center 2 • Mat B

Student 5
EMC 3527 • Center 2 • Mat B

Student 5
EMC 3527 • Center 2 • Mat B

Student 5
EMC 3527 • Center 2 • Mat B

Student 5
EMC 3527 • Center 2 • Mat B

Name ______________________

Practice It!

Listen to the clue.
Draw a line to the word that the clue describes.
Then circle the letters in the word that have the **long *e*** sound.

1. one part of your face	• sweep
2. one way to clean	• peach
3. one part of a tree	• weep
4. one plant in the sea	• cheek
5. one sweet treat	• bean
6. one green food	• leaf
7. one way to show how you feel	• beak
8. one part of a hen	• seaweed

Read It!

Write the word on the line that best completes the sentence.

1. Some weeds make me ________________.
   sneeze **please**

2. Can you ________________ a peach on that tree?
   beach **reach**

3. I want to ________________ late this weekend.
   sleeve **sleep**

4. Fish are a good ________________ for a seal.
   meal **mean**

5. Kareem is the oldest player on our ________________.
   meat **team**

6. I need to put ________________ in my tea.
   cream **dream**

7. Our teacher likes to ________________ us with a smile.
   green **greet**

8. Lee feels ________________ after he has been sick.
   wheat **weak**

center 3

INTERMEDIATE

Long i Digraphs ie · igh

For the Teacher

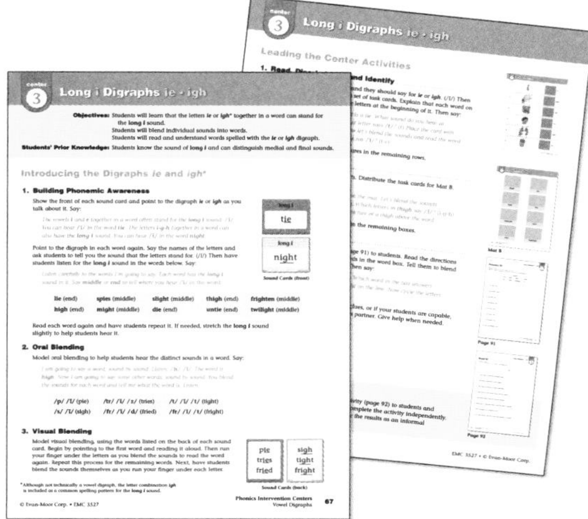

Lesson Plan

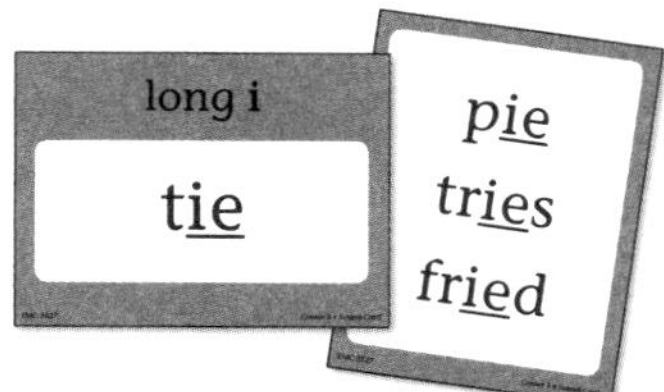

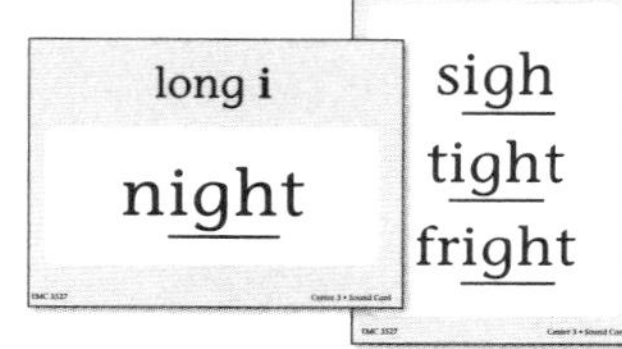

Sound Cards

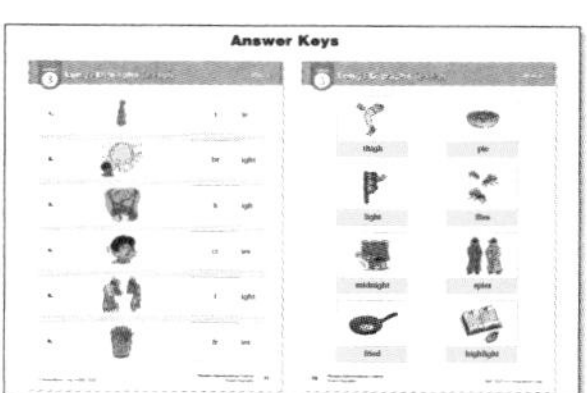

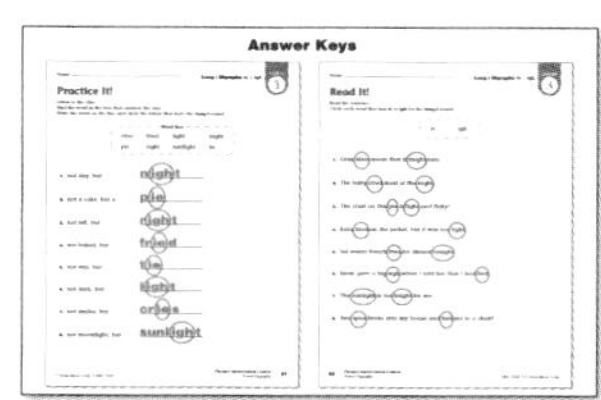

Answer Keys

For the Student

front (Mat A)

back (Mat B)

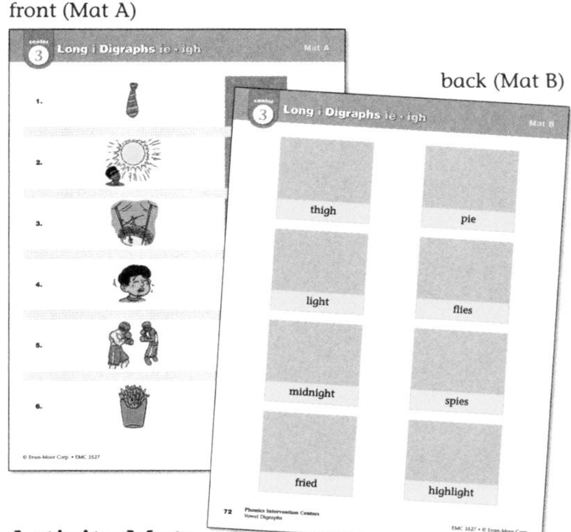

Activity Mats

Task Cards

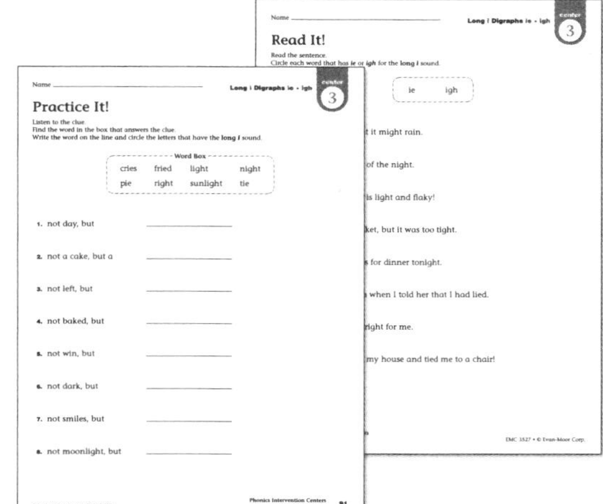

Practice and Assessment Activities

center

3 Long i Digraphs ie • igh

Objectives: Students will learn that the letters ***ie*** or ***igh**** together in a word can stand for the **long *i*** sound.
Students will blend individual sounds into words.
Students will read and understand words spelled with the ***ie*** or ***igh*** digraph.

Students' Prior Knowledge: Students know the sound of **long *i*** and can distinguish medial and final sounds.

Introducing the Digraphs *ie* and *igh**

1. Building Phonemic Awareness

Show the front of each sound card and point to the digraph ***ie*** or ***igh*** as you talk about it. Say:

*The vowels **i** and **e** together in a word often stand for the **long i** sound: /ī/. You can hear /ī/ in the word **tie**. The letters **i-g-h** together in a word can also have the **long i** sound. You can hear /ī/ in the word **night**.*

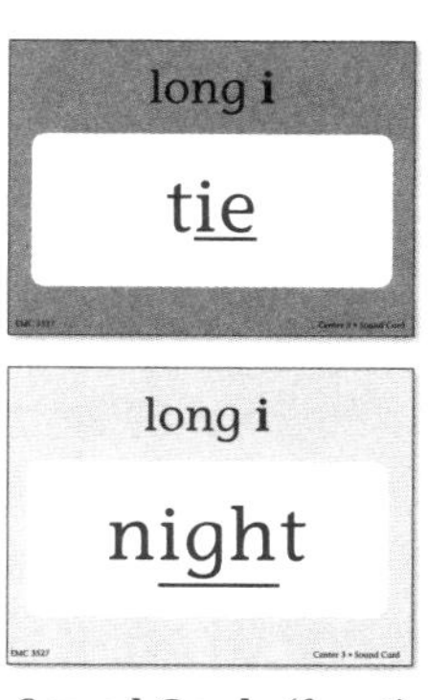

Sound Cards (front)

Point to the digraph in each word again. Say the names of the letters and ask students to tell you the sound that the letters stand for. (/ī/) Then have students listen for the **long *i*** sound in the words below. Say:

*Listen carefully to the words I'm going to say. Each word has the **long i** sound in it. Say **middle** or **end** to tell where you hear /ī/ in the word:*

lie (end)	**spies** (middle)	**slight** (middle)	**thigh** (end)	**frighten** (middle)
high (end)	**might** (middle)	**die** (end)	**untie** (end)	**twilight** (middle)

Read each word again and have students repeat it. If needed, stretch the **long *i*** sound slightly to help students hear it.

2. Oral Blending

Model oral blending to help students hear the distinct sounds in a word. Say:

*I am going to say a word, sound by sound. Listen: /**h**/ /ī/. The word is **high**. Now I am going to say some other words, sound by sound. You blend the sounds for each word and tell me what the word is. Listen:*

/p/ /ī/ (pie)	**/tr/ /ī/ /z/** (tries)	**/t/ /ī/ /t/** (tight)
/s/ /ī/ (sigh)	**/fr/ /ī/ /d/** (fried)	**/fr/ /ī/ /t/** (fright)

3. Visual Blending

Model visual blending, using the words listed on the back of each sound card. Begin by pointing to the first word and reading it aloud. Then run your finger under the letters as you blend the sounds to read the word again. Repeat this process for the remaining words. Next, have students blend the sounds themselves as you run your finger under each letter.

Sound Cards (back)

*Although not technically a vowel digraph, the letter combination ***igh*** is included as a common spelling pattern for the **long *i*** sound.

Leading the Center Activities

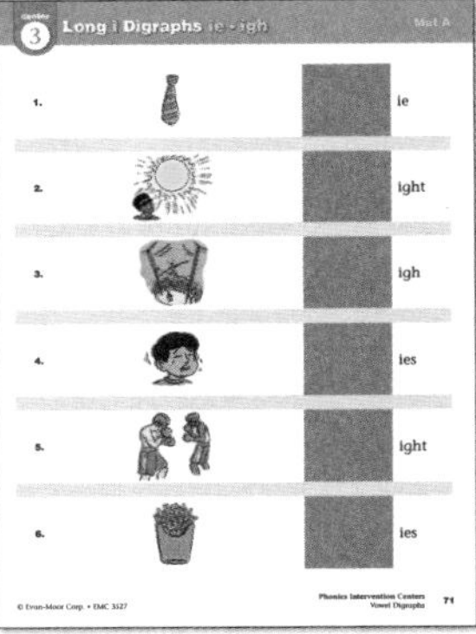
Long i Digraphs ie • igh
Mat A

1. ie
2. ight
3. igh
4. ies
5. ight
6. ies

Mat A

1. Read, Discriminate, and Identify

Ask students to tell you the sound they should say for ***ie*** or ***igh***. (/ī/) Then give each student Mat A and a set of task cards. Explain that each word on the mat is missing one or more letters at the beginning of it. Then say:

> *Look at the picture in row 1. It is a tie. What sound do you hear at the beginning of* ***tie****?* (/t/) *What letter says* **/t/***?* (t) *Place the card with the letter* **t** *on it in the box. Now let's blend the sounds and read the word:* **/t/ /ī/ *tie***. *Which letters in* ***tie*** *say* **/ī/***?* (i-e)

Repeat this process with the pictures in the remaining rows.

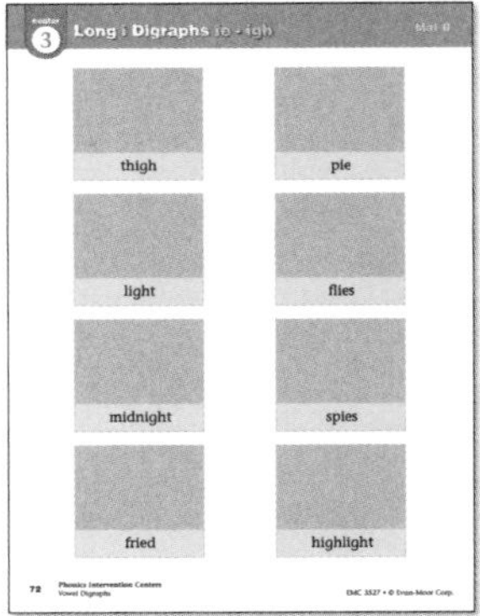
Long i Digraphs ie • igh
Mat B

thigh	pie
light	flies
midnight	spies
fried	highlight

Mat B

2. Read and Understand

Have students turn over their mats. Distribute the task cards for Mat B. Then say:

> *Look at the word in the first box on the mat. Let's blend the sounds to read the word:* **/th/ /ī/ *thigh***. *Which letters in* ***thigh*** *say* **/ī/***?* (i-g-h) *Now place the card that shows a picture of a thigh above the word.*

Repeat this process with the words in the remaining boxes.

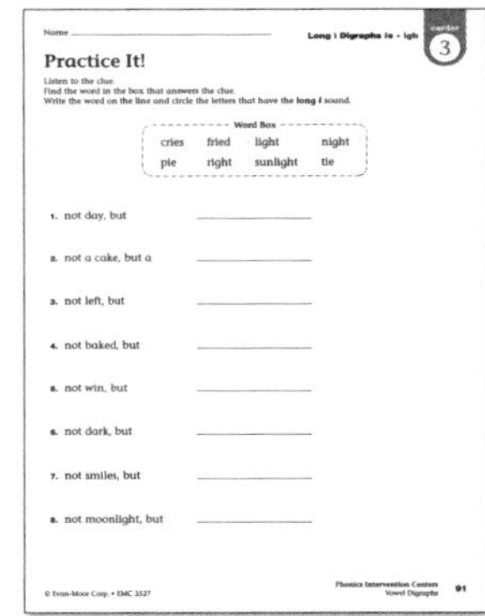
Name
Long i Digraphs ie • igh
Practice It!
Listen to the clue.
Find the word in the box that answers the clue.
Write the word on the line and circle the letters that have the long i sound.

Word Box
cries fried light night
pie right sunlight tie

1. not day, but
2. not a cake, but a
3. not left, but
4. not baked, but
5. not win, but
6. not dark, but
7. not smiles, but
8. not moonlight, but

Page 91

3. Practice the Skill

Distribute the Practice It! activity (page 91) to students. Read the directions aloud and have students say the words in the word box. Tell them to blend the sounds as they read each word. Then say:

> *Listen to the first clue:* ***not day, but***. *Which word in the box answers the clue?* (night) *Write the word* ***night*** *on the line. Now circle the letters in* ***night*** *that say* **/ī/**. (igh)

Repeat this process for the remaining clues, or if your students are capable, have them complete the activity with a partner. Give help when needed. Then go over the answers as a group.

Name
Long i Digraphs ie • igh
Read It!
Read the sentence.
Circle each word that has ie or igh for the long i sound.

ie igh

1. Gray skies mean that it might rain.
2. The baby cried most of the night.
3. The crust on this pie is light and flaky!
4. Kara tried on the jacket, but it was too tight.
5. Sal wants french fries for dinner tonight.
6. Mom gave a big sigh when I told her that I had lied.
7. The sunlight is too bright for me.
8. Two spies broke into my house and tied me to a chair!

Page 92

Apply and Assess

After the lesson, distribute the Read It! activity (page 92) to students and read the directions aloud. Have students complete the activity independently. Then listen to them read the sentences. Use the results as an informal assessment of students' skill mastery.

long i

tie

Center 3 • Sound Card

EMC 3527

long i

night

Center 3 • Sound Card

EMC 3527

Answer Keys

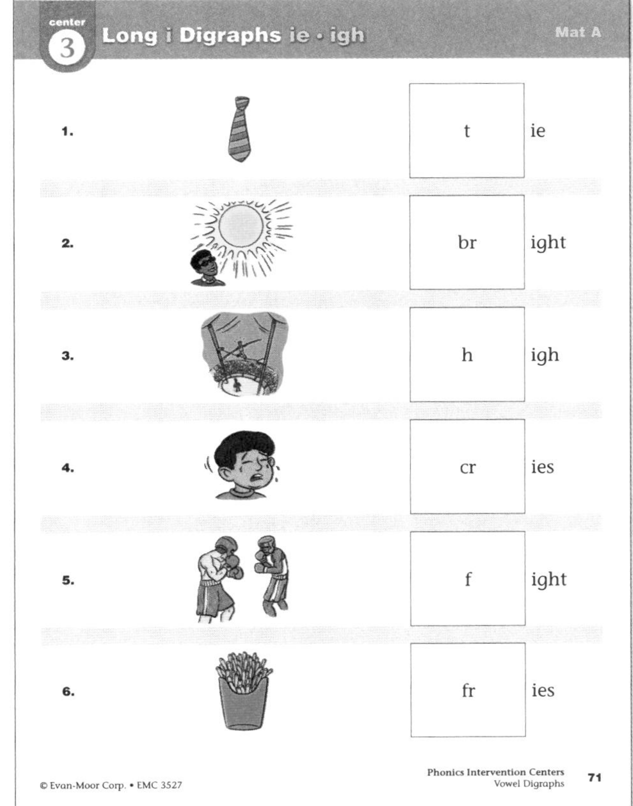

center 3 **Long i Digraphs ie • igh** Mat A

1.		t	ie
2.		br	ight
3.		h	igh
4.		cr	ies
5.		f	ight
6.		fr	ies

© Evan-Moor Corp. • EMC 3527

Phonics Intervention Centers
Vowel Digraphs 71

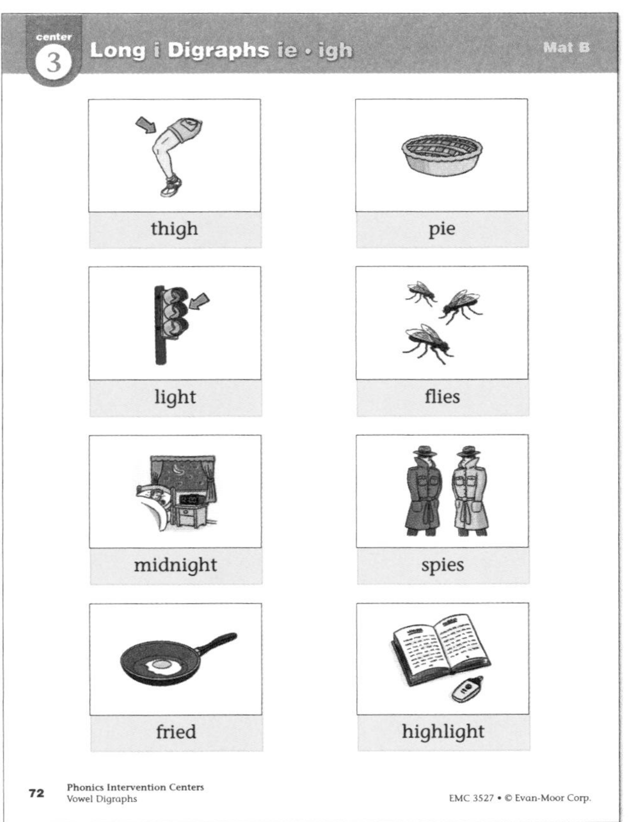

center 3 **Long i Digraphs ie • igh** Mat B

thigh	pie
light	flies
midnight	spies
fried	highlight

72 Phonics Intervention Centers
Vowel Digraphs

EMC 3527 • © Evan-Moor Corp.

sigh

tight

fright

EMC 3527 Center 3 • Sound Card

pie

tries

fried

EMC 3527 Center 3 • Sound Card

Answer Keys

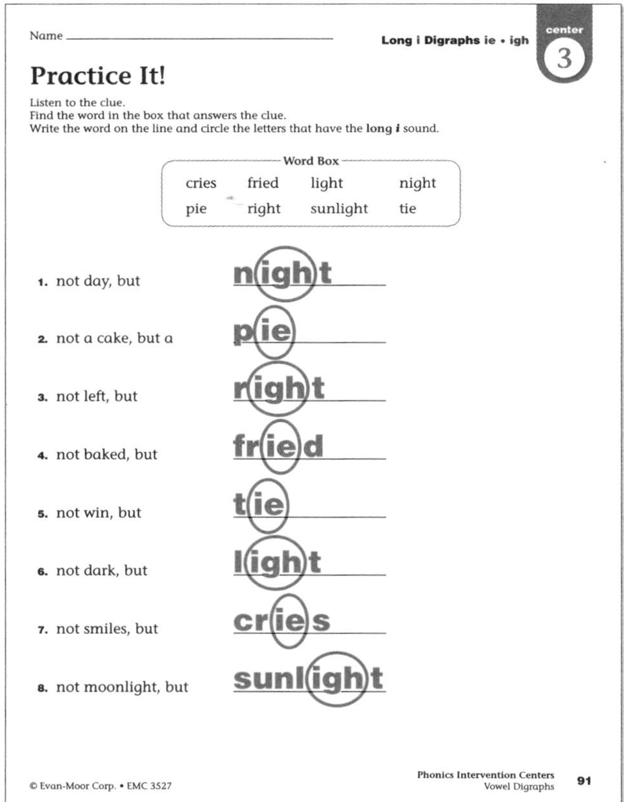

Name ______________________ **Long i Digraphs ie • igh** center 3

Practice It!

Listen to the clue.
Find the word in the box that answers the clue.
Write the word on the line and circle the letters that have the **long *i*** sound.

Word Box

cries	fried	light	night
pie	right	sunlight	tie

1. not day, but night
2. not a cake, but a pie
3. not left, but right
4. not baked, but fried
5. not win, but tie
6. not dark, but light
7. not smiles, but cries
8. not moonlight, but sunlight

© Evan-Moor Corp. • EMC 3527 Phonics Intervention Centers Vowel Digraphs 91

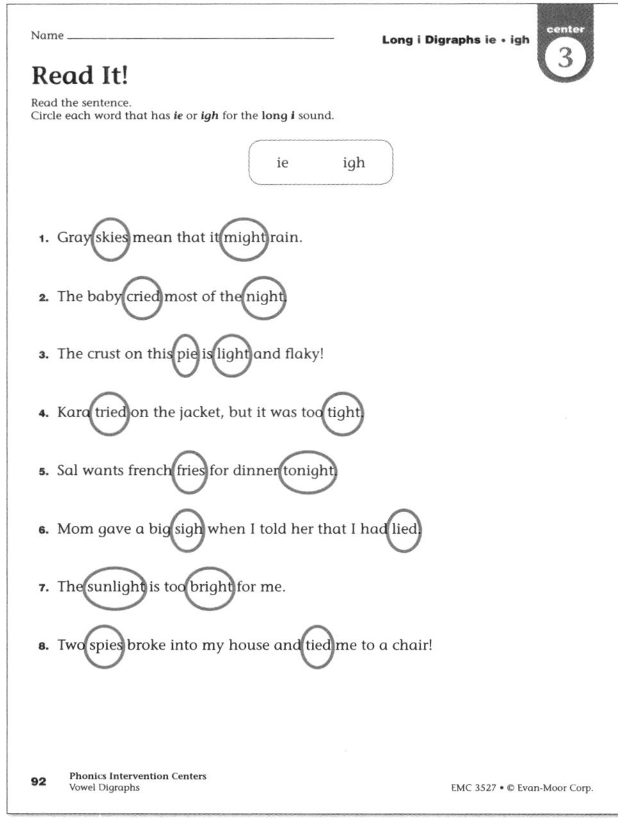

Name ______________________ **Long i Digraphs ie • igh** center 3

Read It!

Read the sentence.
Circle each word that has ***ie*** or ***igh*** for the **long *i*** sound.

ie igh

1. Gray skies mean that it might rain.
2. The baby cried most of the night.
3. The crust on this pie is light and flaky!
4. Kara tried on the jacket, but it was too tight.
5. Sal wants french fries for dinner tonight.
6. Mom gave a big sigh when I told her that I had lied.
7. The sunlight is too bright for me.
8. Two spies broke into my house and tied me to a chair!

92 Phonics Intervention Centers Vowel Digraphs EMC 3527 • © Evan-Moor Corp.

center 3

Long i Digraphs ie • igh

Mat A

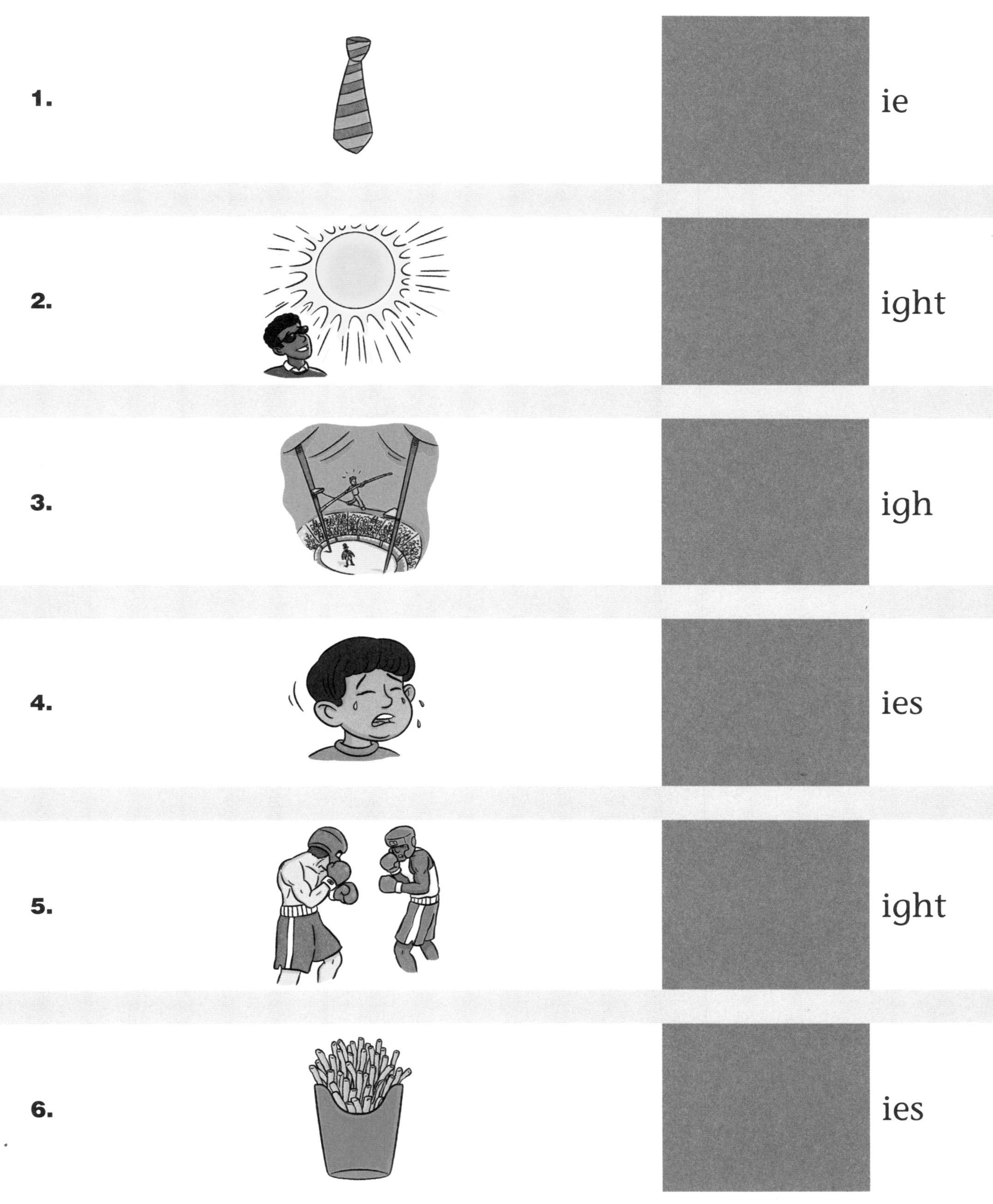

Long i Digraphs ie • igh

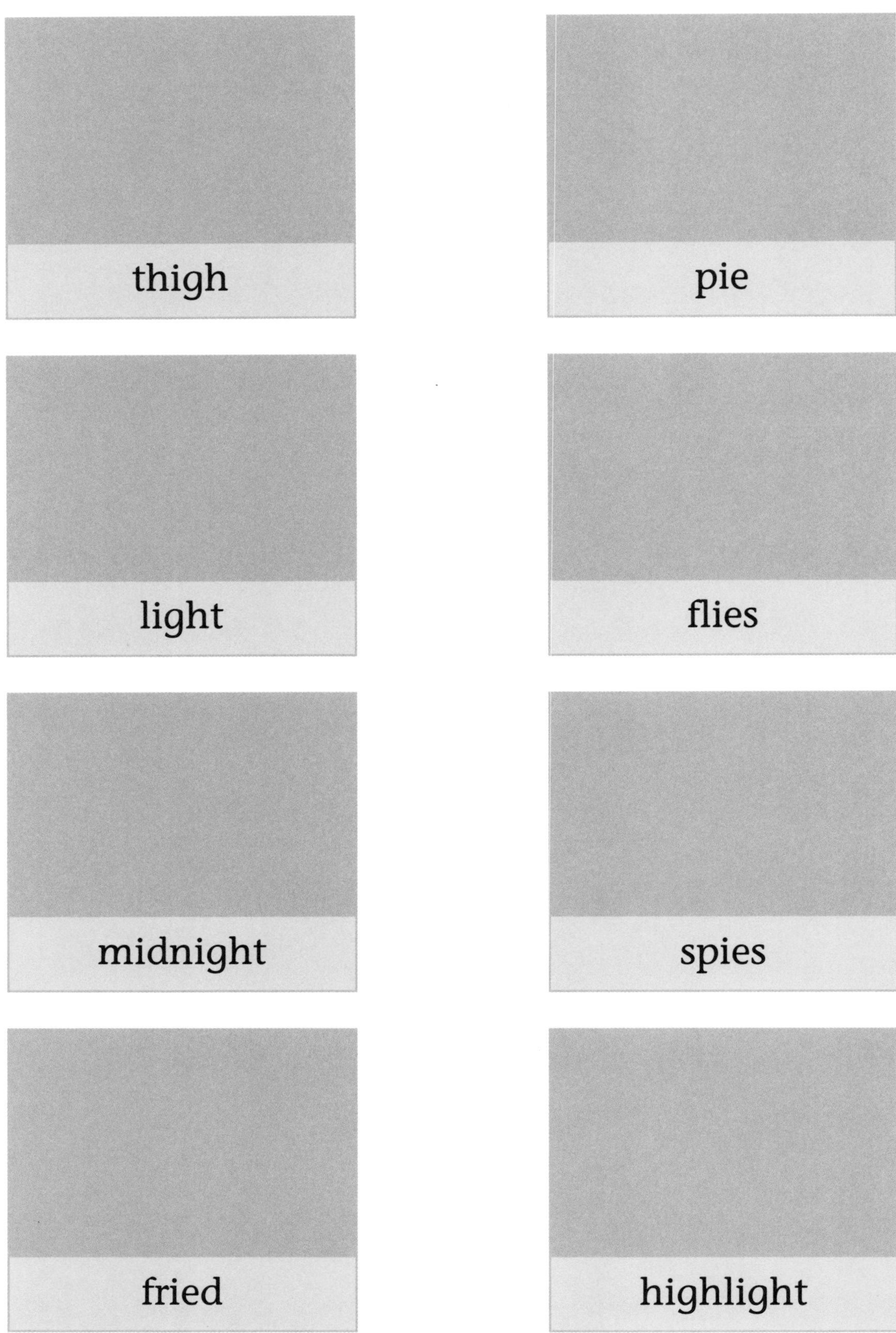

center 3

Long i Digraphs ie • igh

Mat A

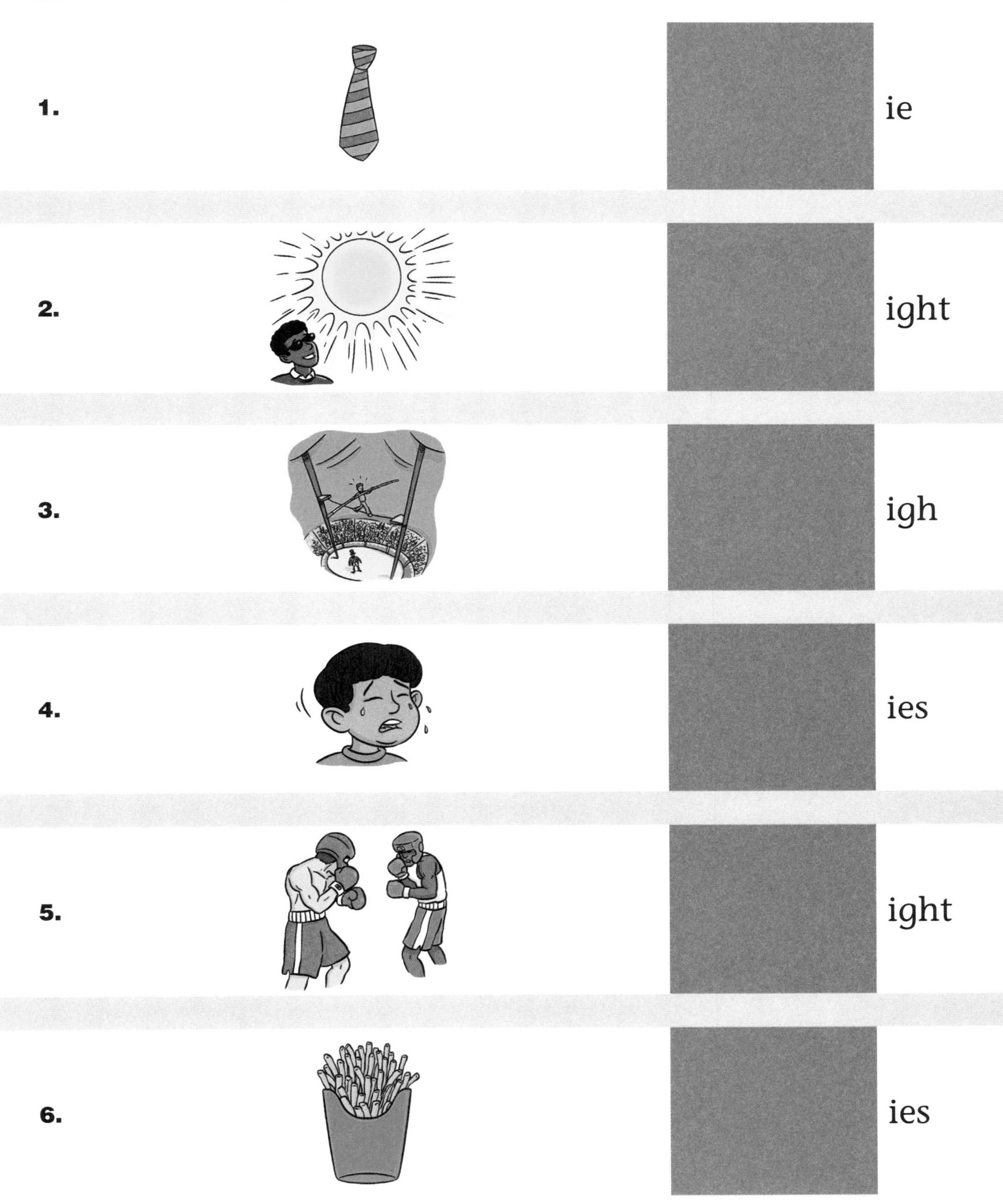

Long i Digraphs ie • igh

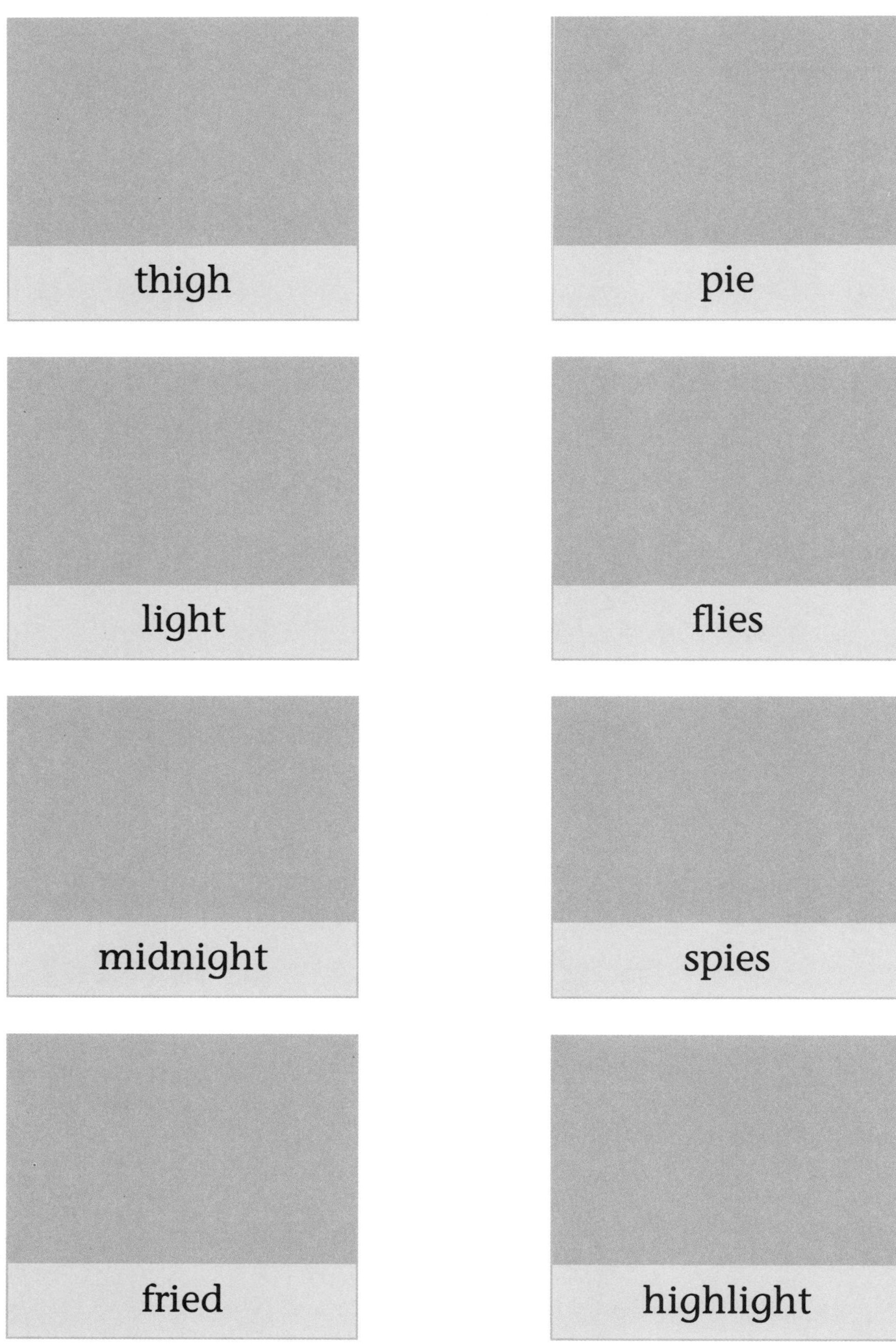

Long i Digraphs ie • igh

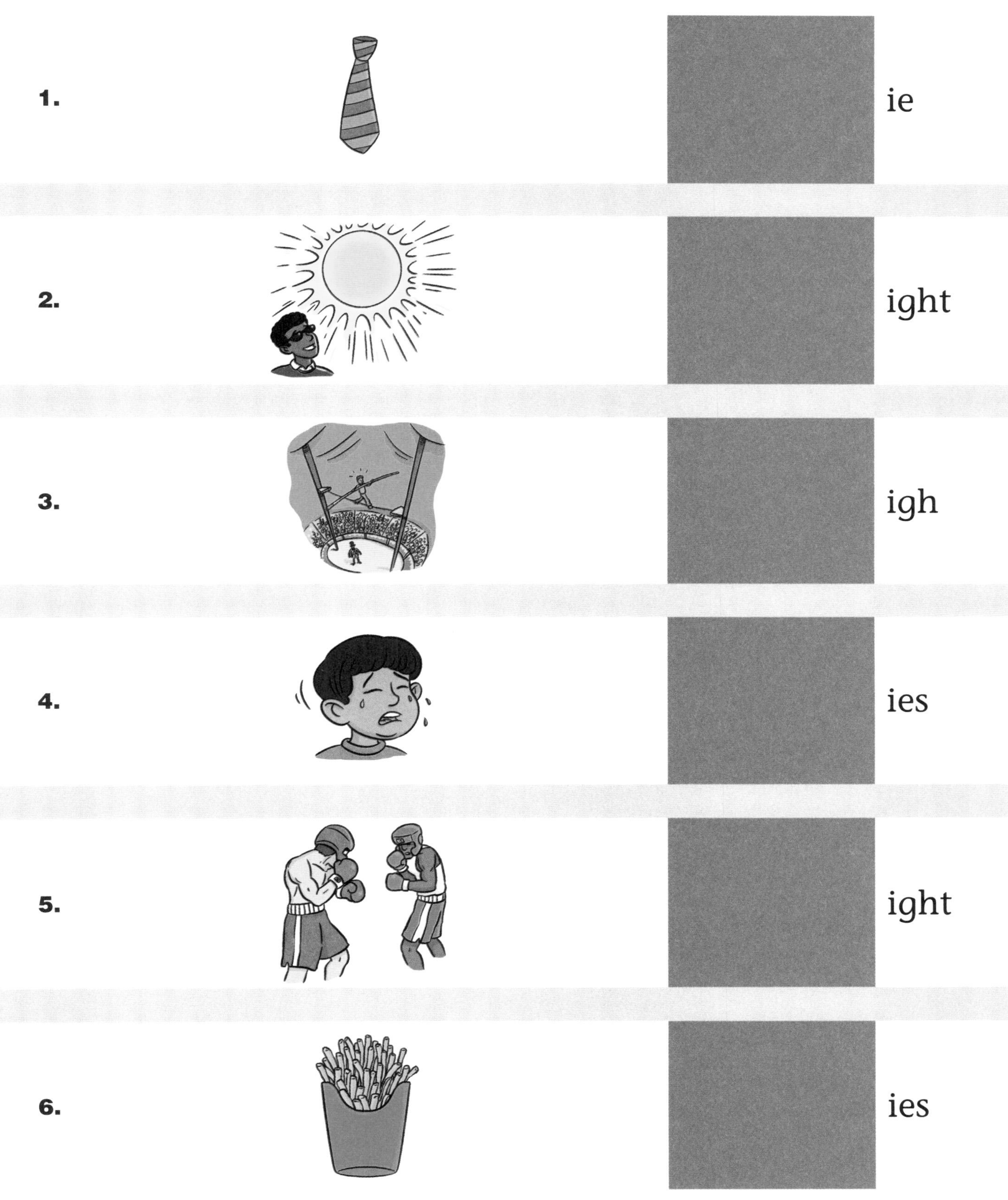

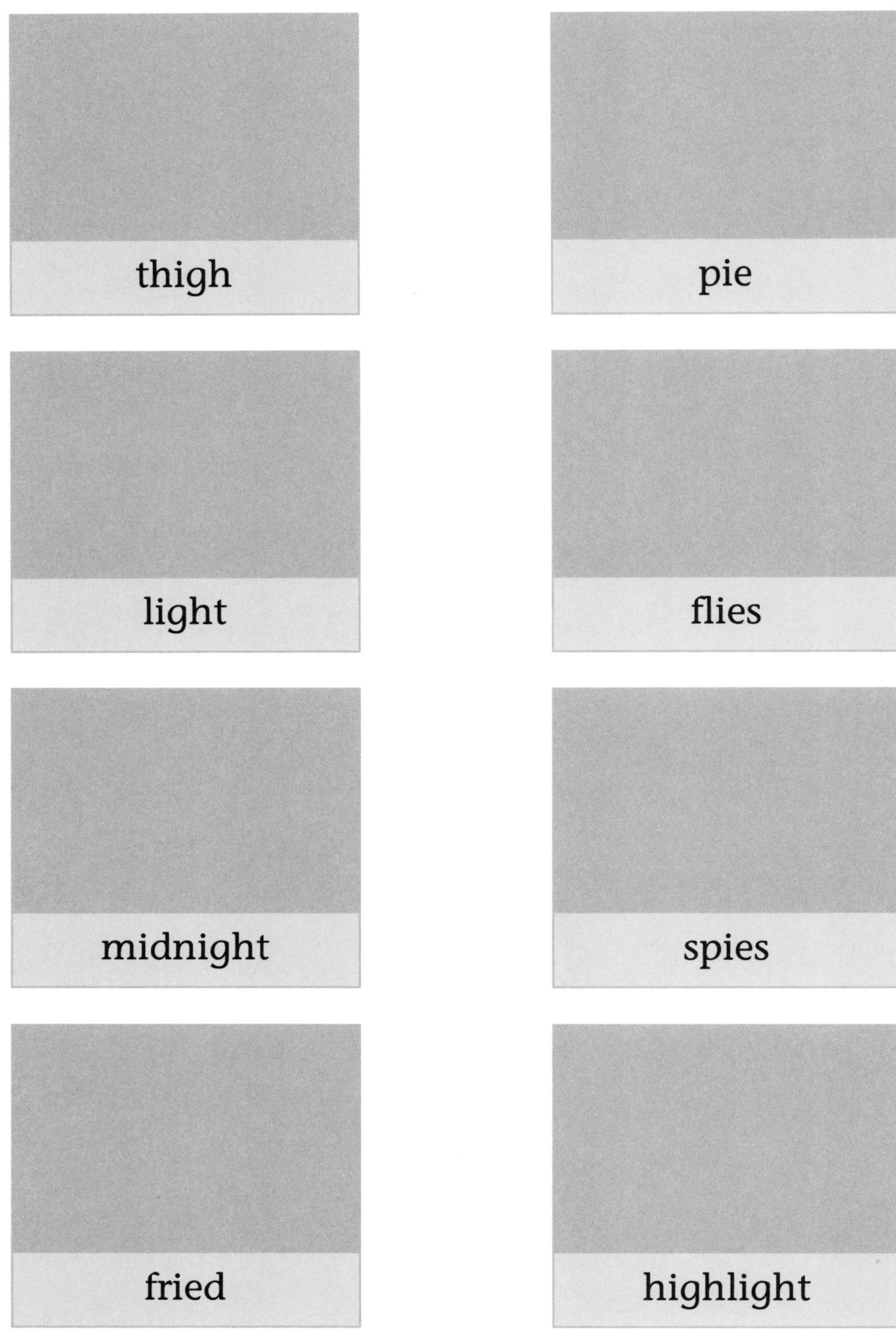
thigh
pie
light
flies
midnight
spies
fried
highlight

Long i Digraphs ie • igh

Mat A

1.  ie

2.  ight

3.  igh

4.  ies

5.  ight

6.  ies

Long i Digraphs ie • igh

Mat B

thigh	pie
light	flies
midnight	spies
fried	highlight

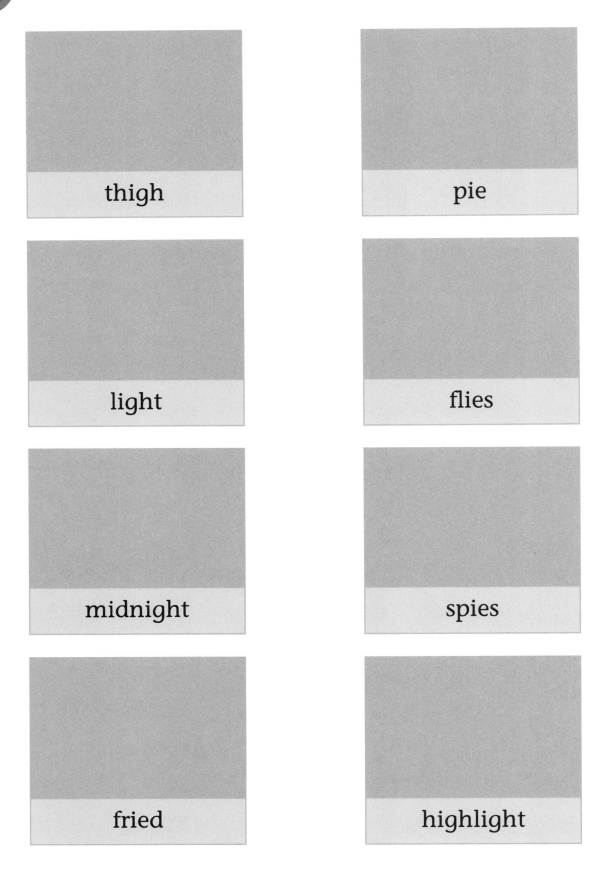

Long i Digraphs ie • igh

Mat A

1.  ie

2.  ight

3. 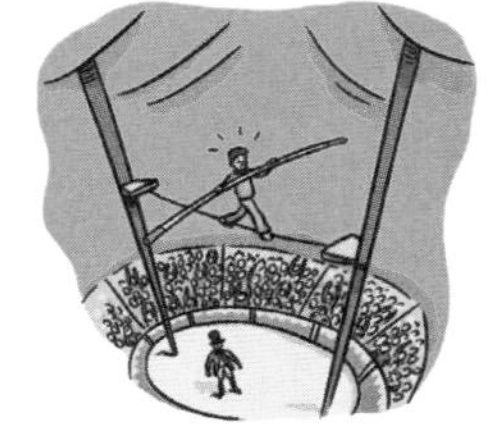 igh

4.  ies

5.  ight

6.  ies

Long i Digraphs ie • igh

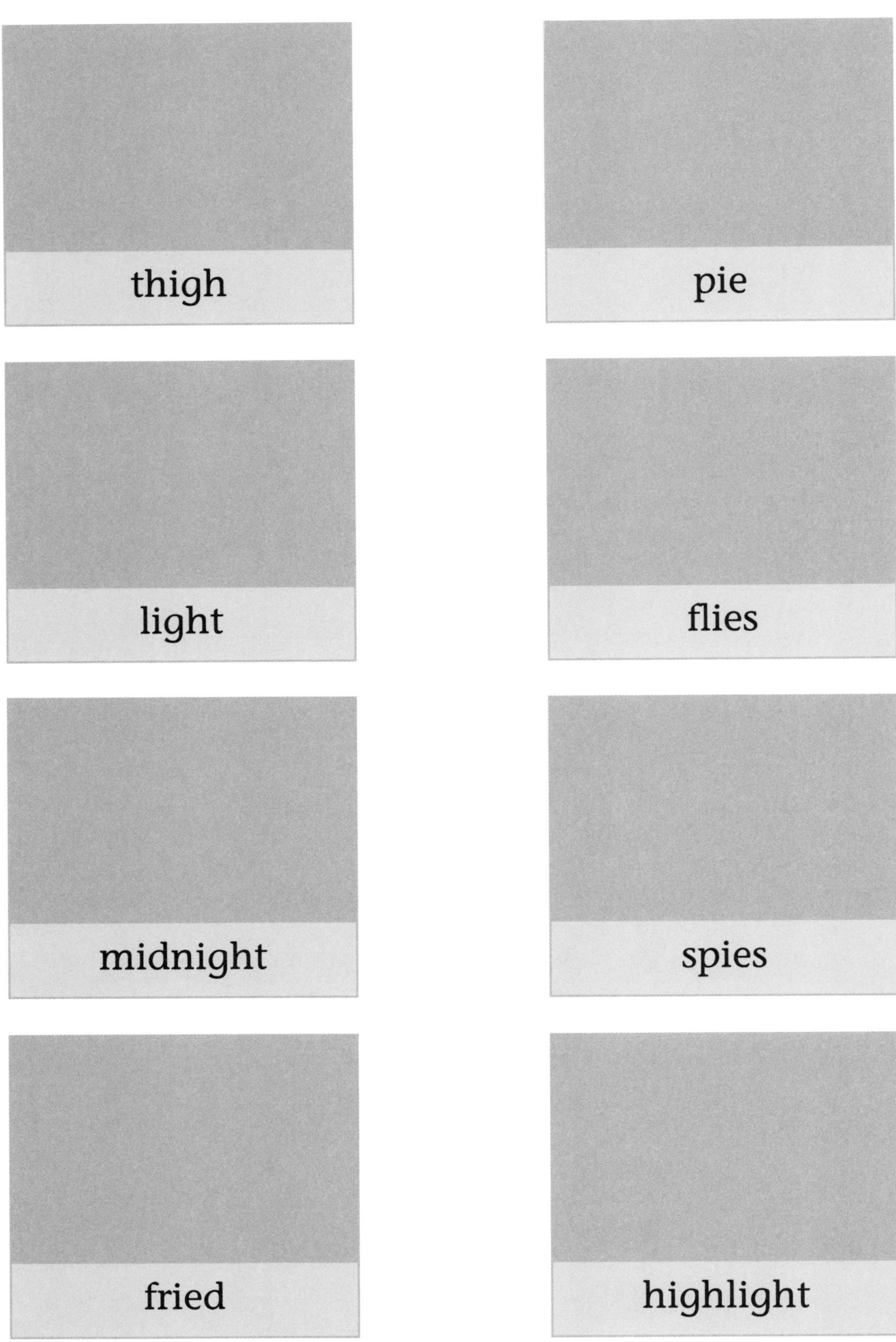

center 3 Long i Digraphs ie • igh

Mat A

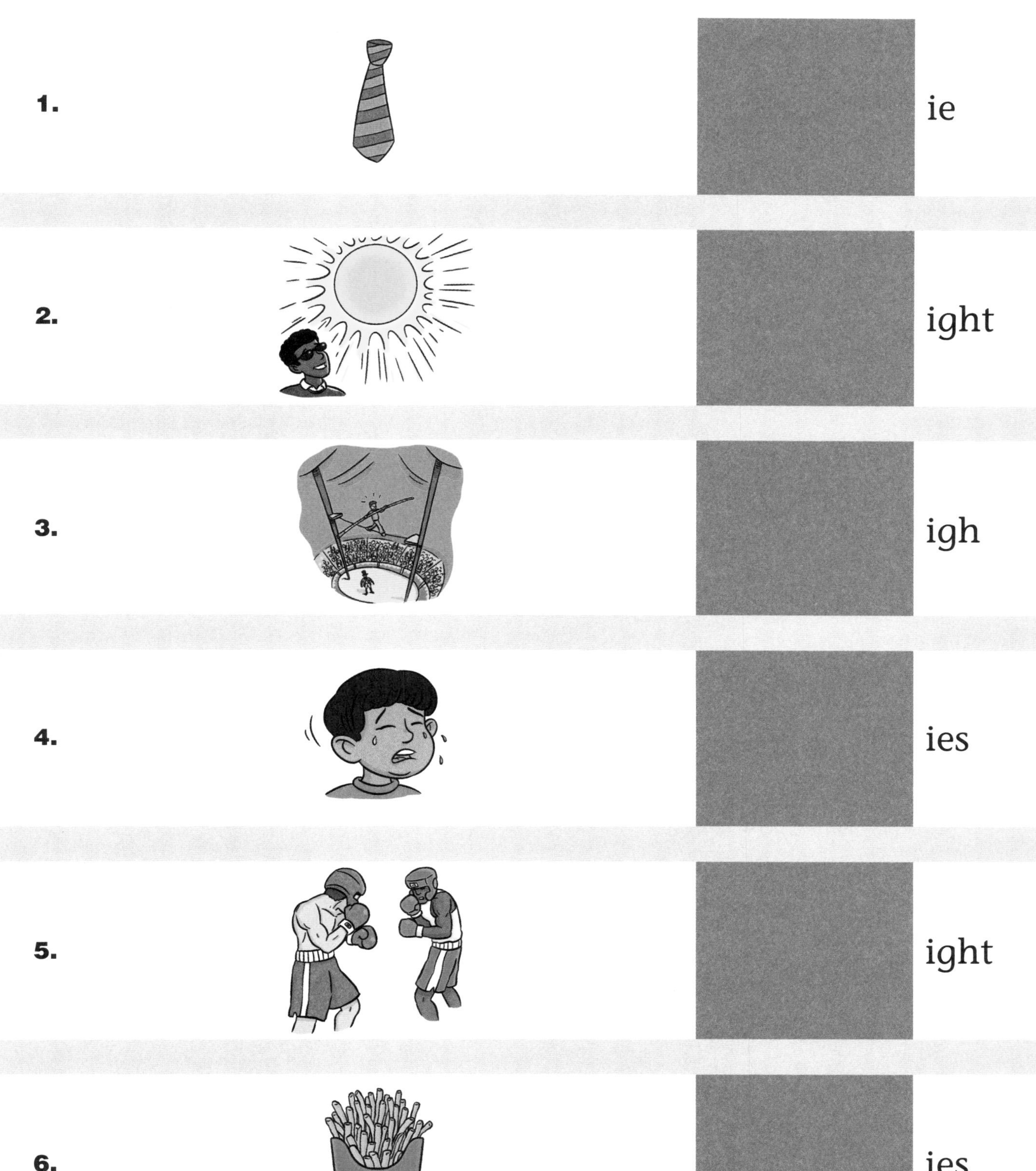

Long i Digraphs ie • igh

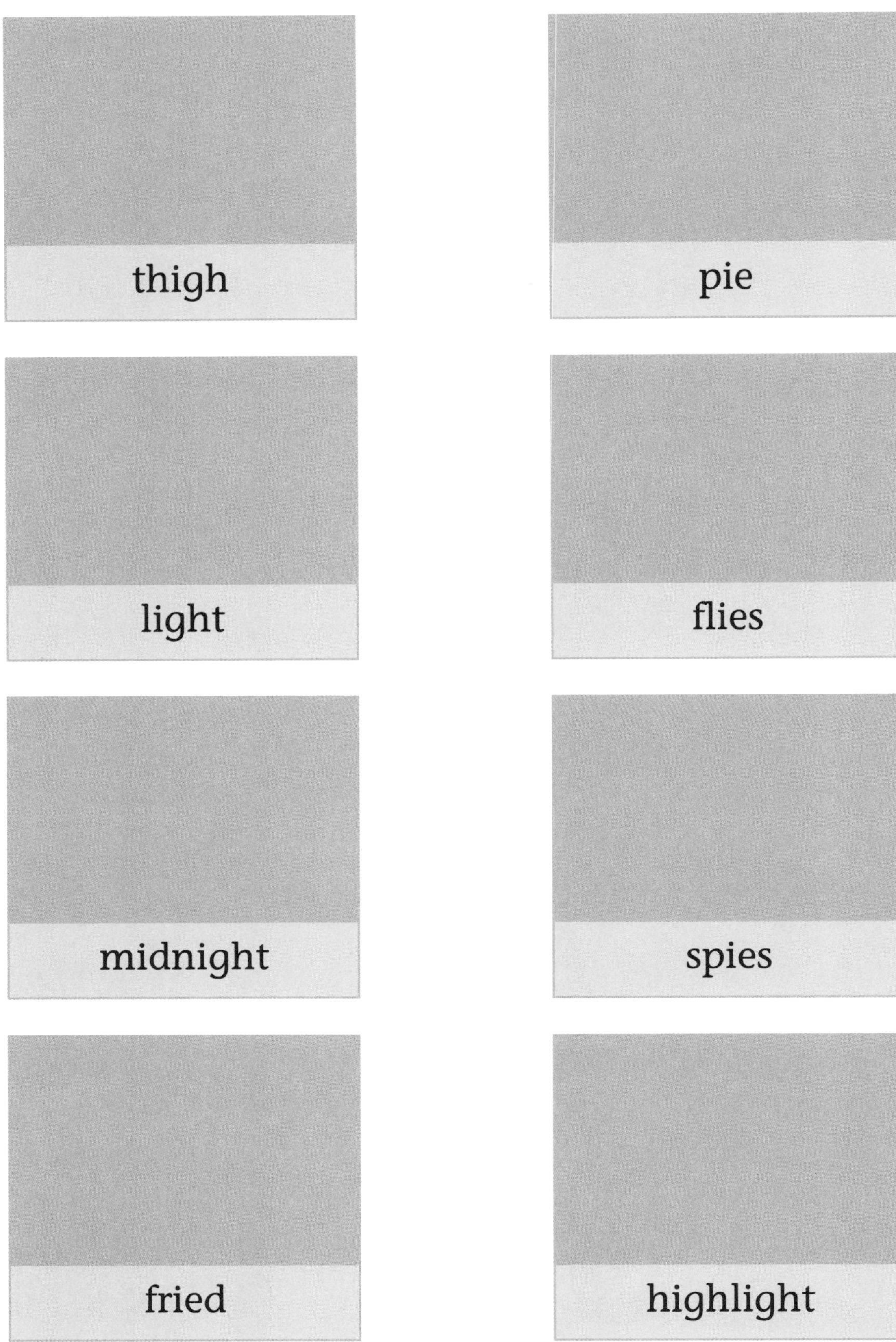

Task Cards

Student 1	Student 2	Student 3	Student 4	Student 5	Student 6
br	br	br	br	br	br
cr	cr	cr	cr	cr	cr
fr	fr	fr	fr	fr	fr
h	h	h	h	h	h
f	f	f	f	f	f
t	t	t	t	t	t

center 3

Task Cards

Mat A

Student 6 EMC 3527 Center 3 • Mat A	**Student 6** EMC 3527 Center 3 • Mat A	**Student 6** EMC 3527 Center 3 • Mat A	**Student 6** EMC 3527 Center 3 • Mat A	**Student 6** EMC 3527 Center 3 • Mat A	**Student 6** EMC 3527 Center 3 • Mat A
Student 5 EMC 3527 Center 3 • Mat A	**Student 5** EMC 3527 Center 3 • Mat A	**Student 5** EMC 3527 Center 3 • Mat A	**Student 5** EMC 3527 Center 3 • Mat A	**Student 5** EMC 3527 Center 3 • Mat A	**Student 5** EMC 3527 Center 3 • Mat A
Student 4 EMC 3527 Center 3 • Mat A	**Student 4** EMC 3527 Center 3 • Mat A	**Student 4** EMC 3527 Center 3 • Mat A	**Student 4** EMC 3527 Center 3 • Mat A	**Student 4** EMC 3527 Center 3 • Mat A	**Student 4** EMC 3527 Center 3 • Mat A
Student 3 EMC 3527 Center 3 • Mat A	**Student 3** EMC 3527 Center 3 • Mat A	**Student 3** EMC 3527 Center 3 • Mat A	**Student 3** EMC 3527 Center 3 • Mat A	**Student 3** EMC 3527 Center 3 • Mat A	**Student 3** EMC 3527 Center 3 • Mat A
Student 2 EMC 3527 Center 3 • Mat A	**Student 2** EMC 3527 Center 3 • Mat A	**Student 2** EMC 3527 Center 3 • Mat A	**Student 2** EMC 3527 Center 3 • Mat A	**Student 2** EMC 3527 Center 3 • Mat A	**Student 2** EMC 3527 Center 3 • Mat A
Student 1 EMC 3527 Center 3 • Mat A	**Student 1** EMC 3527 Center 3 • Mat A	**Student 1** EMC 3527 Center 3 • Mat A	**Student 1** EMC 3527 Center 3 • Mat A	**Student 1** EMC 3527 Center 3 • Mat A	**Student 1** EMC 3527 Center 3 • Mat A

Task Cards

Student 2

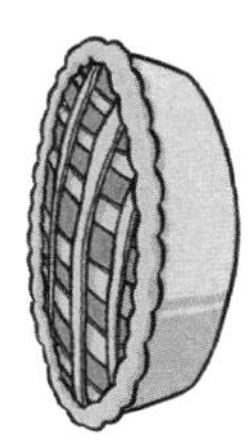

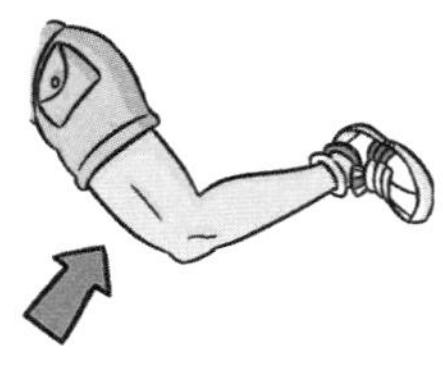

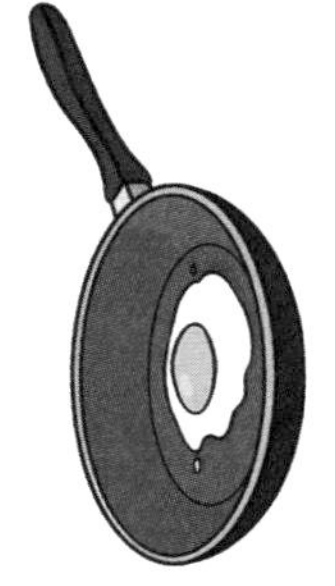

Student 1

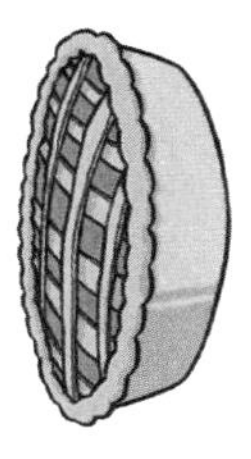

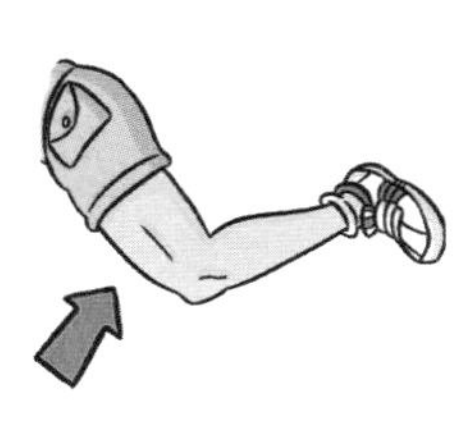
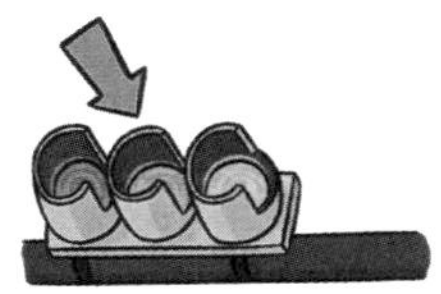

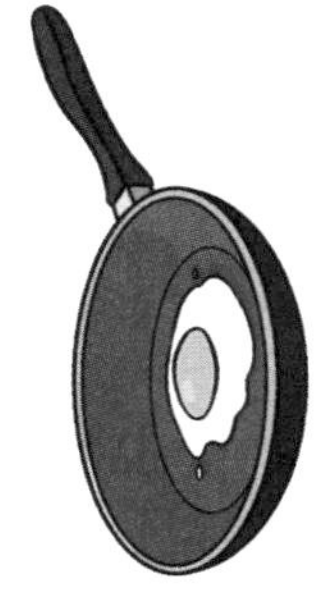

Task Cards

Student 2
EMC 3527 • Center 3 • Mat B

Student 2
EMC 3527 • Center 3 • Mat B

Student 2
EMC 3527 • Center 3 • Mat B

Student 2
EMC 3527 • Center 3 • Mat B

Student 2
EMC 3527 • Center 3 • Mat B

Student 2
EMC 3527 • Center 3 • Mat B

Student 2
EMC 3527 • Center 3 • Mat B

Student 2
EMC 3527 • Center 3 • Mat B

Student 1
EMC 3527 • Center 3 • Mat B

Student 1
EMC 3527 • Center 3 • Mat B

Student 1
EMC 3527 • Center 3 • Mat B

Student 1
EMC 3527 • Center 3 • Mat B

Student 1
EMC 3527 • Center 3 • Mat B

Student 1
EMC 3527 • Center 3 • Mat B

Student 1
EMC 3527 • Center 3 • Mat B

Student 1
EMC 3527 • Center 3 • Mat B

Task Cards

Student 4

Student 3

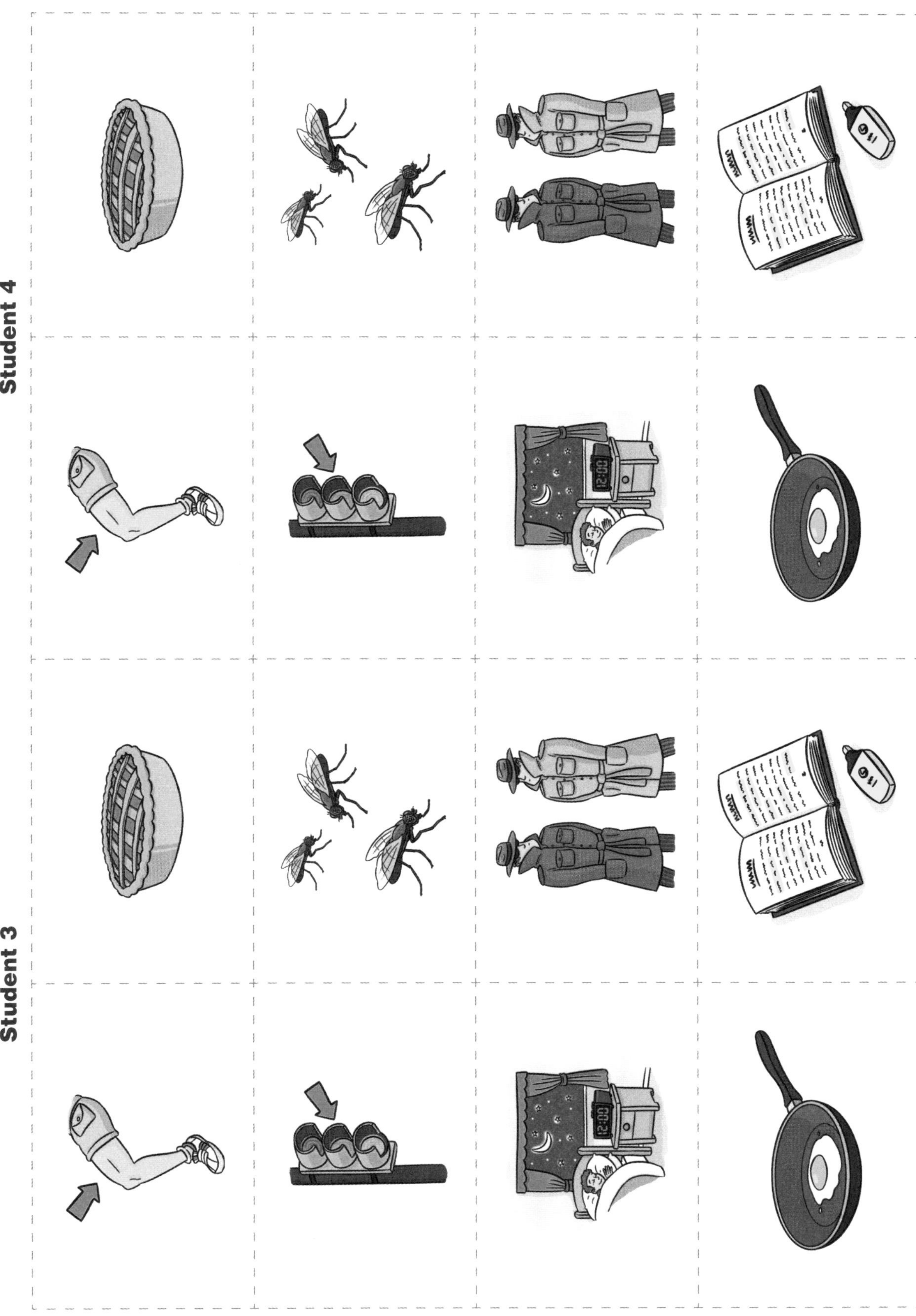

Student 4
EMC 3527 • Center 3 • Mat B

Student 4
EMC 3527 • Center 3 • Mat B

Student 4
EMC 3527 • Center 3 • Mat B

Student 4
EMC 3527 • Center 3 • Mat B

Student 4
EMC 3527 • Center 3 • Mat B

Student 4
EMC 3527 • Center 3 • Mat B

Student 4
EMC 3527 • Center 3 • Mat B

Student 4
EMC 3527 • Center 3 • Mat B

Student 3
EMC 3527 • Center 3 • Mat B

Student 3
EMC 3527 • Center 3 • Mat B

Student 3
EMC 3527 • Center 3 • Mat B

Student 3
EMC 3527 • Center 3 • Mat B

Student 3
EMC 3527 • Center 3 • Mat B

Student 3
EMC 3527 • Center 3 • Mat B

Student 3
EMC 3527 • Center 3 • Mat B

Student 3
EMC 3527 • Center 3 • Mat B

Task Cards

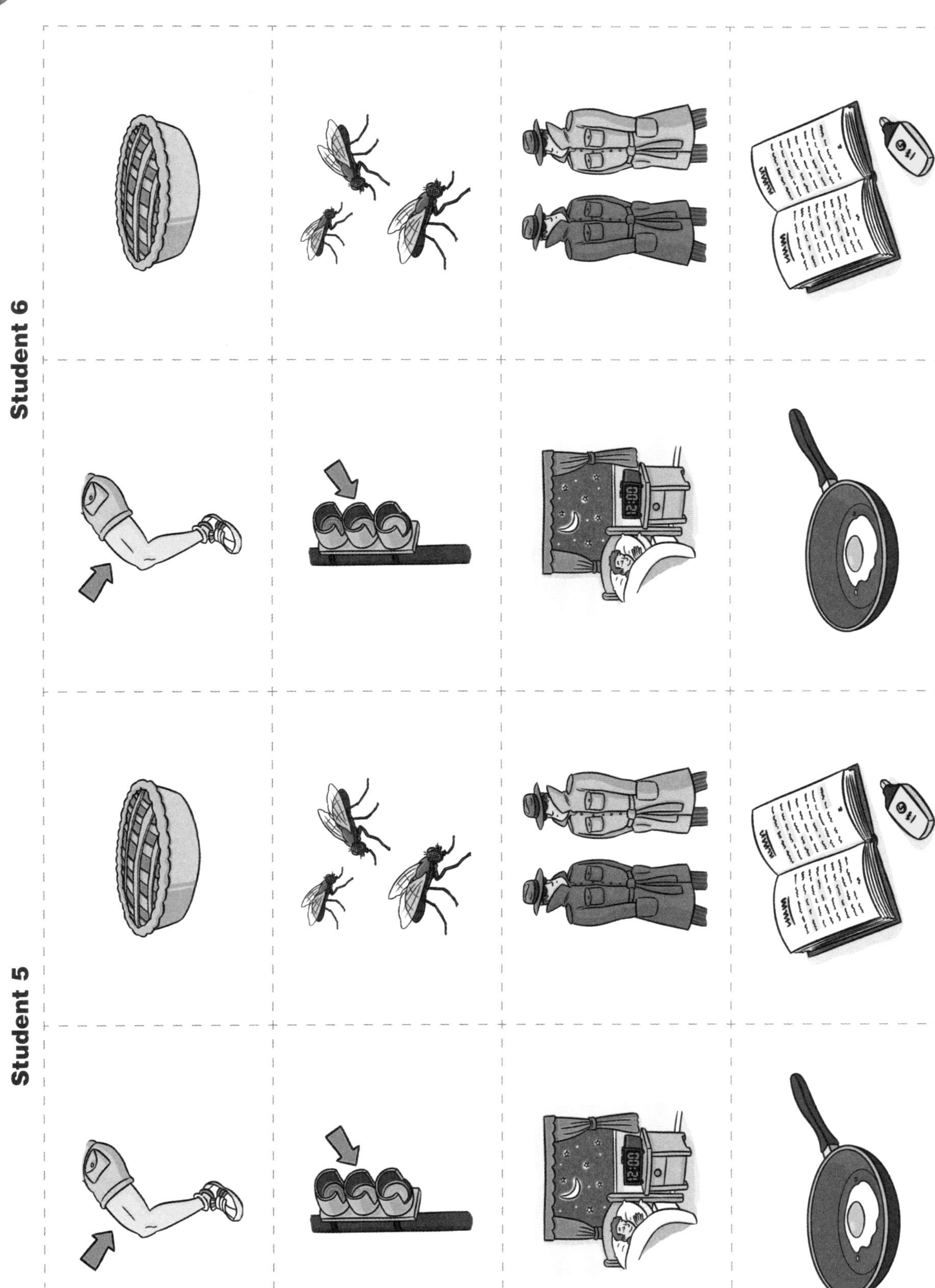

center 3

Task Cards

Mat B

Student 6
EMC 3527 • Center 3 • Mat B

Student 6
EMC 3527 • Center 3 • Mat B

Student 6
EMC 3527 • Center 3 • Mat B

Student 6
EMC 3527 • Center 3 • Mat B

Student 6
EMC 3527 • Center 3 • Mat B

Student 6
EMC 3527 • Center 3 • Mat B

Student 6
EMC 3527 • Center 3 • Mat B

Student 6
EMC 3527 • Center 3 • Mat B

Student 5
EMC 3527 • Center 3 • Mat B

Student 5
EMC 3527 • Center 3 • Mat B

Student 5
EMC 3527 • Center 3 • Mat B

Student 5
EMC 3527 • Center 3 • Mat B

Student 5
EMC 3527 • Center 3 • Mat B

Student 5
EMC 3527 • Center 3 • Mat B

Student 5
EMC 3527 • Center 3 • Mat B

Student 5
EMC 3527 • Center 3 • Mat B

Name ______________________

Practice It!

Listen to the clue.
Find the word in the box that answers the clue.
Write the word on the line and circle the letters that have the **long *i*** sound.

Word Box

cries	fried	light	night
pie	right	sunlight	tie

1. not day, but ______________

2. not a cake, but a ______________

3. not left, but ______________

4. not baked, but ______________

5. not win, but ______________

6. not dark, but ______________

7. not smiles, but ______________

8. not moonlight, but ______________

Name ____________________

Read It!

Read the sentence.
Circle each word that has ***ie*** or ***igh*** for the **long *i*** sound.

ie igh

1. Gray skies mean that it might rain.

2. The baby cried most of the night.

3. The crust on this pie is light and flaky!

4. Kara tried on the jacket, but it was too tight.

5. Sal wants french fries for dinner tonight.

6. Mom gave a big sigh when I told her that I had lied.

7. The sunlight is too bright for me.

8. Two spies broke into my house and tied me to a chair!

INTERMEDIATE

Long o Digraphs oa • ow

For the Teacher

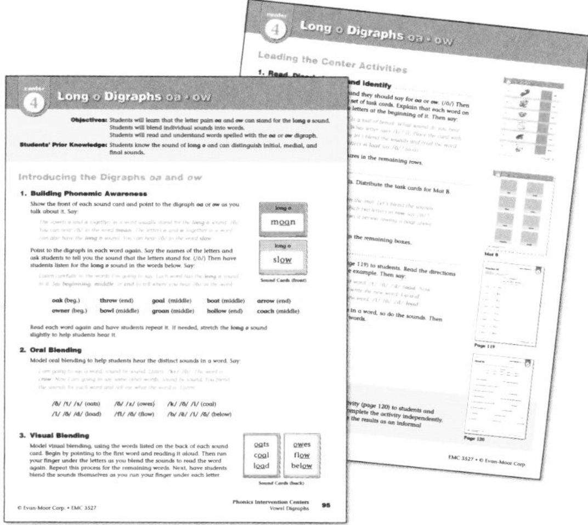

Lesson Plan

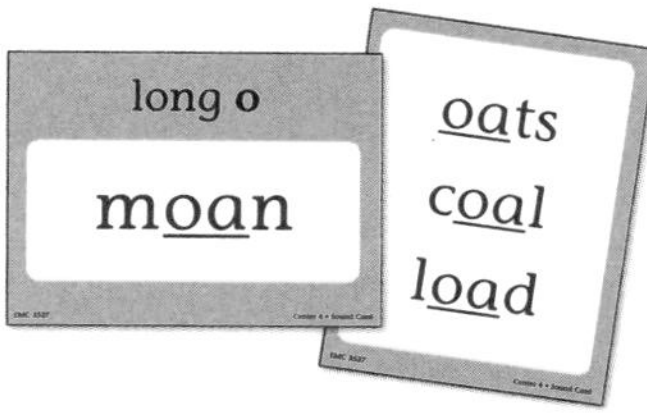

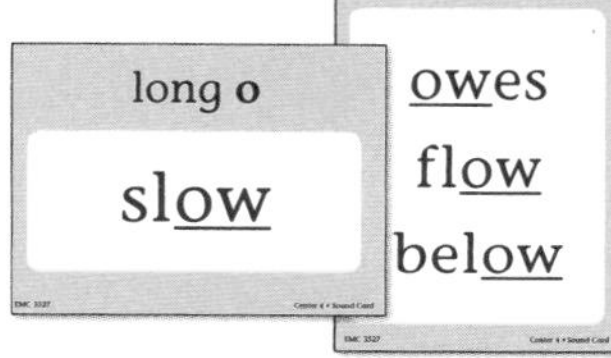

Sound Cards

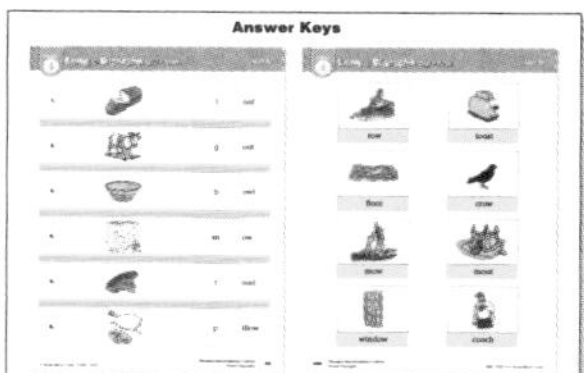

Answer Keys

For the Student

front (Mat A)

back (Mat B)

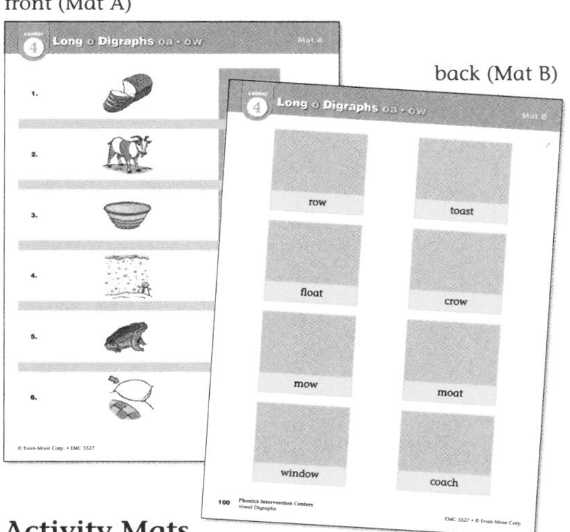

Activity Mats

Task Cards

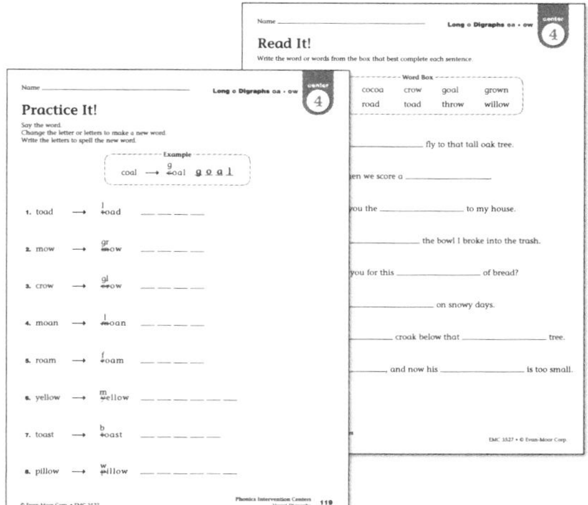

Practice and Assessment Activities

Long o Digraphs oa • ow

Objectives: Students will learn that the letter pairs ***oa*** and ***ow*** can stand for the **long *o*** sound.
Students will blend individual sounds into words.
Students will read and understand words spelled with the ***oa*** or ***ow*** digraph.

Students' Prior Knowledge: Students know the sound of **long *o*** and can distinguish initial, medial, and final sounds.

Introducing the Digraphs *oa* and *ow*

1. Building Phonemic Awareness

Show the front of each sound card and point to the digraph ***oa*** or ***ow*** as you talk about it. Say:

*The vowels **o** and **a** together in a word usually stand for the **long o** sound: /ō/. You can hear /ō/ in the word **moan**. The letters **o** and **w** together in a word can also have the **long o** sound. You can hear /ō/ in the word **slow**.*

Sound Cards (front)

Point to the digraph in each word again. Say the names of the letters and ask students to tell you the sound that the letters stand for. (/ō/) Then have students listen for the **long *o*** sound in the words below. Say:

*Listen carefully to the words I'm going to say. Each word has the **long o** sound in it. Say **beginning**, **middle**, or **end** to tell where you hear /ō/ in the word.*

oak (beg.)	**throw** (end)	**goal** (middle)	**boat** (middle)	**arrow** (end)
owner (beg.)	**bowl** (middle)	**groan** (middle)	**hollow** (end)	**coach** (middle)

Read each word again and have students repeat it. If needed, stretch the **long *o*** sound slightly to help students hear it.

2. Oral Blending

Model oral blending to help students hear the distinct sounds in a word. Say:

*I am going to say a word, sound by sound. Listen: /kr/ /ō/. The word is **crow**. Now I am going to say some other words, sound by sound. You blend the sounds for each word and tell me what the word is. Listen:*

/ō/ /t/ /s/ (oats)	**/ō/ /z/** (owes)	**/k/ /ō/ /l/** (coal)
/l/ /ō/ /d/ (load)	**/fl/ /ō/** (flow)	**/b/ /ē/ /l/ /ō/** (below)

3. Visual Blending

Model visual blending, using the words listed on the back of each sound card. Begin by pointing to the first word and reading it aloud. Then run your finger under the letters as you blend the sounds to read the word again. Repeat this process for the remaining words. Next, have students blend the sounds themselves as you run your finger under each letter.

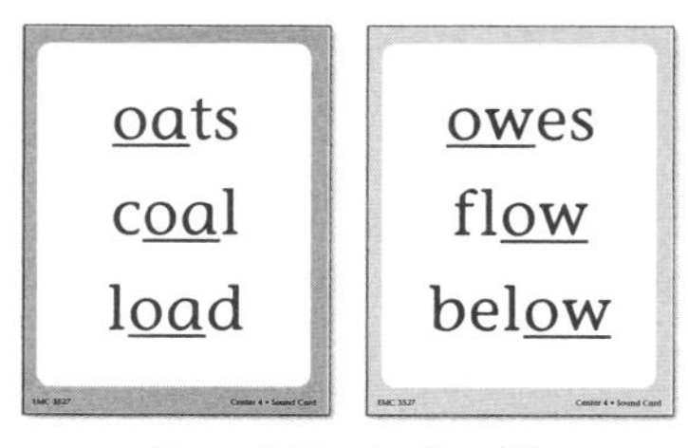

Sound Cards (back)

Leading the Center Activities

1. Read, Discriminate, and Identify

Ask students to tell you the sound they should say for ***oa*** or ***ow***. (/ō/) Then give each student Mat A and a set of task cards. Explain that each word on the mat is missing one or more letters at the beginning of it. Then say:

> *Look at the picture in row 1. It is a loaf of bread. What sound do you hear at the beginning of **loaf**?* (/l/) *What letter says /l/?* (l) *Place the card with the letter **l** on it in the box. Now let's blend the sounds and read the word: /l/ /ō/ /f/ **loaf**. Which two letters in **loaf** say /ō/?* (o-a)

Repeat this process with the pictures in the remaining rows.

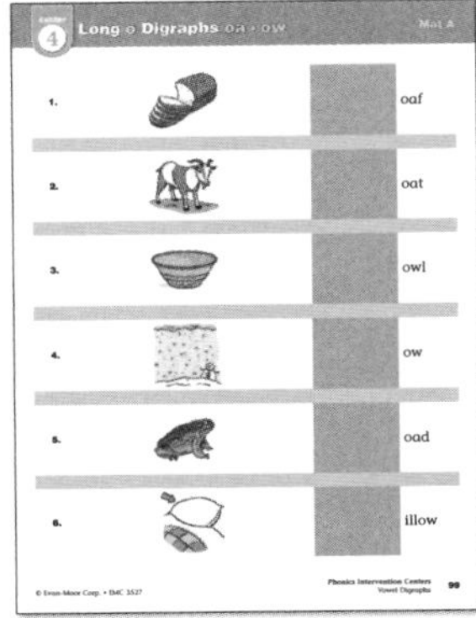

Mat A

2. Read and Understand

Have students turn over their mats. Distribute the task cards for Mat B. Then say:

> *Look at the word in the first box on the mat. Let's blend the sounds to read the word: /r/ /ō/ **row**. Which two letters in **row** say /ō/?* (o-w) *Now place the card that shows a person rowing a boat above the word.*

Repeat this process with the words in the remaining boxes.

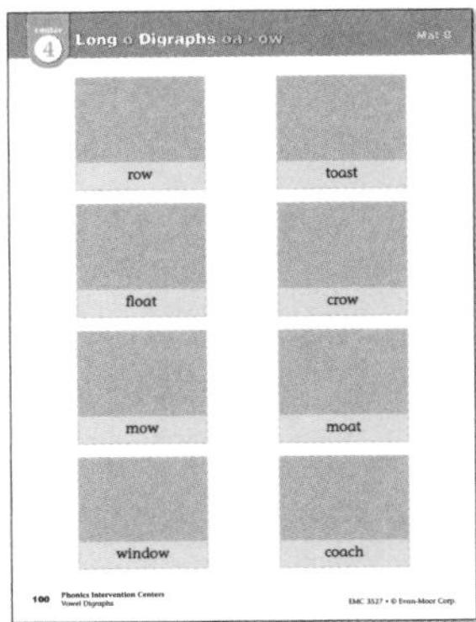

Mat B

3. Practice the Skill

Distribute the Practice It! activity (page 119) to students. Read the directions aloud and guide students through the example. Then say:

> *Let's blend the sounds to read the first word: /t/ /ō/ /d/ **toad**. Now let's change the **t** in **toad** to an **l** and write the new word: **l-o-a-d**. Now blend the sounds and read the new word: /l/ /ō/ /d/ **load**.*

Remind students that as letters change in a word, so do the sounds. Then repeat this process with the remaining words.

Page 119

Apply and Assess

After the lesson, distribute the Read It! activity (page 120) to students and read the directions aloud. Have students complete the activity independently. Then listen to them read the sentences. Use the results as an informal assessment of students' skill mastery.

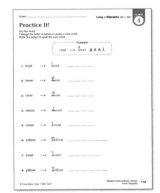

Page 120

long o

moan

Center 4 • Sound Card

EMC 3527

long o

slow

Center 4 • Sound Card

EMC 3527

Answer Keys

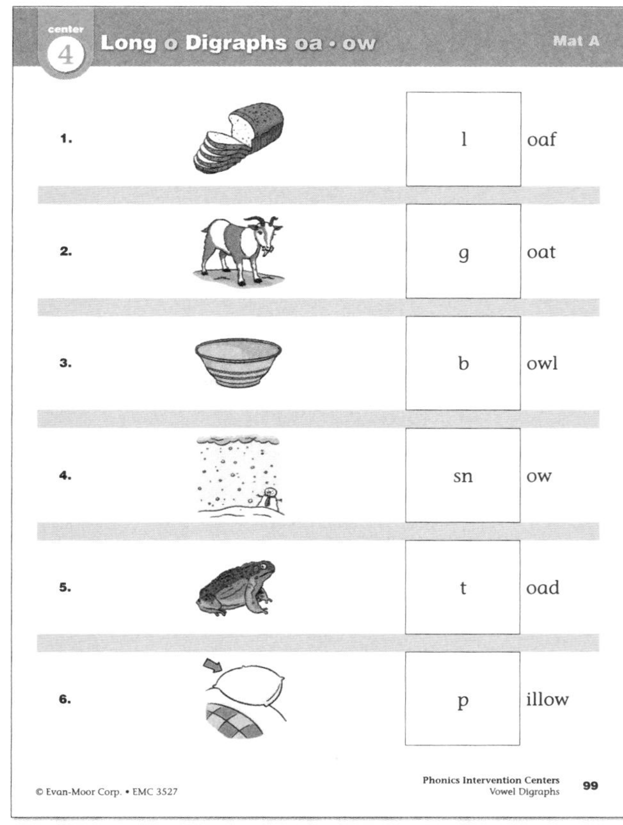

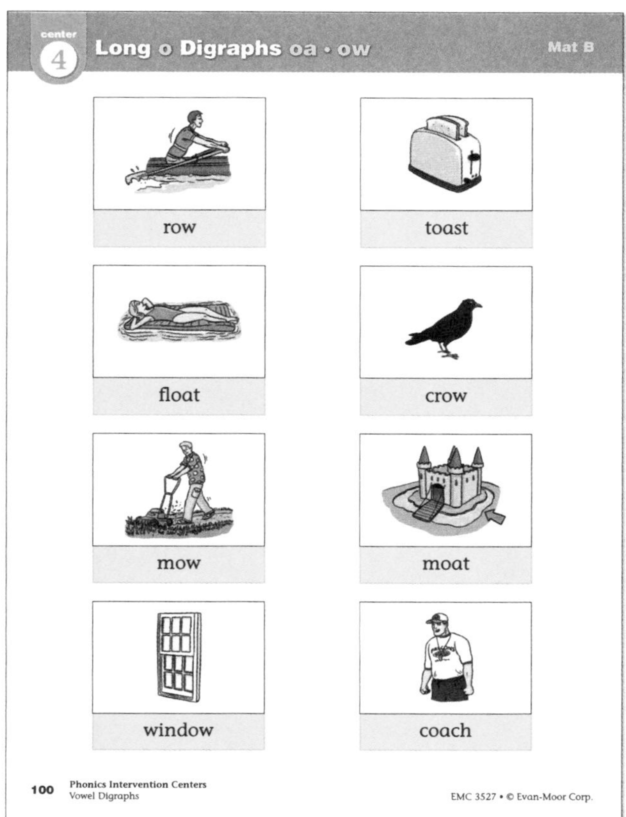

owes

flow

below

EMC 3527 Center 4 • Sound Card

oats

coal

load

EMC 3527 Center 4 • Sound Card

Answer Keys

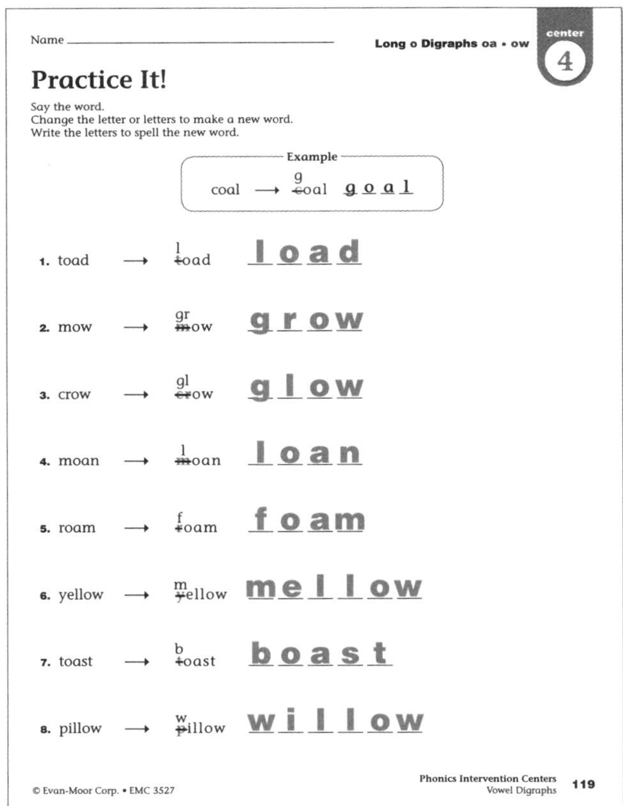

Name ______________________ **Long o Digraphs oa • ow** center 4

Practice It!

Say the word.
Change the letter or letters to make a new word.
Write the letters to spell the new word.

Example

coal → g coal g o a l

1. toad → l toad l o a d
2. mow → gr mow g r o w
3. crow → gl crow g l o w
4. moan → l moan l o a n
5. roam → f roam f o a m
6. yellow → m yellow m e l l o w
7. toast → b toast b o a s t
8. pillow → w pillow w i l l o w

© Evan-Moor Corp. • EMC 3527 Phonics Intervention Centers Vowel Digraphs 119

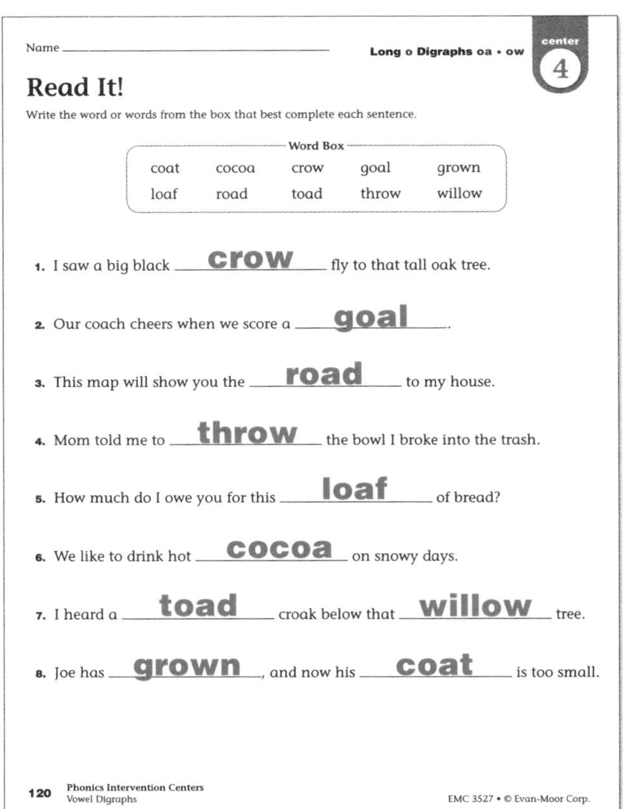

Name ______________________ **Long o Digraphs oa • ow** center 4

Read It!

Write the word or words from the box that best complete each sentence.

Word Box

coat	cocoa	crow	goal	grown
loaf	road	toad	throw	willow

1. I saw a big black **crow** fly to that tall oak tree.
2. Our coach cheers when we score a **goal**.
3. This map will show you the **road** to my house.
4. Mom told me to **throw** the bowl I broke into the trash.
5. How much do I owe you for this **loaf** of bread?
6. We like to drink hot **cocoa** on snowy days.
7. I heard a **toad** croak below that **willow** tree.
8. Joe has **grown**, and now his **coat** is too small.

120 Phonics Intervention Centers Vowel Digraphs EMC 3527 • © Evan-Moor Corp.

Long o Digraphs oa • ow

Mat A

1.  oaf

2.  oat

3.  owl

4.  ow

5.  oad

6. 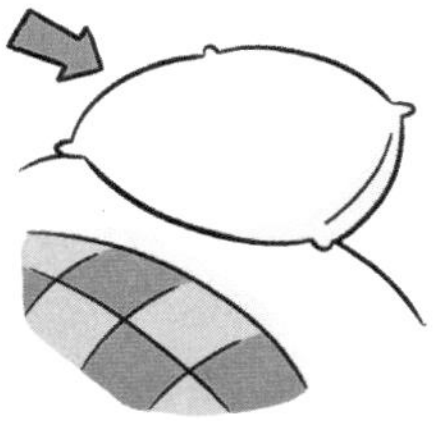 illow

Long o Digraphs oa • ow

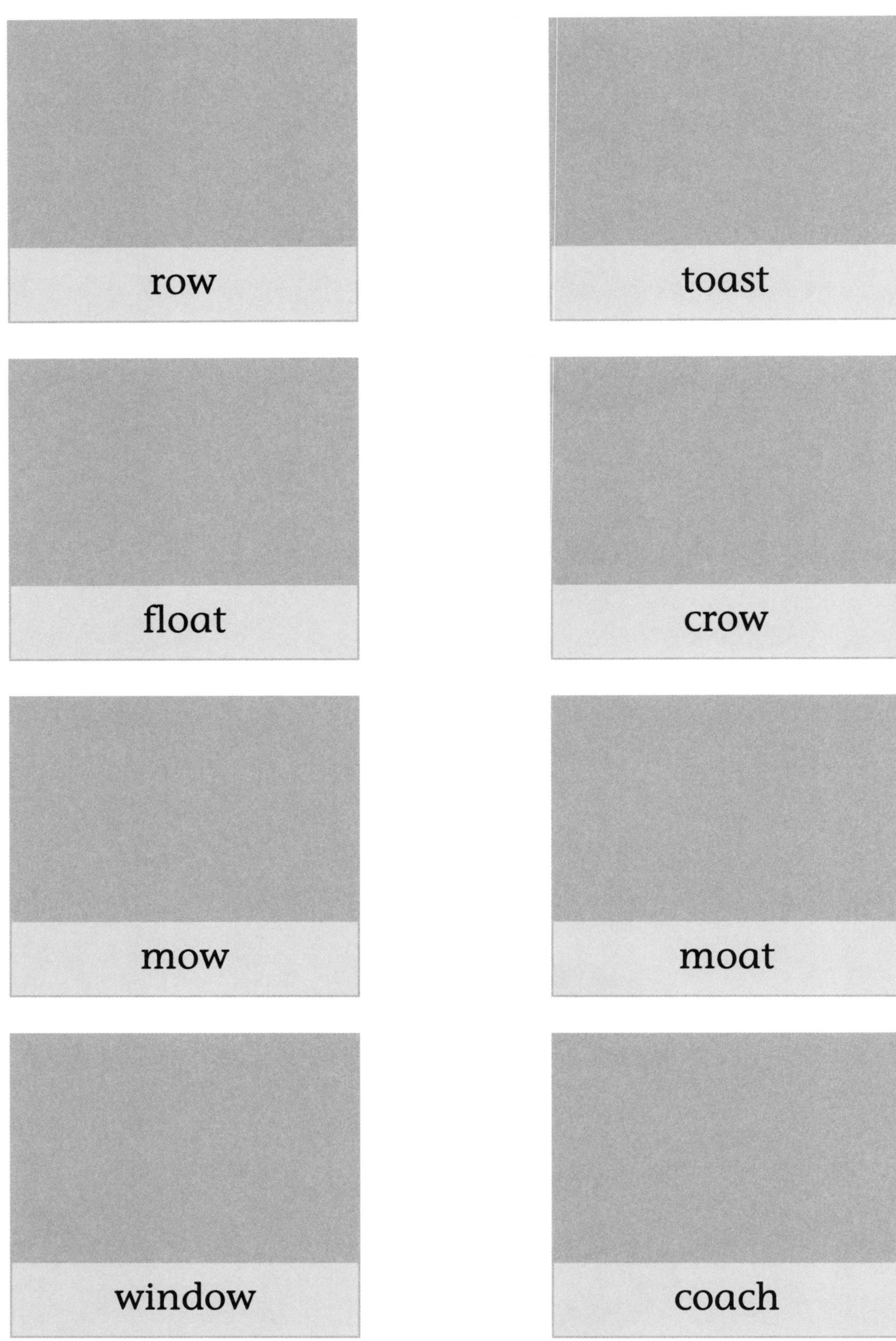

Long o Digraphs oa • ow

Mat A

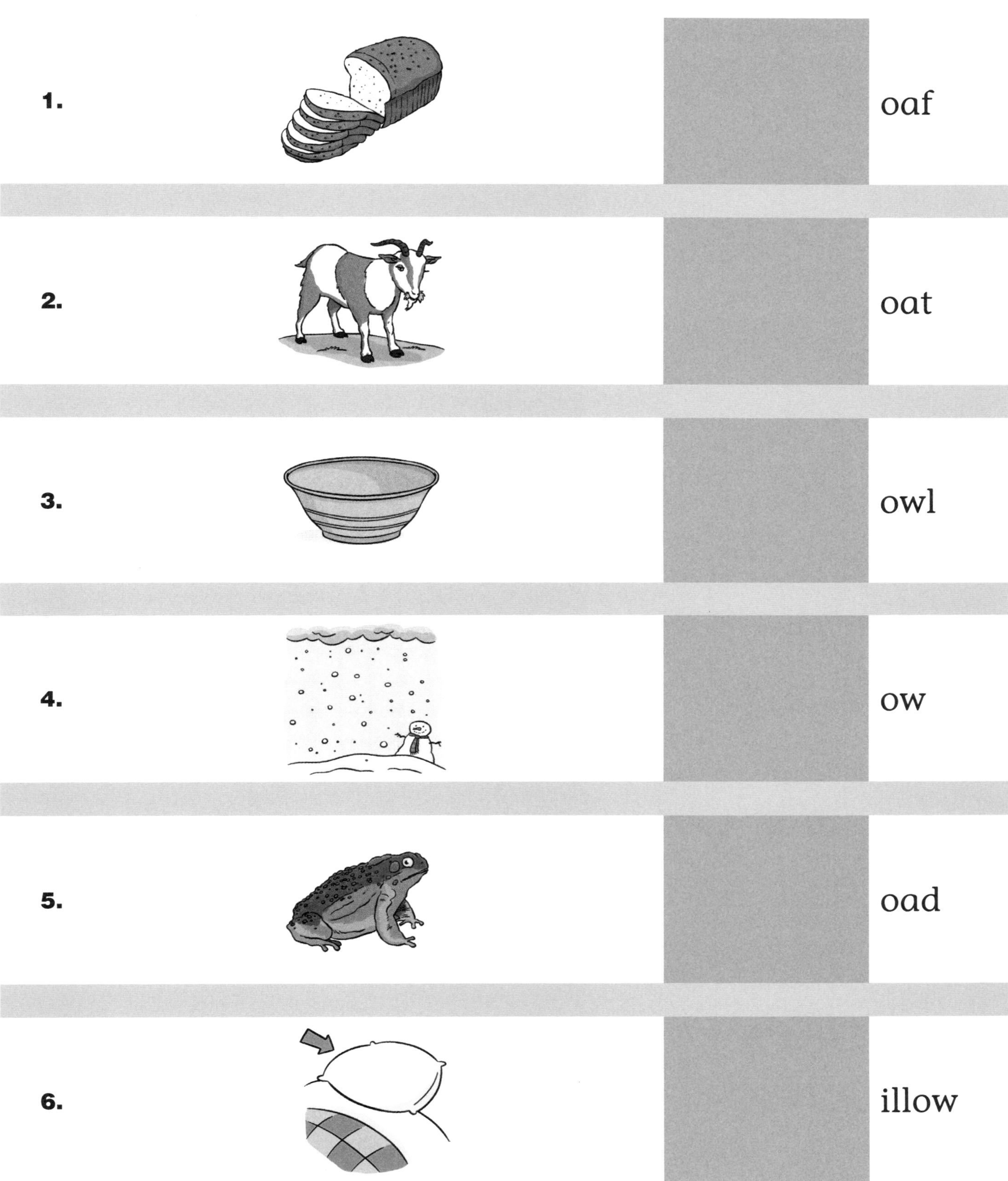

Long o Digraphs oa • ow

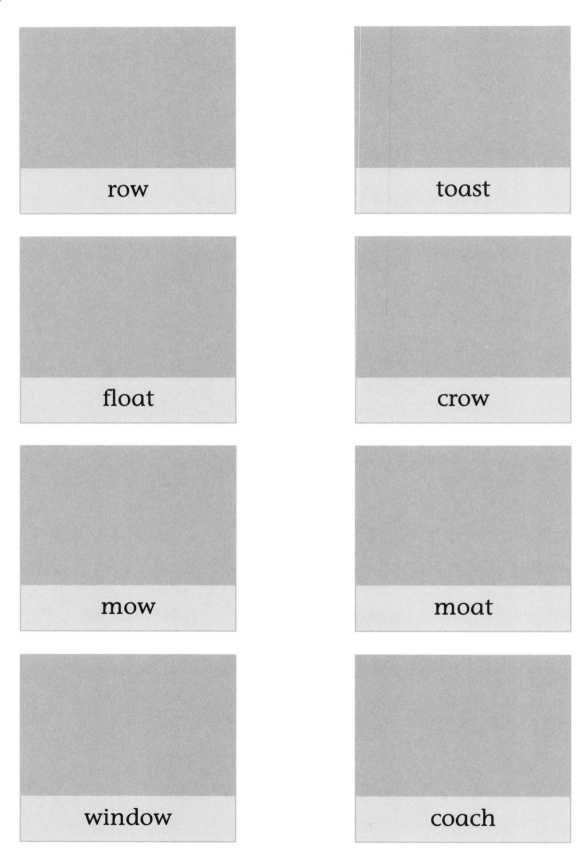

row	toast
float	crow
mow	moat
window	coach

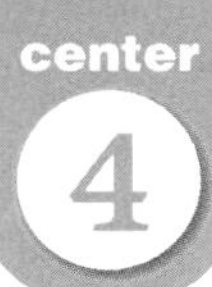

Long o Digraphs oa • ow

Mat A

1. oaf

2. oat

3. owl

4. ow

5. oad

6. illow

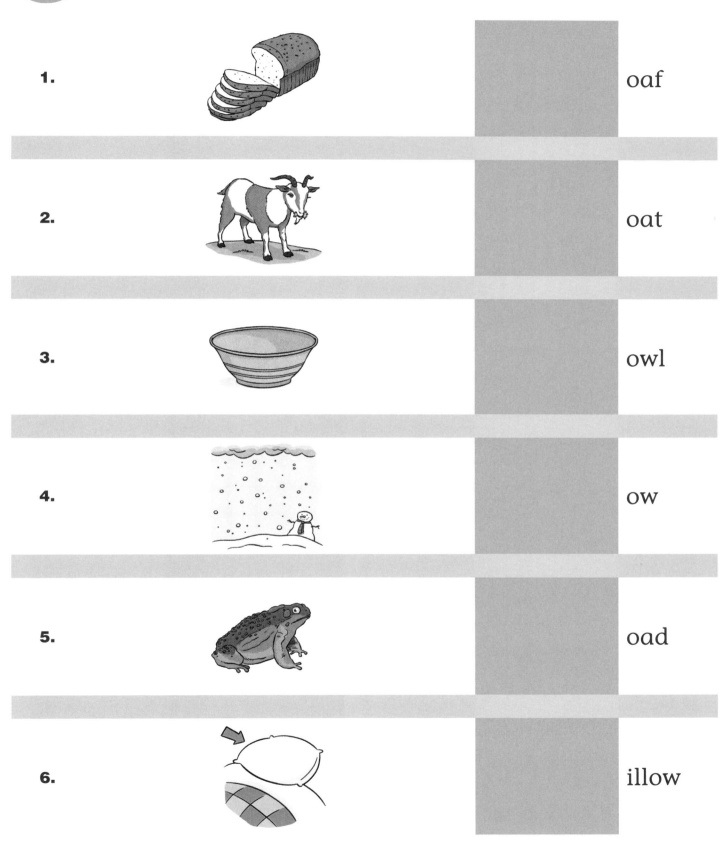

Long o Digraphs oa • ow

Mat B

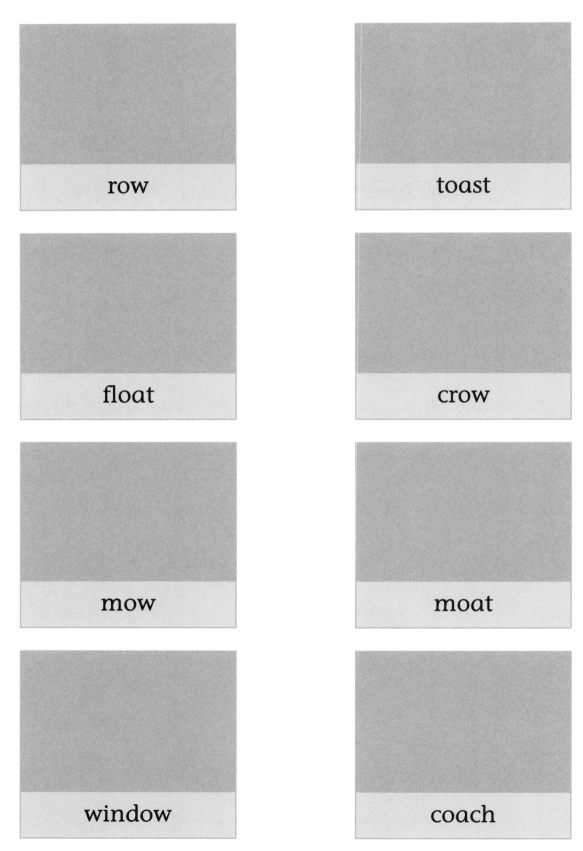

row	toast
float	crow
mow	moat
window	coach

Long o Digraphs oa • ow

1. oaf

2. oat

3. owl

4. ow

5. oad

6. illow

Long o Digraphs oa • ow

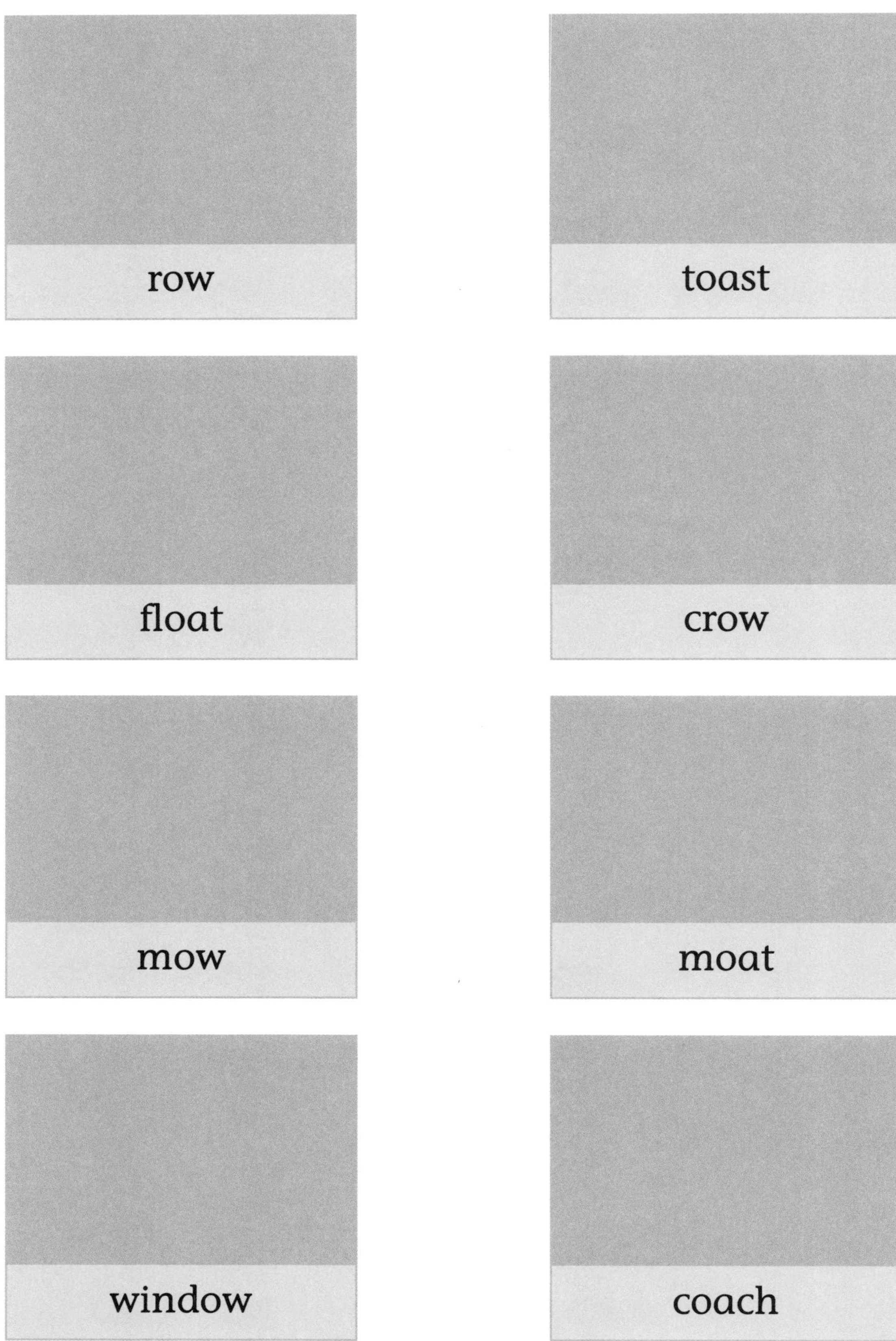

Long o Digraphs oa • ow

1.  oaf

2.  oat

3.  owl

4.  ow

5.  oad

6. 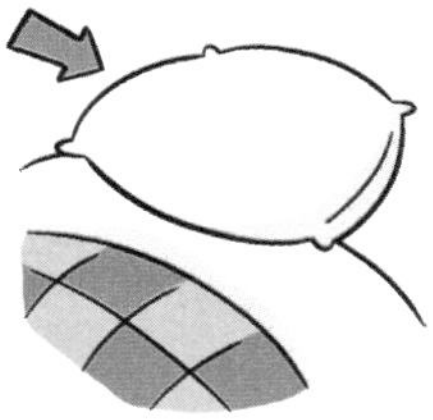 illow

Long o Digraphs oa • ow

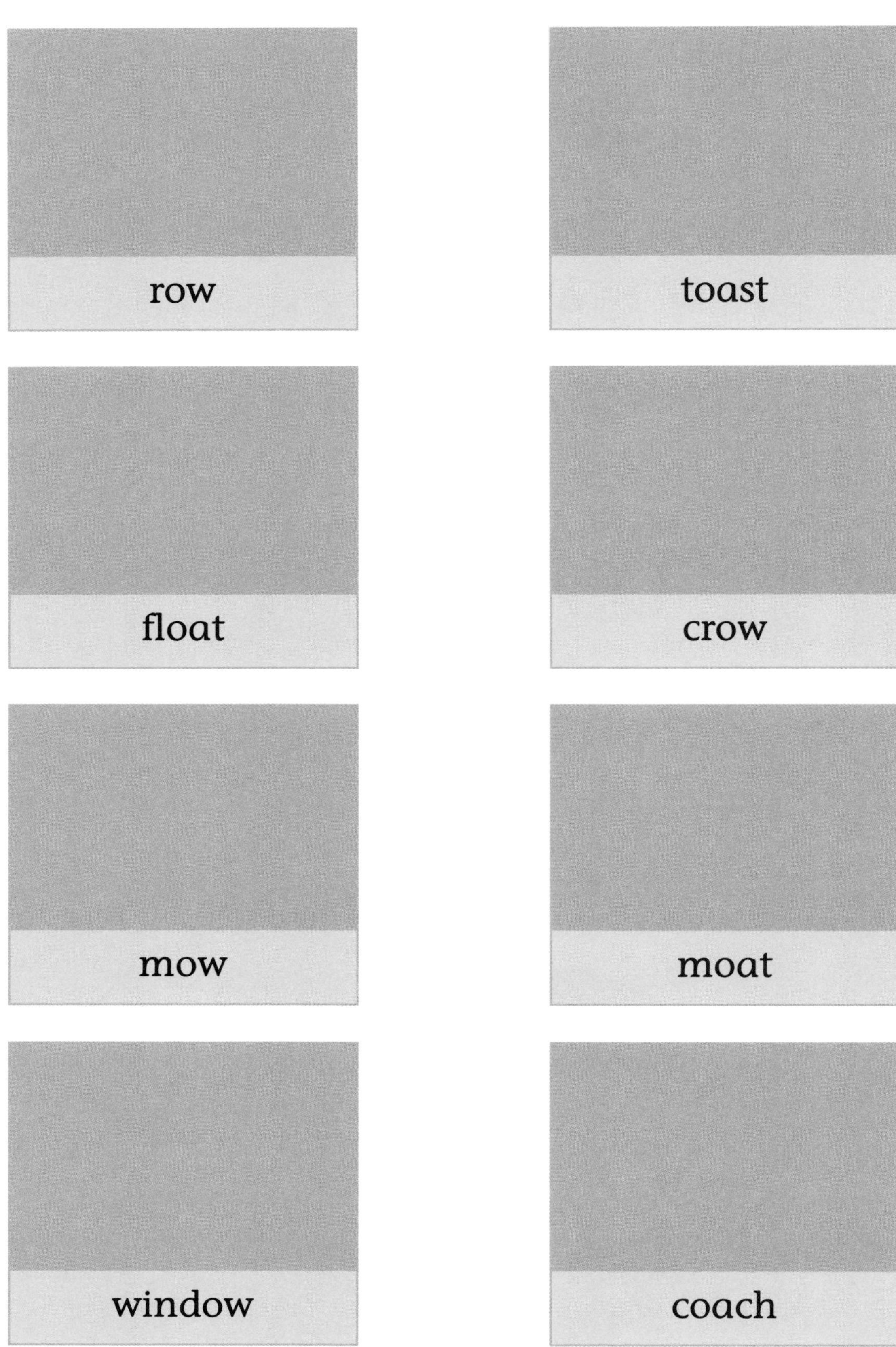

Long o Digraphs oa • ow

Mat A

1.  oaf

2.  oat

3.  owl

4.  ow

5.  oad

6. 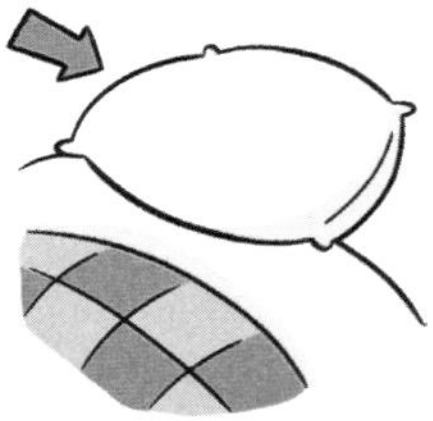 illow

Long o Digraphs oa • ow

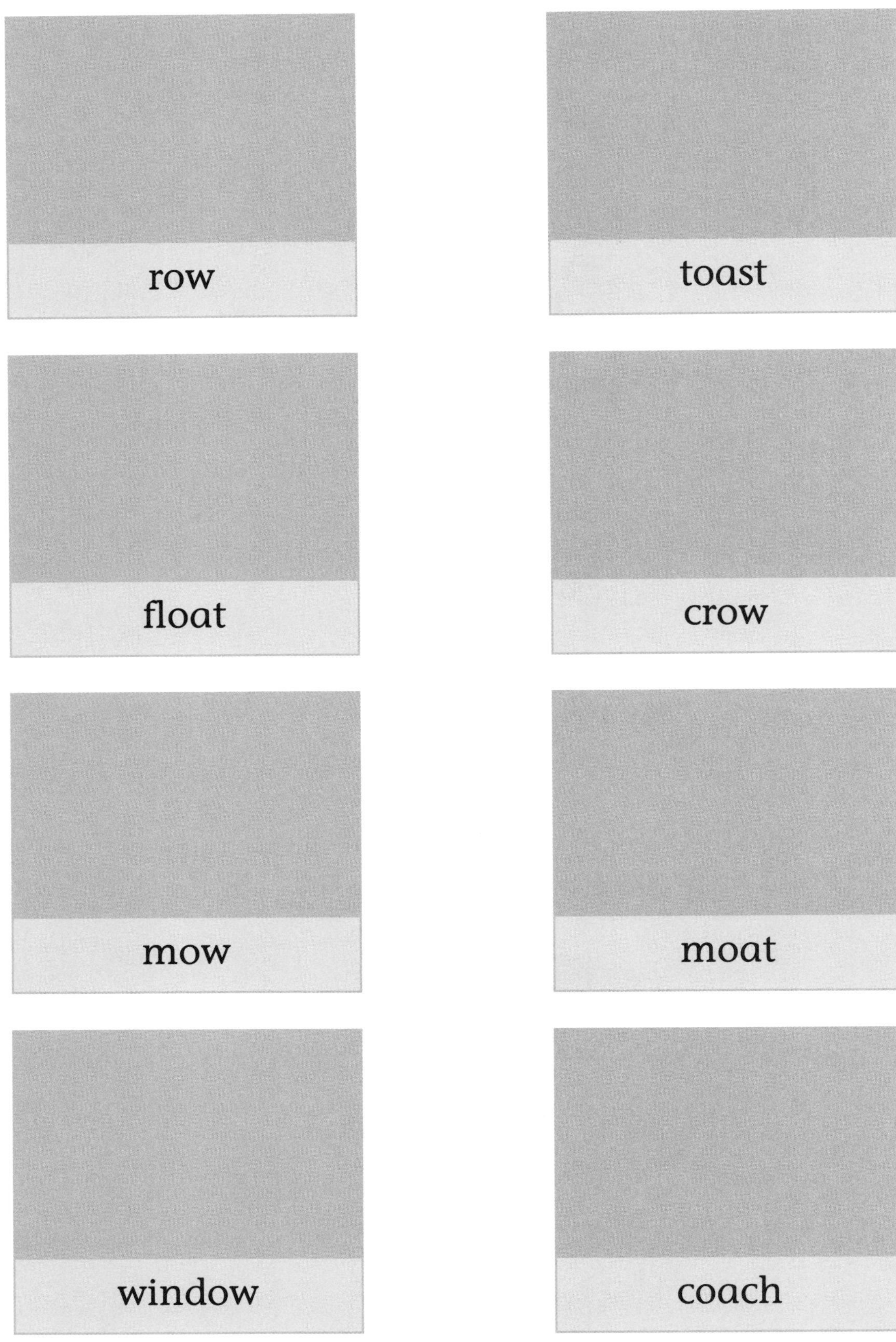

center 4

Task Cards

Mat A

Student 1	Student 2	Student 3	Student 4	Student 5	Student 6
b	b	b	b	b	b
g	g	g	g	g	g
l	l	l	l	l	l
p	p	p	p	p	p
sn	sn	sn	sn	sn	sn
t	t	t	t	t	t

Student 6
EMC 3527
Center 4 • Mat A

Student 5
EMC 3527
Center 4 • Mat A

Student 4
EMC 3527
Center 4 • Mat A

Student 3
EMC 3527
Center 4 • Mat A

Student 2
EMC 3527
Center 4 • Mat A

Student 1
EMC 3527
Center 4 • Mat A

Student 6
EMC 3527
Center 4 • Mat A

Student 5
EMC 3527
Center 4 • Mat A

Student 4
EMC 3527
Center 4 • Mat A

Student 3
EMC 3527
Center 4 • Mat A

Student 2
EMC 3527
Center 4 • Mat A

Student 1
EMC 3527
Center 4 • Mat A

Student 6
EMC 3527
Center 4 • Mat A

Student 5
EMC 3527
Center 4 • Mat A

Student 4
EMC 3527
Center 4 • Mat A

Student 3
EMC 3527
Center 4 • Mat A

Student 2
EMC 3527
Center 4 • Mat A

Student 1
EMC 3527
Center 4 • Mat A

Student 6
EMC 3527
Center 4 • Mat A

Student 5
EMC 3527
Center 4 • Mat A

Student 4
EMC 3527
Center 4 • Mat A

Student 3
EMC 3527
Center 4 • Mat A

Student 2
EMC 3527
Center 4 • Mat A

Student 1
EMC 3527
Center 4 • Mat A

Student 6
EMC 3527
Center 4 • Mat A

Student 5
EMC 3527
Center 4 • Mat A

Student 4
EMC 3527
Center 4 • Mat A

Student 3
EMC 3527
Center 4 • Mat A

Student 2
EMC 3527
Center 4 • Mat A

Student 1
EMC 3527
Center 4 • Mat A

Student 6
EMC 3527
Center 4 • Mat A

Student 5
EMC 3527
Center 4 • Mat A

Student 4
EMC 3527
Center 4 • Mat A

Student 3
EMC 3527
Center 4 • Mat A

Student 2
EMC 3527
Center 4 • Mat A

Student 1
EMC 3527
Center 4 • Mat A

Task Cards

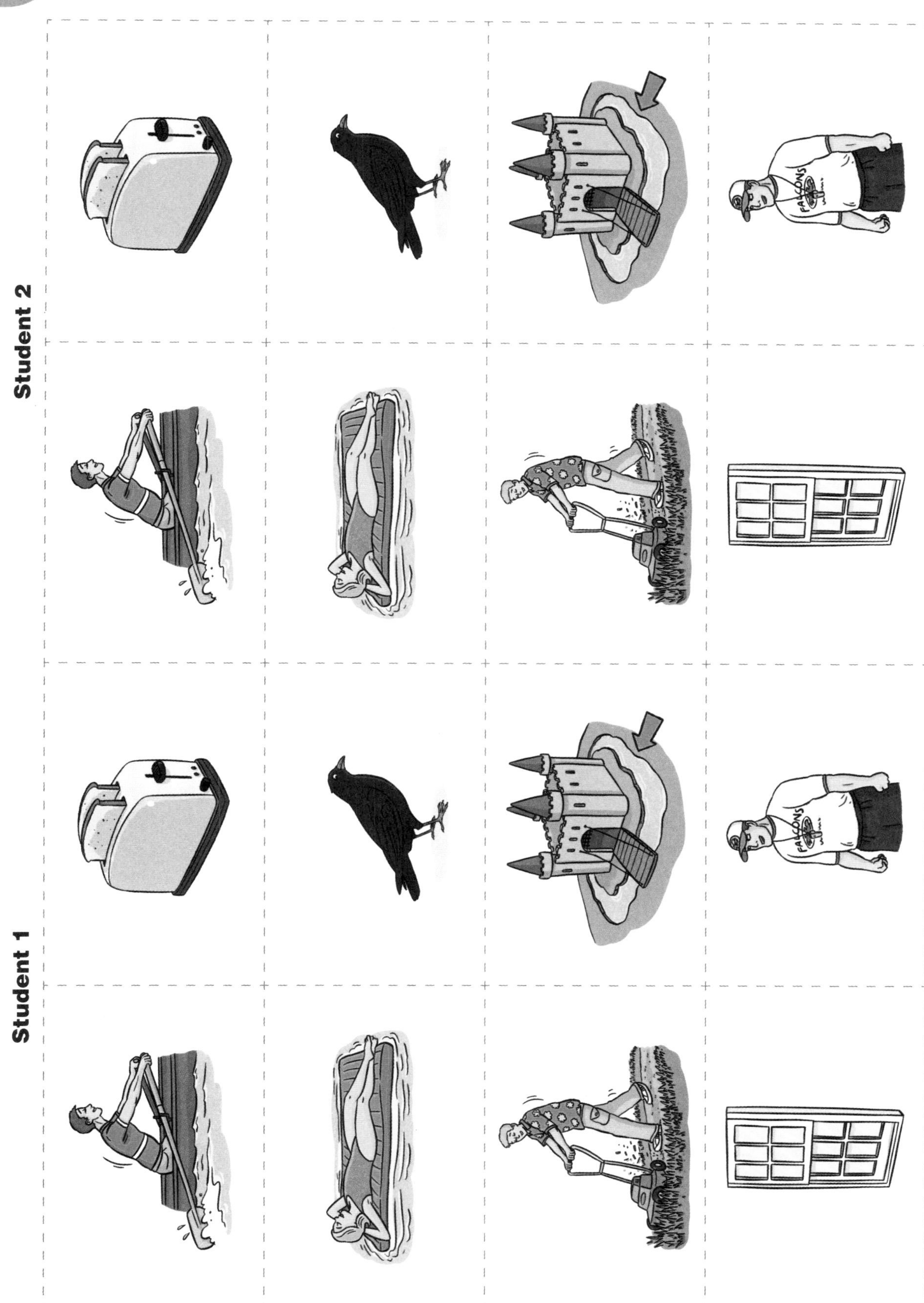

Task Cards

Student 2
EMC 3527 • Center 4 • Mat B

Student 2
EMC 3527 • Center 4 • Mat B

Student 2
EMC 3527 • Center 4 • Mat B

Student 2
EMC 3527 • Center 4 • Mat B

Student 2
EMC 3527 • Center 4 • Mat B

Student 2
EMC 3527 • Center 4 • Mat B

Student 2
EMC 3527 • Center 4 • Mat B

Student 2
EMC 3527 • Center 4 • Mat B

Student 1
EMC 3527 • Center 4 • Mat B

Student 1
EMC 3527 • Center 4 • Mat B

Student 1
EMC 3527 • Center 4 • Mat B

Student 1
EMC 3527 • Center 4 • Mat B

Student 1
EMC 3527 • Center 4 • Mat B

Student 1
EMC 3527 • Center 4 • Mat B

Student 1
EMC 3527 • Center 4 • Mat B

Student 1
EMC 3527 • Center 4 • Mat B

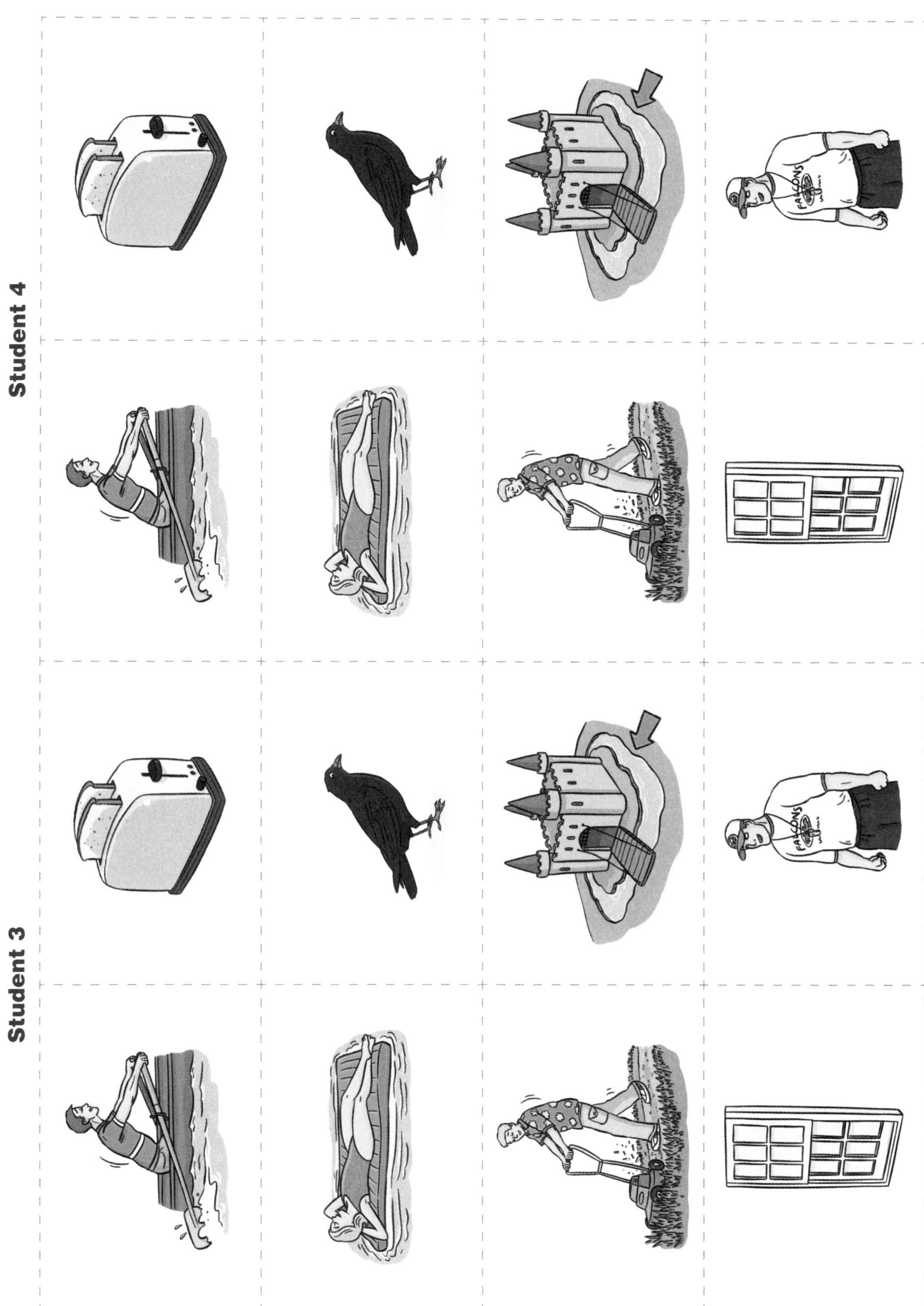
Student 4
Student 3

Student 4

EMC 3527 • Center 4 • Mat B

Student 4

EMC 3527 • Center 4 • Mat B

Student 4

EMC 3527 • Center 4 • Mat B

Student 4

EMC 3527 • Center 4 • Mat B

Student 4

EMC 3527 • Center 4 • Mat B

Student 4

EMC 3527 • Center 4 • Mat B

Student 4

EMC 3527 • Center 4 • Mat B

Student 4

EMC 3527 • Center 4 • Mat B

Student 3

EMC 3527 • Center 4 • Mat B

Student 3

EMC 3527 • Center 4 • Mat B

Student 3

EMC 3527 • Center 4 • Mat B

Student 3

EMC 3527 • Center 4 • Mat B

Student 3

EMC 3527 • Center 4 • Mat B

Student 3

EMC 3527 • Center 4 • Mat B

Student 3

EMC 3527 • Center 4 • Mat B

Student 3

EMC 3527 • Center 4 • Mat B

Task Cards

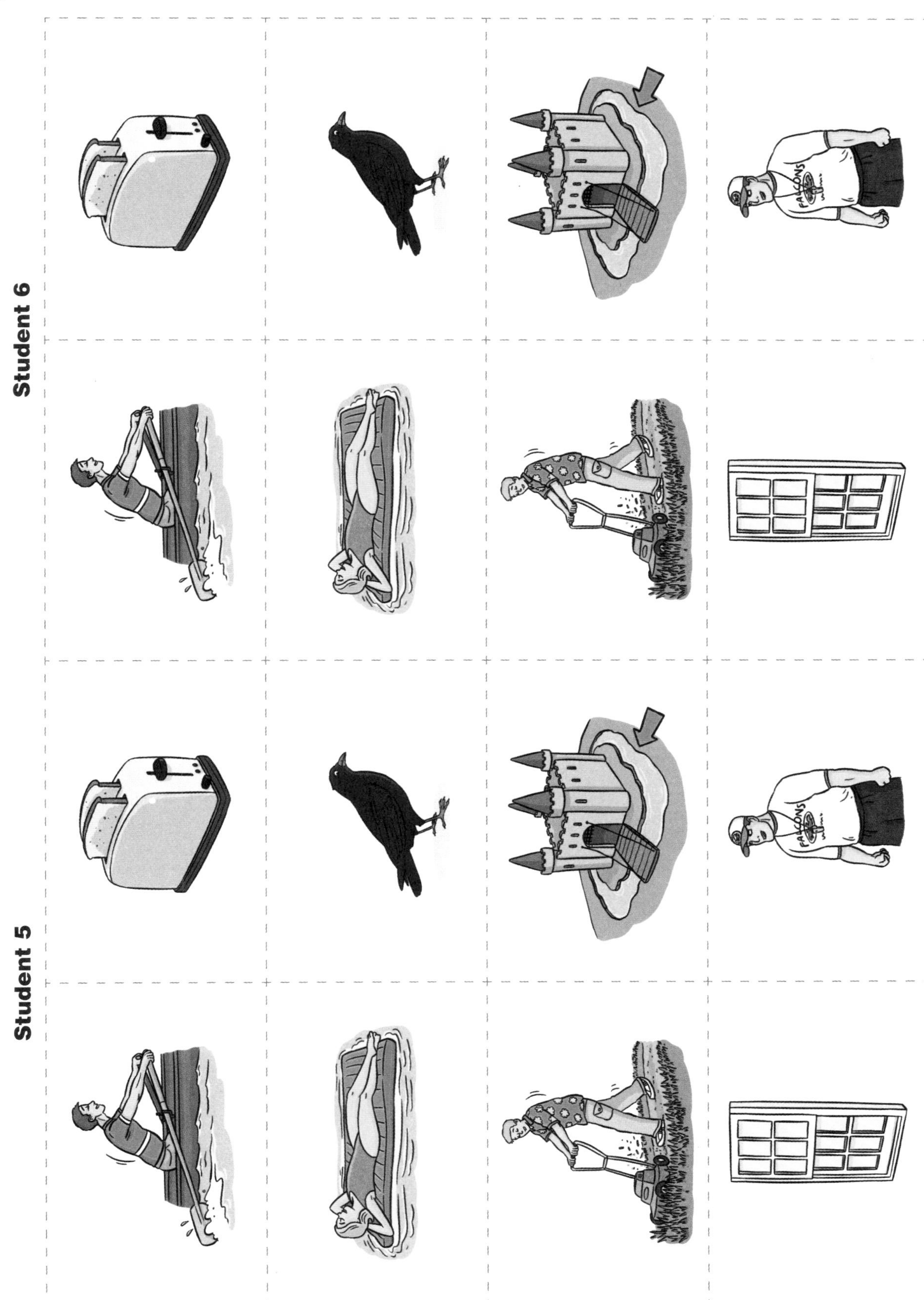

Student 6
EMC 3527 • Center 4 • Mat B

Student 6
EMC 3527 • Center 4 • Mat B

Student 6
EMC 3527 • Center 4 • Mat B

Student 6
EMC 3527 • Center 4 • Mat B

Student 6
EMC 3527 • Center 4 • Mat B

Student 6
EMC 3527 • Center 4 • Mat B

Student 6
EMC 3527 • Center 4 • Mat B

Student 6
EMC 3527 • Center 4 • Mat B

Student 5
EMC 3527 • Center 4 • Mat B

Student 5
EMC 3527 • Center 4 • Mat B

Student 5
EMC 3527 • Center 4 • Mat B

Student 5
EMC 3527 • Center 4 • Mat B

Student 5
EMC 3527 • Center 4 • Mat B

Student 5
EMC 3527 • Center 4 • Mat B

Student 5
EMC 3527 • Center 4 • Mat B

Student 5
EMC 3527 • Center 4 • Mat B

Name ______________________________

Practice It!

Say the word.
Change the letter or letters to make a new word.
Write the letters to spell the new word.

Example

coal ⟶ ~~c~~oal (g) **g o a l**

1. toad ⟶ ~~t~~oad (l) ___ ___ ___ ___

2. mow ⟶ ~~m~~ow (gr) ___ ___ ___ ___

3. crow ⟶ ~~cr~~ow (gl) ___ ___ ___ ___

4. moan ⟶ ~~m~~oan (l) ___ ___ ___ ___

5. roam ⟶ ~~r~~oam (f) ___ ___ ___ ___

6. yellow ⟶ ~~y~~ellow (m) ___ ___ ___ ___ ___ ___

7. toast ⟶ ~~t~~oast (b) ___ ___ ___ ___ ___

8. pillow ⟶ ~~p~~illow (w) ___ ___ ___ ___ ___ ___

Name ___________________________________

Read It!

Write the word or words from the box that best complete each sentence.

Word Box

coat	cocoa	crow	goal	grown
loaf	road	toad	throw	willow

1. I saw a big black ____________ fly to that tall oak tree.

2. Our coach cheers when we score a ____________.

3. This map will show you the ____________ to my house.

4. Mom told me to ____________ the bowl I broke into the trash.

5. How much do I owe you for this ____________ of bread?

6. We like to drink hot ____________ on snowy days.

7. I heard a ____________ croak below that ____________ tree.

8. Joe has ____________, and now his ____________ is too small.

center 5

INTERMEDIATE

Long u Digraphs ew • ue

For the Teacher

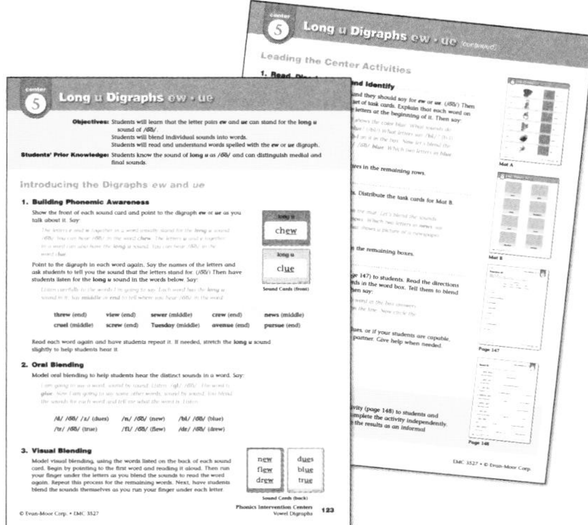

Lesson Plan

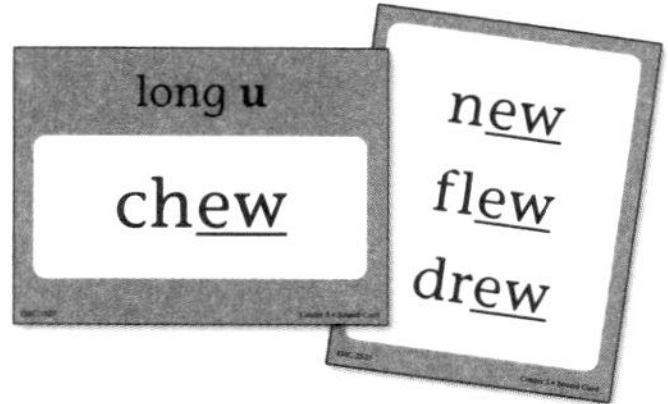

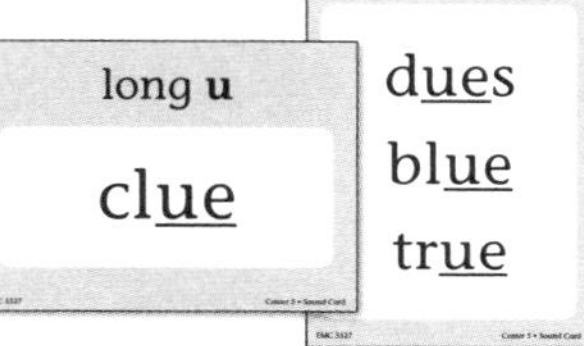

Sound Cards

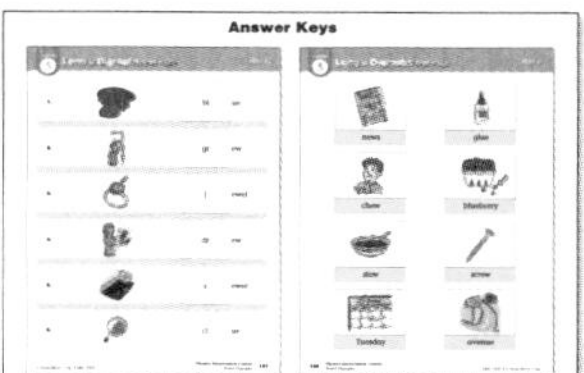

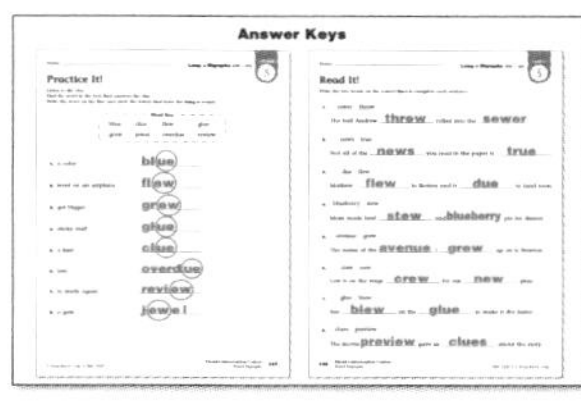

Answer Keys

For the Student

front (Mat A)

back (Mat B)

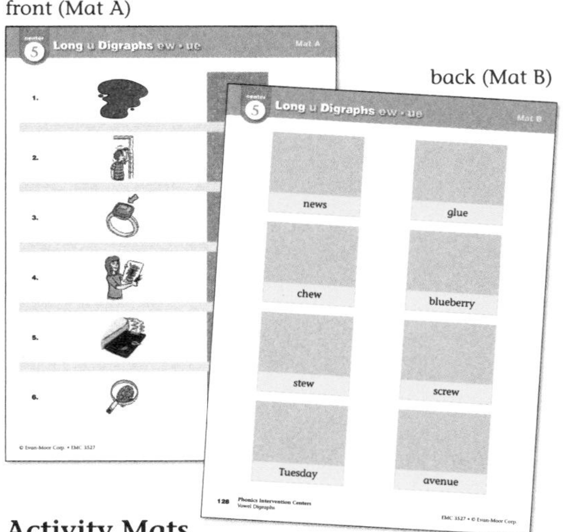

Activity Mats

Task Cards

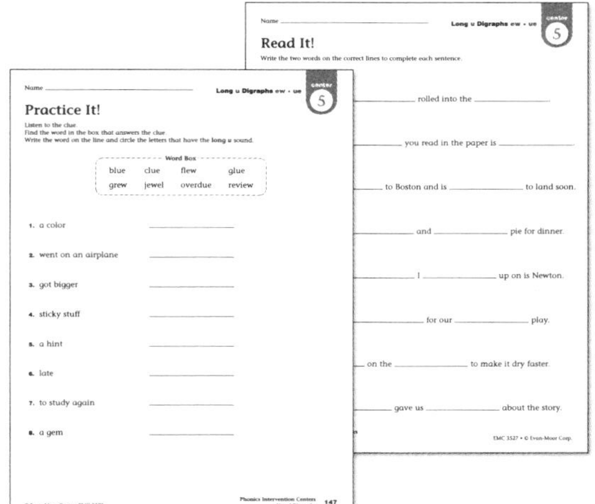

Practice and Assessment Activities

Long u Digraphs ew • ue

Objectives: Students will learn that the letter pairs ***ew*** and ***ue*** can stand for the **long *u*** sound of /o͞o/.
Students will blend individual sounds into words.
Students will read and understand words spelled with the ***ew*** or ***ue*** digraph.

Students' Prior Knowledge: Students know the sound of **long *u*** as /o͞o/ and can distinguish medial and final sounds.

Introducing the Digraphs *ew* and *ue*

1. Building Phonemic Awareness

Show the front of each sound card and point to the digraph ***ew*** or ***ue*** as you talk about it. Say:

*The letters **e** and **w** together in a word usually stand for the **long u** sound: /o͞o/. You can hear /o͞o/ in the word **chew**. The letters **u** and **e** together in a word can also have the **long u** sound. You can hear /o͞o/ in the word **clue**.*

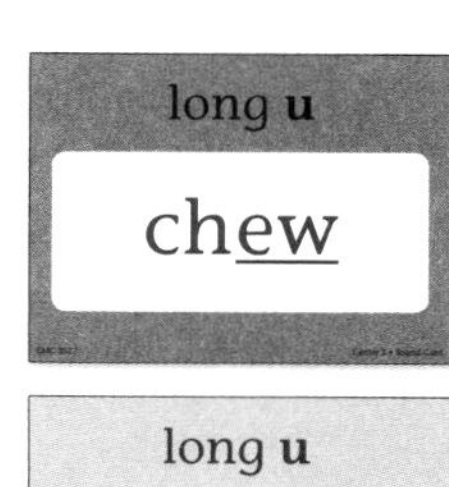

Sound Cards (front)

Point to the digraph in each word again. Say the names of the letters and ask students to tell you the sound that the letters stand for. (/o͞o/) Then have students listen for the **long *u*** sound in the words below. Say:

*Listen carefully to the words I'm going to say. Each word has the **long u** sound in it. Say **middle** or **end** to tell where you hear /o͞o/ in the word:*

threw (end)	**view** (end)	**sewer** (middle)	**crew** (end)	**news** (middle)
cruel (middle)	**screw** (end)	**Tuesday** (middle)	**avenue** (end)	**pursue** (end)

Read each word again and have students repeat it. If needed, stretch the **long *u*** sound slightly to help students hear it.

2. Oral Blending

Model oral blending to help students hear the distinct sounds in a word. Say:

*I am going to say a word, sound by sound. Listen: /gl/ /o͞o/. The word is **glue**. Now I am going to say some other words, sound by sound. You blend the sounds for each word and tell me what the word is. Listen:*

/d/ /o͞o/ /z/ (dues)	**/n/ /o͞o/** (new)	**/bl/ /o͞o/** (blue)
/tr/ /o͞o/ (true)	**/fl/ /o͞o/** (flew)	**/dr/ /o͞o/** (drew)

3. Visual Blending

Model visual blending, using the words listed on the back of each sound card. Begin by pointing to the first word and reading it aloud. Then run your finger under the letters as you blend the sounds to read the word again. Repeat this process for the remaining words. Next, have students blend the sounds themselves as you run your finger under each letter.

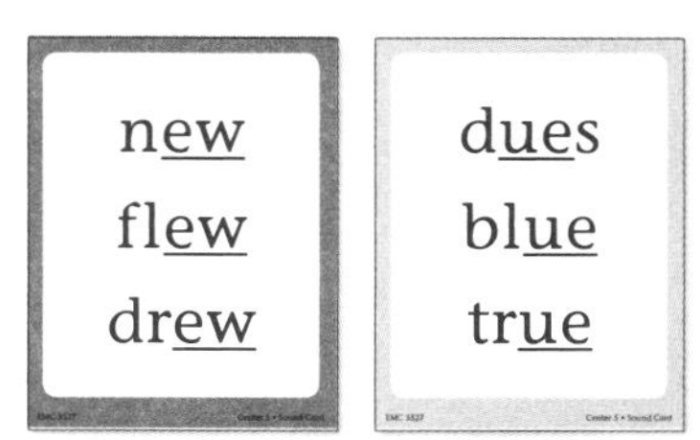

Sound Cards (back)

Leading the Center Activities

1. Read, Discriminate, and Identify

Ask students to tell you the sound they should say for ***ew*** or ***ue***. (/o͞o/) Then give each student Mat A and a set of task cards. Explain that each word on the mat is missing one or more letters at the beginning of it. Then say:

> *Look at the picture in row 1. It shows the color blue. What sounds do you hear at the beginning of* ***blue****?* (/bl/) *What letters say* **/bl/***?* (b-l) *Place the card with the letters* ***b-l*** *on it in the box. Now let's blend the sounds and read the word:* **/bl/ /o͞o/** ***blue****. Which two letters in* ***blue*** *say* **/o͞o/***?* (u-e)

Repeat this process with the pictures in the remaining rows.

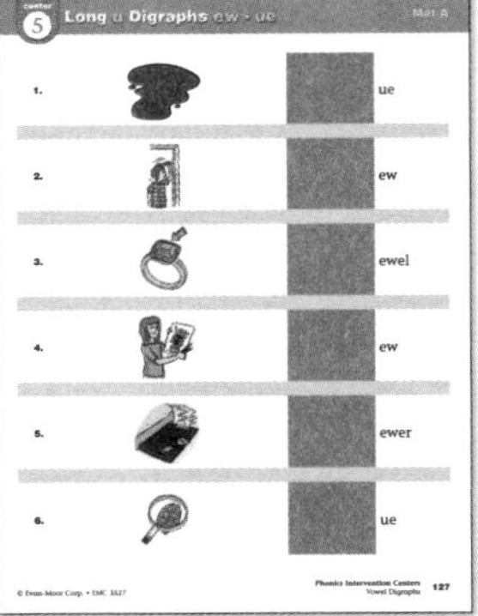

Mat A

2. Read and Understand

Have students turn over their mats. Distribute the task cards for Mat B. Then say:

> *Look at the word in the first box on the mat. Let's blend the sounds to read the word:* **/n/ /o͞o/ /z/** ***news****. Which two letters in* ***news*** *say* **/o͞o/***?* (e-w) *Now place the card that shows a picture of a newspaper above the word.*

Repeat this process with the words in the remaining boxes.

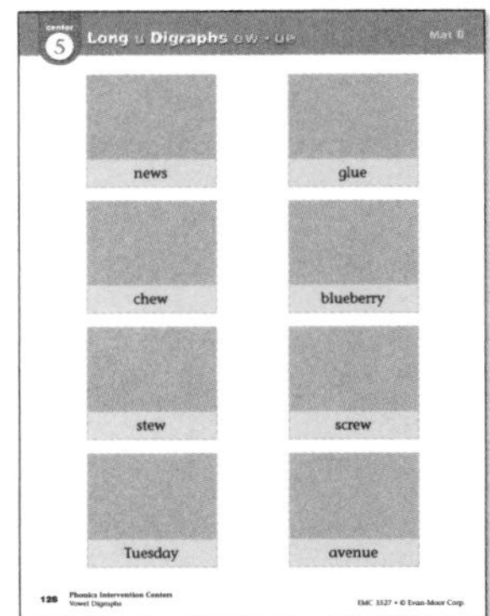

Mat B

3. Practice the Skill

Distribute the Practice It! activity (page 147) to students. Read the directions aloud and have students read the words in the word box. Tell them to blend the sounds as they read each word. Then say:

> *Listen to the first clue:* ***a color****. Which word in the box answers the clue?* (blue) *Write the word* ***blue*** *on the line. Now circle the letters in* ***blue*** *that say* **/o͞o/***.* (ue)

Repeat this process for the remaining clues, or if your students are capable, have them complete the activity with a partner. Give help when needed. Then go over the answers as a group.

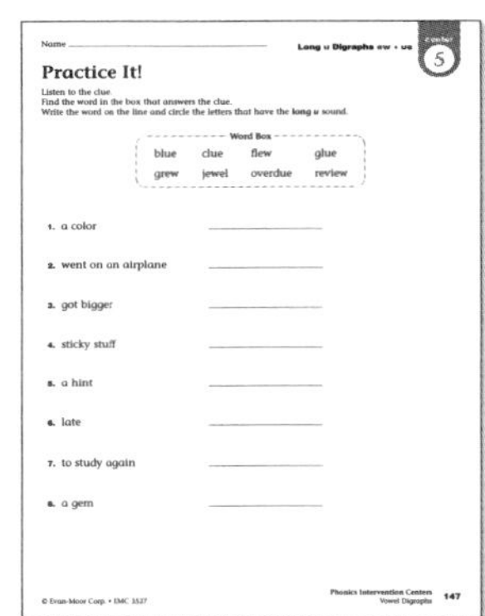

Page 147

Page 148

Apply and Assess

After the lesson, distribute the Read It! activity (page 148) to students and read the directions aloud. Have students complete the activity independently. Then listen to them read the sentences. Use the results as an informal assessment of students' skill mastery.

long **u**

ch<u>ew</u>

Center 5 • Sound Card

EMC 3527

long **u**

cl<u>ue</u>

Center 5 • Sound Card

EMC 3527

Answer Keys

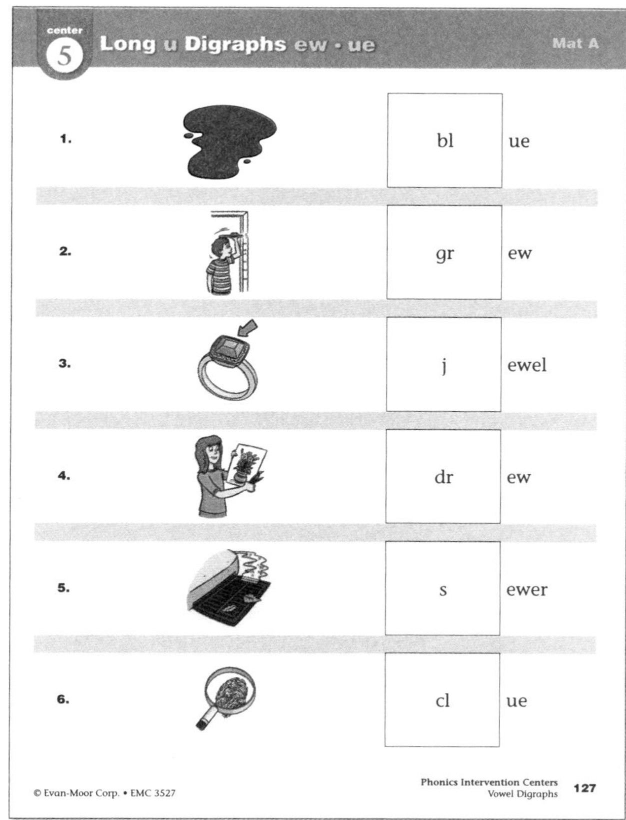

center 5 **Long u Digraphs ew · ue** Mat A

1.	bl	ue
2.	gr	ew
3.	j	ewel
4.	dr	ew
5.	s	ewer
6.	cl	ue

© Evan-Moor Corp. • EMC 3527

Phonics Intervention Centers
Vowel Digraphs 127

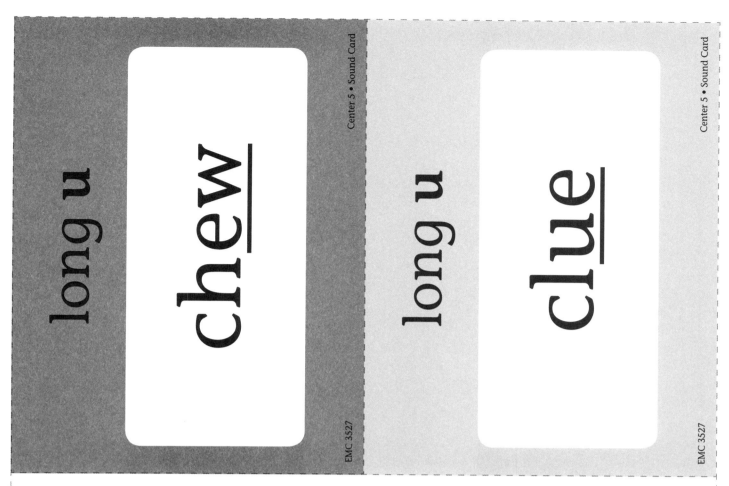

center 5 **Long u Digraphs ew · ue** Mat B

news	glue
chew	blueberry
stew	screw
Tuesday	avenue

128 Phonics Intervention Centers
Vowel Digraphs

EMC 3527 • © Evan-Moor Corp.

dues

blue

true

EMC 3527 Center 5 • Sound Card

new

flew

drew

EMC 3527 Center 5 • Sound Card

Answer Keys

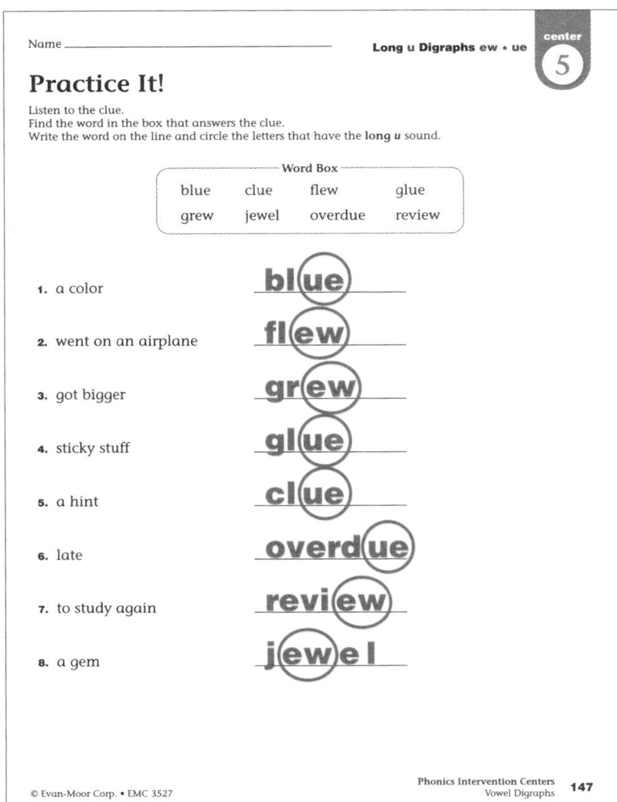

Name ______________

Long u Digraphs ew • ue

center 5

Practice It!

Listen to the clue.
Find the word in the box that answers the clue.
Write the word on the line and circle the letters that have the **long *u*** sound.

Word Box

blue	clue	flew	glue
grew	jewel	overdue	review

1. a color — blue
2. went on an airplane — flew
3. got bigger — grew
4. sticky stuff — glue
5. a hint — clue
6. late — overdue
7. to study again — review
8. a gem — jewel

© Evan-Moor Corp. • EMC 3527 Phonics Intervention Centers Vowel Digraphs 147

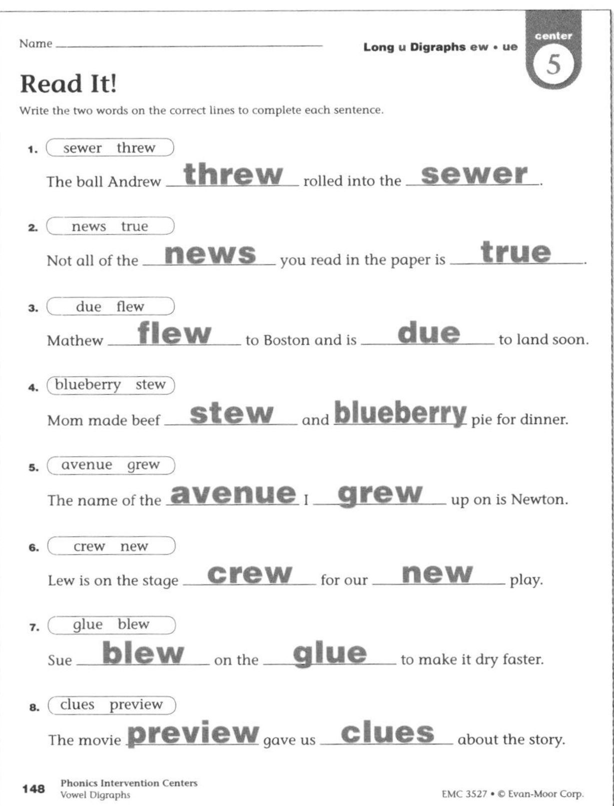

Name ______________

Long u Digraphs ew • ue

center 5

Read It!

Write the two words on the correct lines to complete each sentence.

1. (sewer threw) The ball Andrew threw rolled into the sewer.
2. (news true) Not all of the news you read in the paper is true.
3. (due flew) Mathew flew to Boston and is due to land soon.
4. (blueberry stew) Mom made beef stew and blueberry pie for dinner.
5. (avenue grew) The name of the avenue I grew up on is Newton.
6. (crew new) Lew is on the stage crew for our new play.
7. (glue blew) Sue blew on the glue to make it dry faster.
8. (clues preview) The movie preview gave us clues about the story.

148 Phonics Intervention Centers Vowel Digraphs EMC 3527 • © Evan-Moor Corp.

Long u Digraphs ew • ue

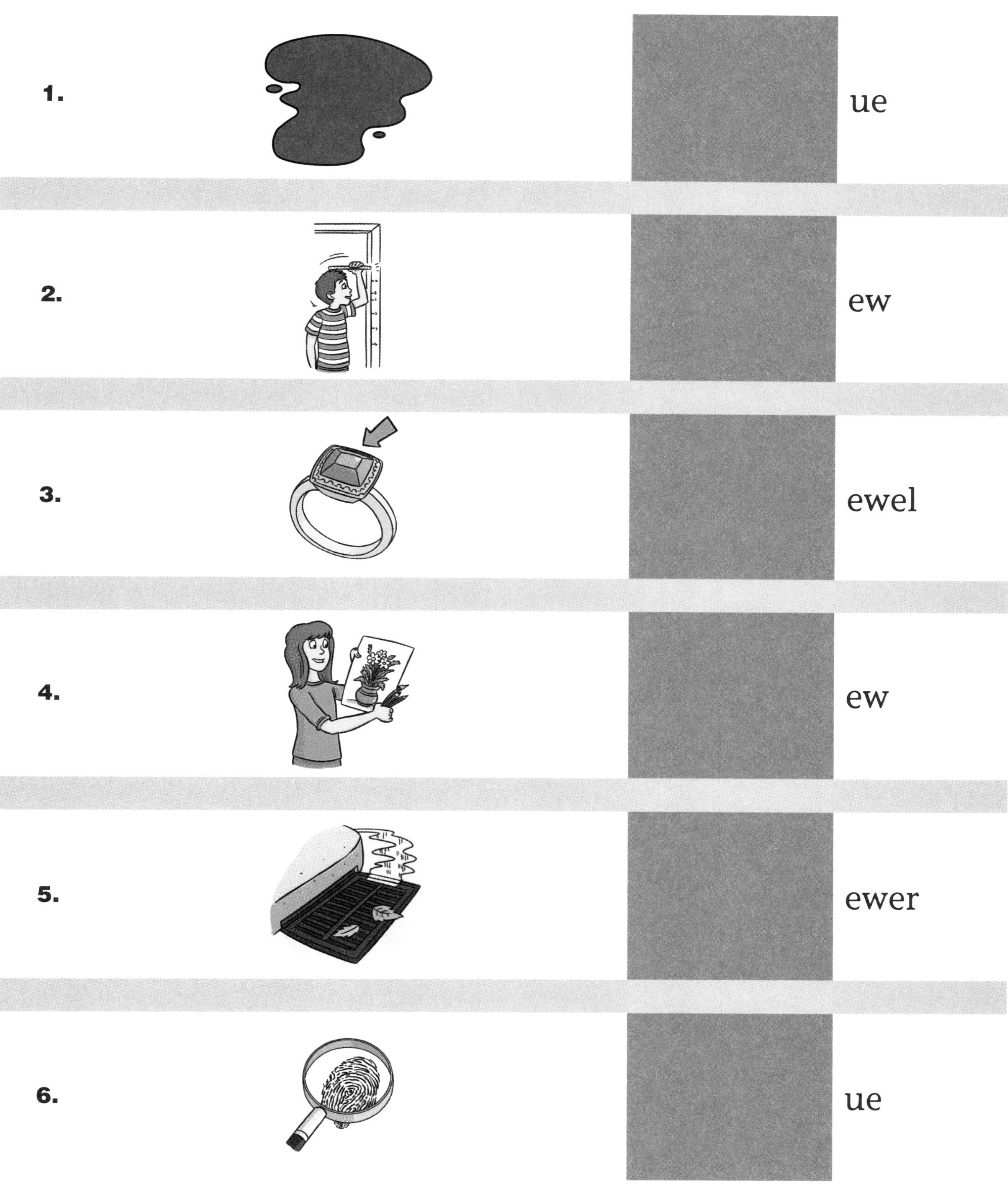

Long u Digraphs ew • ue

Mat B

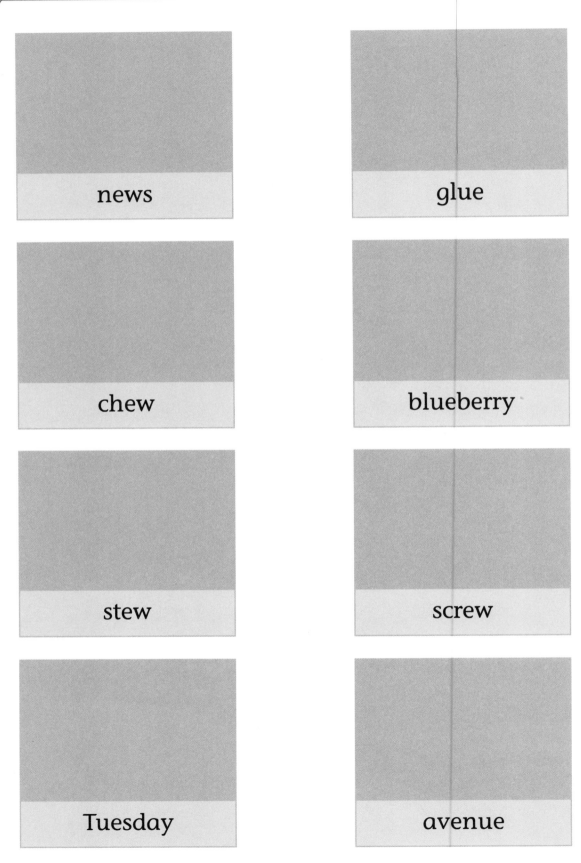

news	glue
chew	blueberry
stew	screw
Tuesday	avenue

Long u Digraphs ew • ue

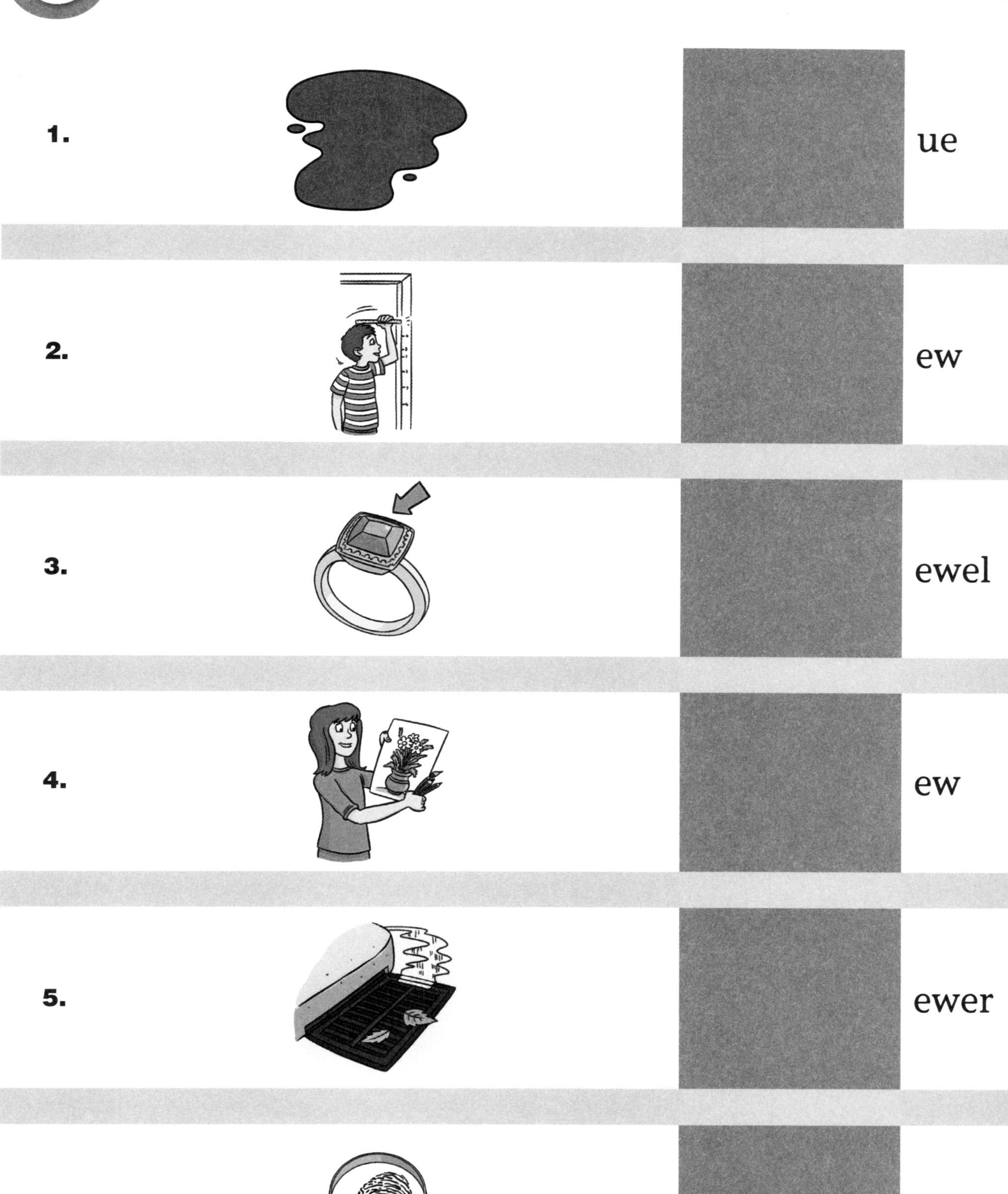

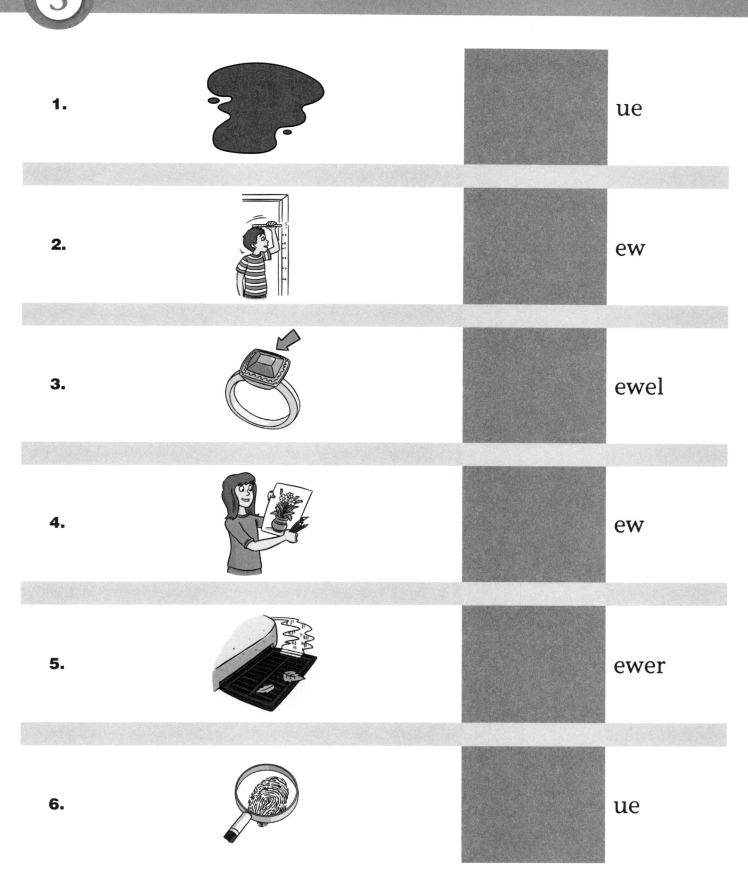

Long u Digraphs ew • ue

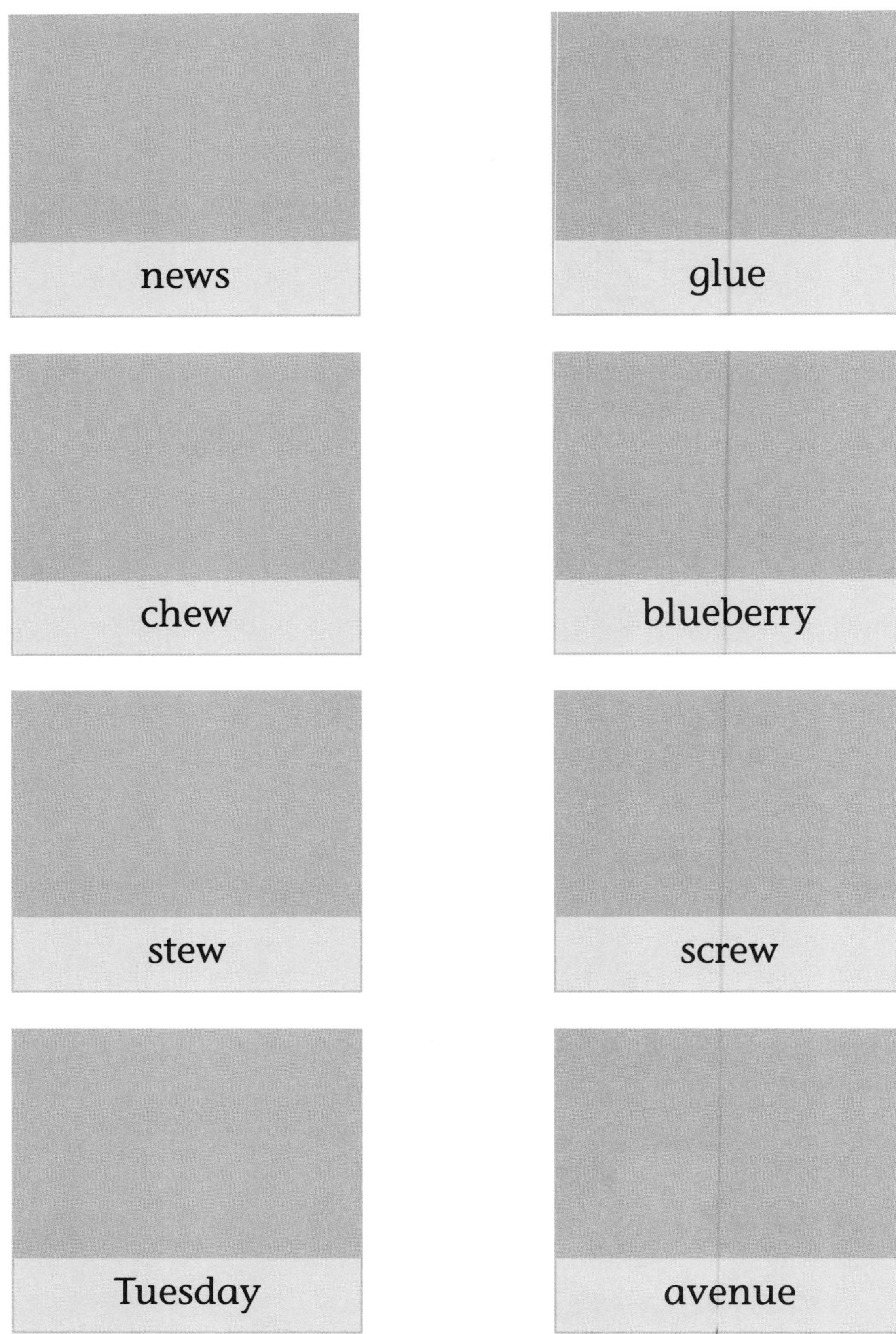

Long u Digraphs ew • ue

Mat A

1. 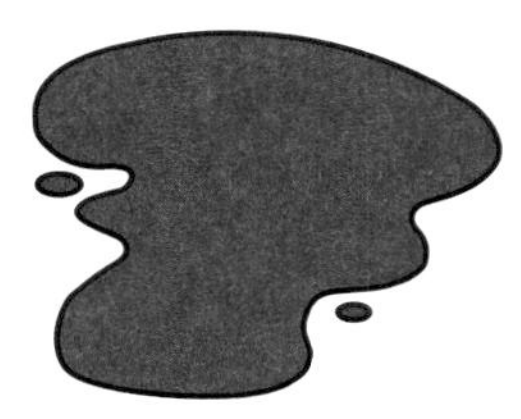 ue

2.  ew

3.  ewel

4.  ew

5. 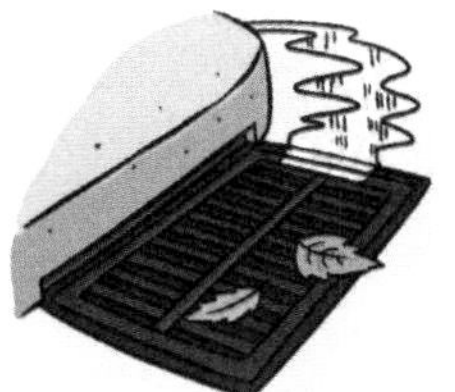 ewer

6.   ue

Long u Digraphs ew • ue

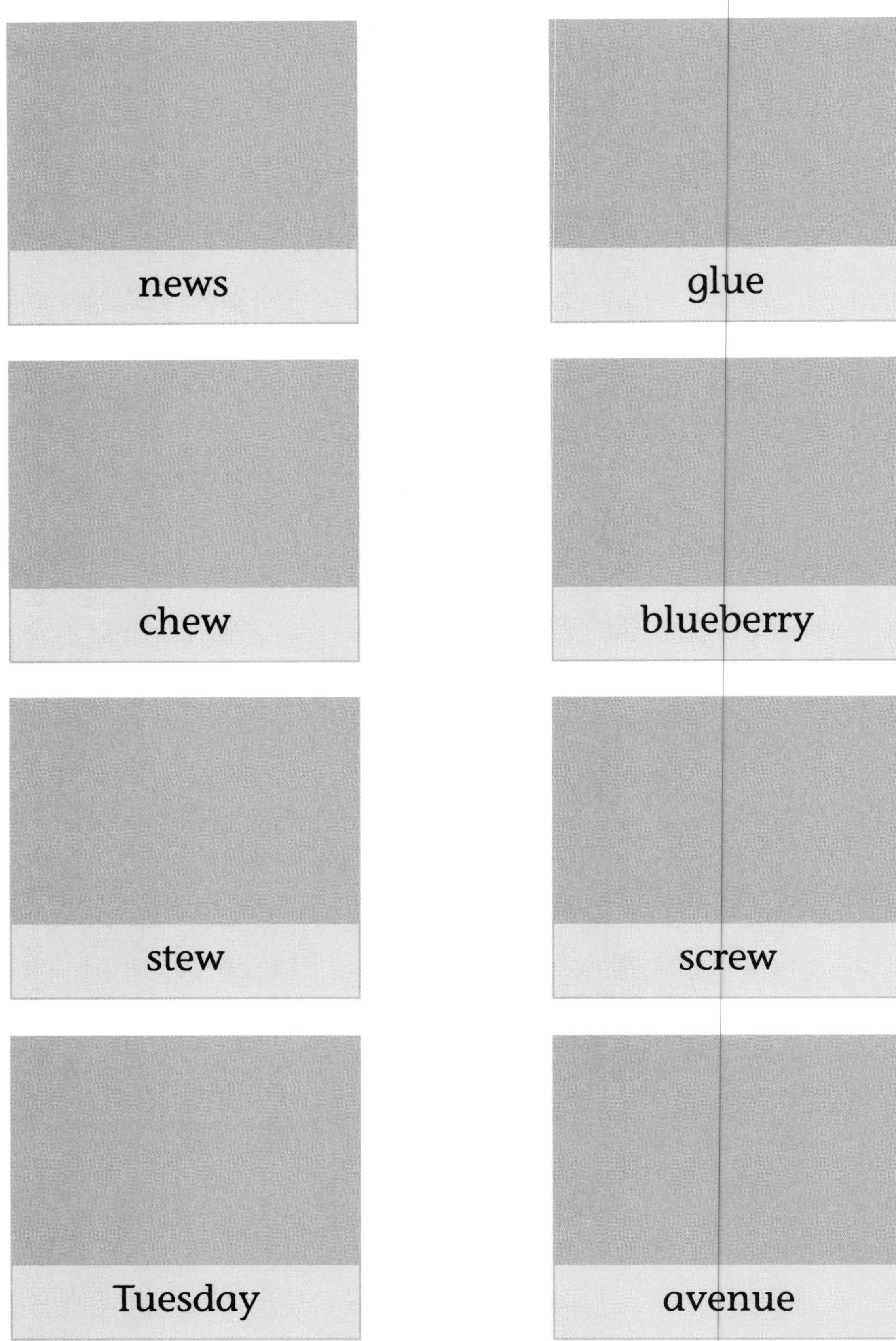

Long u Digraphs ew • ue

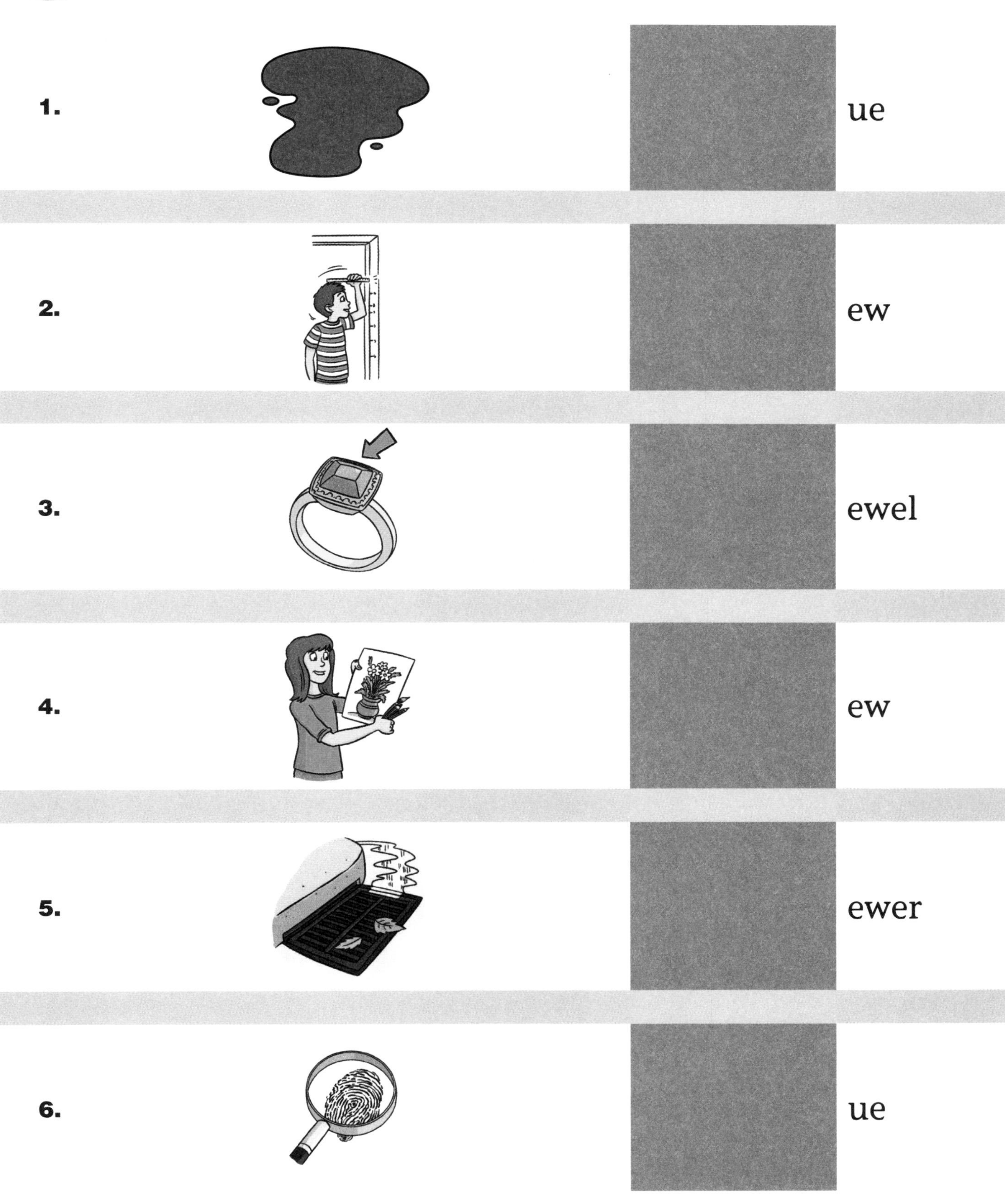

Long u Digraphs ew • ue

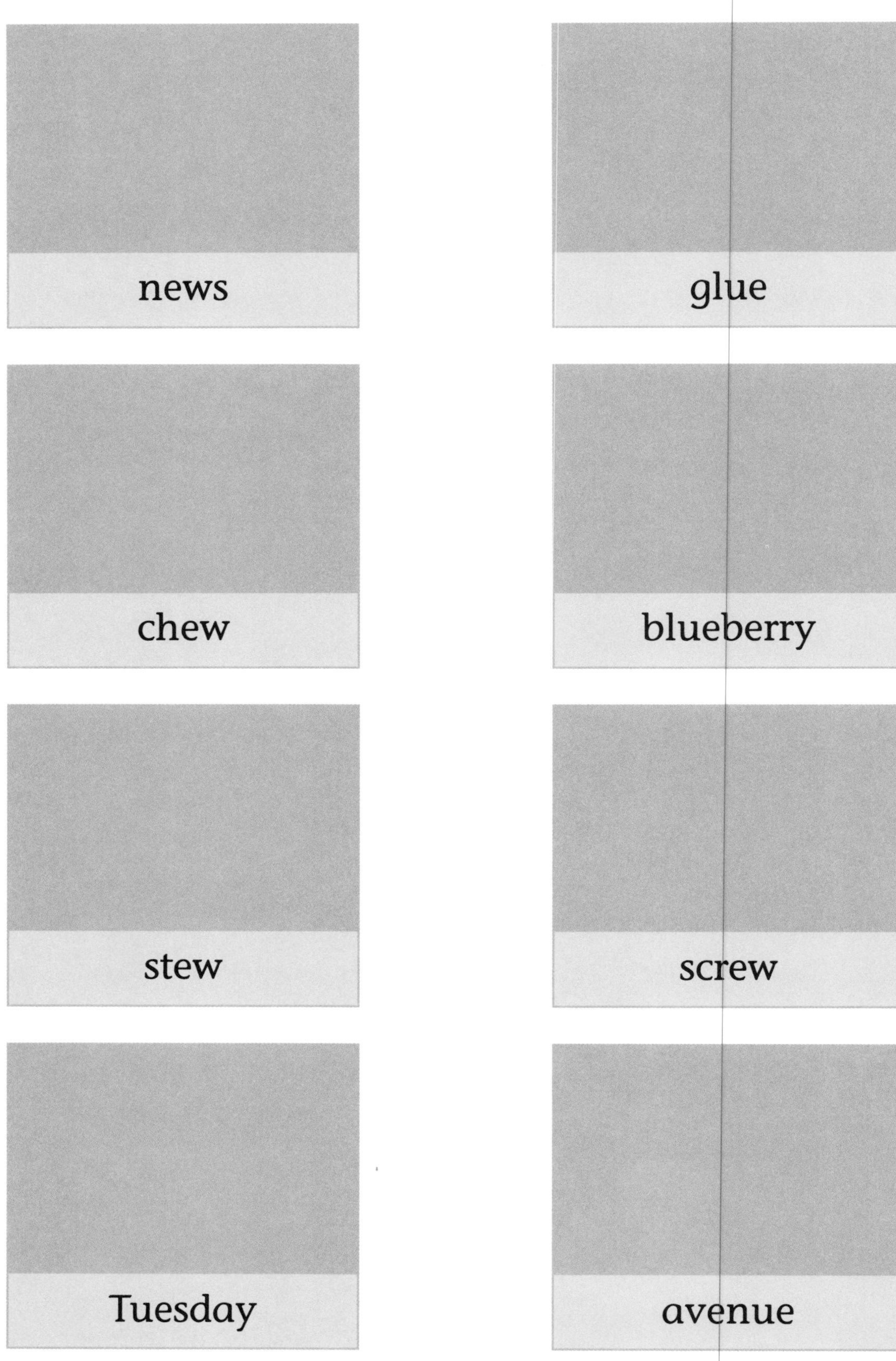

Long u Digraphs ew • ue

Mat A

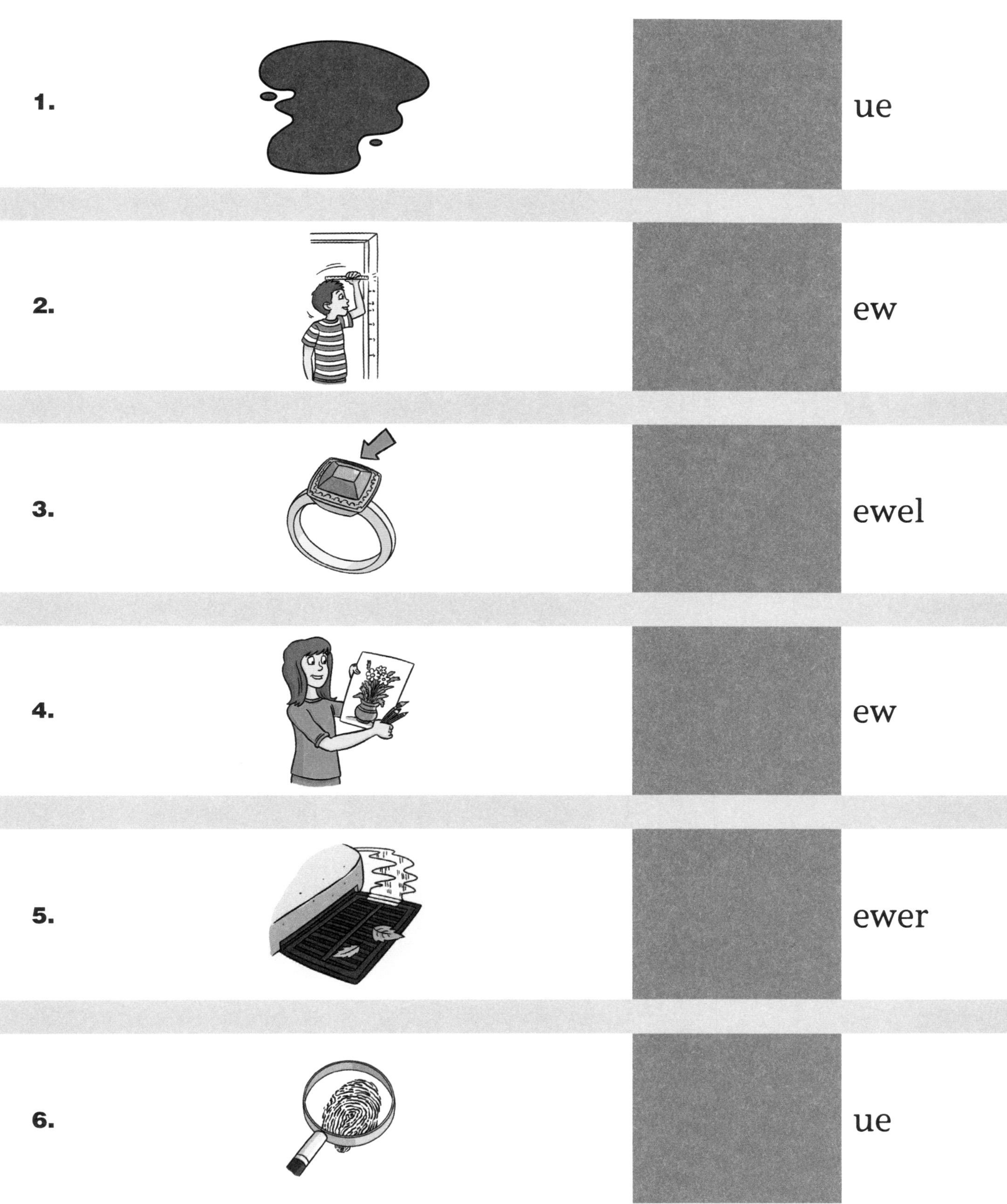

Long u Digraphs ew • ue

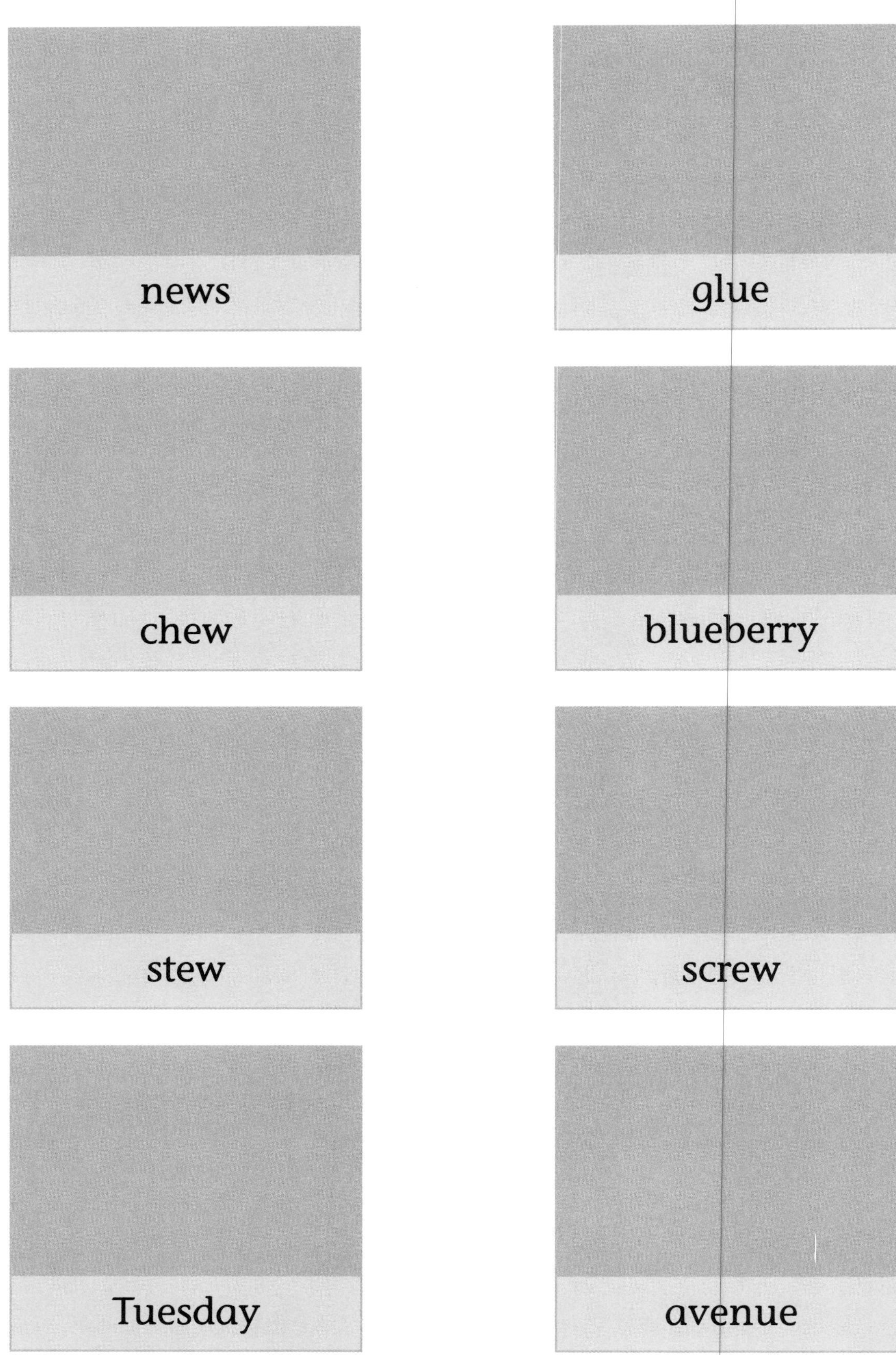

Task Cards

Student 4

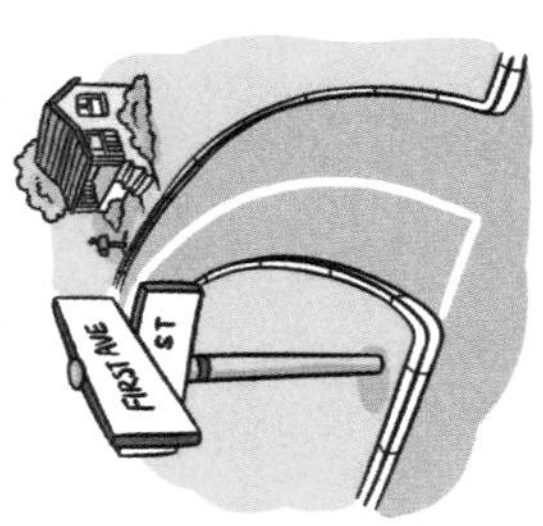

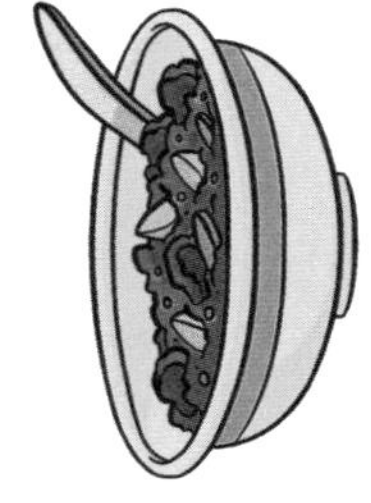

June
Sun Mon Tue Wed
1 2 3
7 8 9 10

Student 3

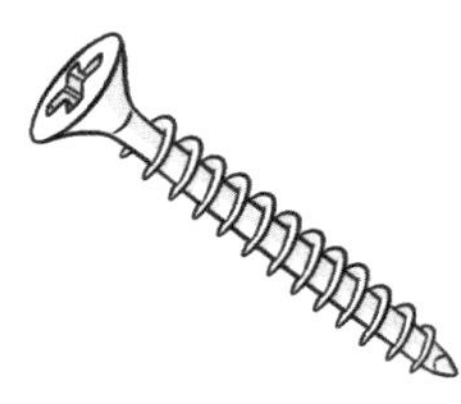

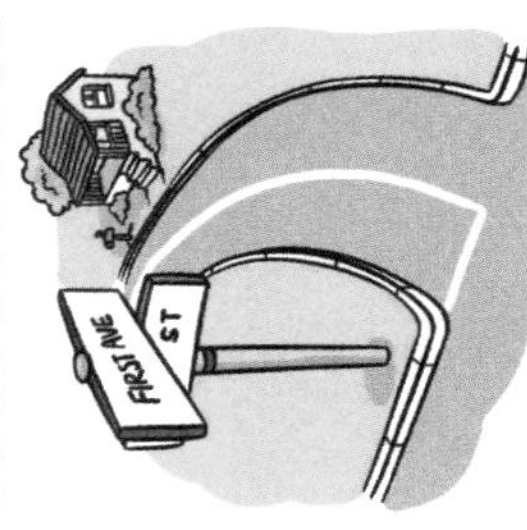

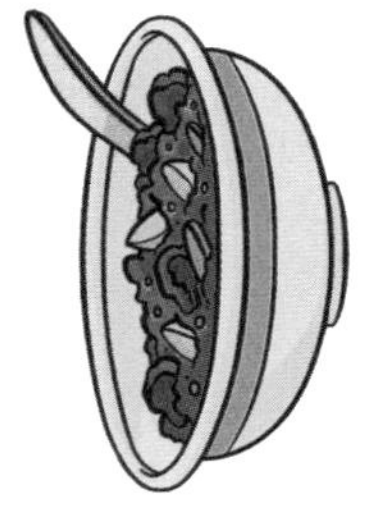

June
Sun Mon Tue Wed
1 2 3
7 8 9 10

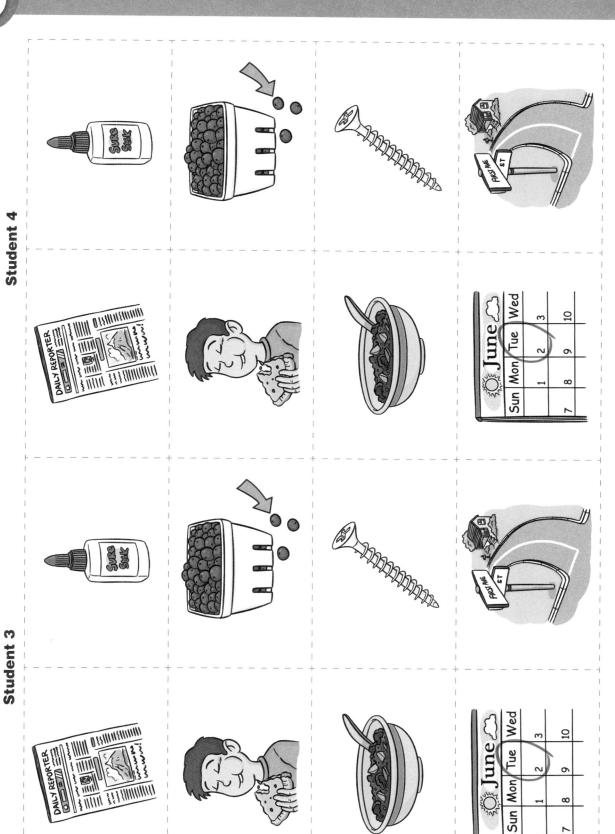

center 5

Task Cards

Mat B

Student 4

EMC 3527 • Center 5 • Mat B

Student 4

EMC 3527 • Center 5 • Mat B

Student 4

EMC 3527 • Center 5 • Mat B

Student 4

EMC 3527 • Center 5 • Mat B

Student 4

EMC 3527 • Center 5 • Mat B

Student 4

EMC 3527 • Center 5 • Mat B

Student 4

EMC 3527 • Center 5 • Mat B

Student 4

EMC 3527 • Center 5 • Mat B

Student 3

EMC 3527 • Center 5 • Mat B

Student 3

EMC 3527 • Center 5 • Mat B

Student 3

EMC 3527 • Center 5 • Mat B

Student 3

EMC 3527 • Center 5 • Mat B

Student 3

EMC 3527 • Center 5 • Mat B

Student 3

EMC 3527 • Center 5 • Mat B

Student 3

EMC 3527 • Center 5 • Mat B

Student 3

EMC 3527 • Center 5 • Mat B

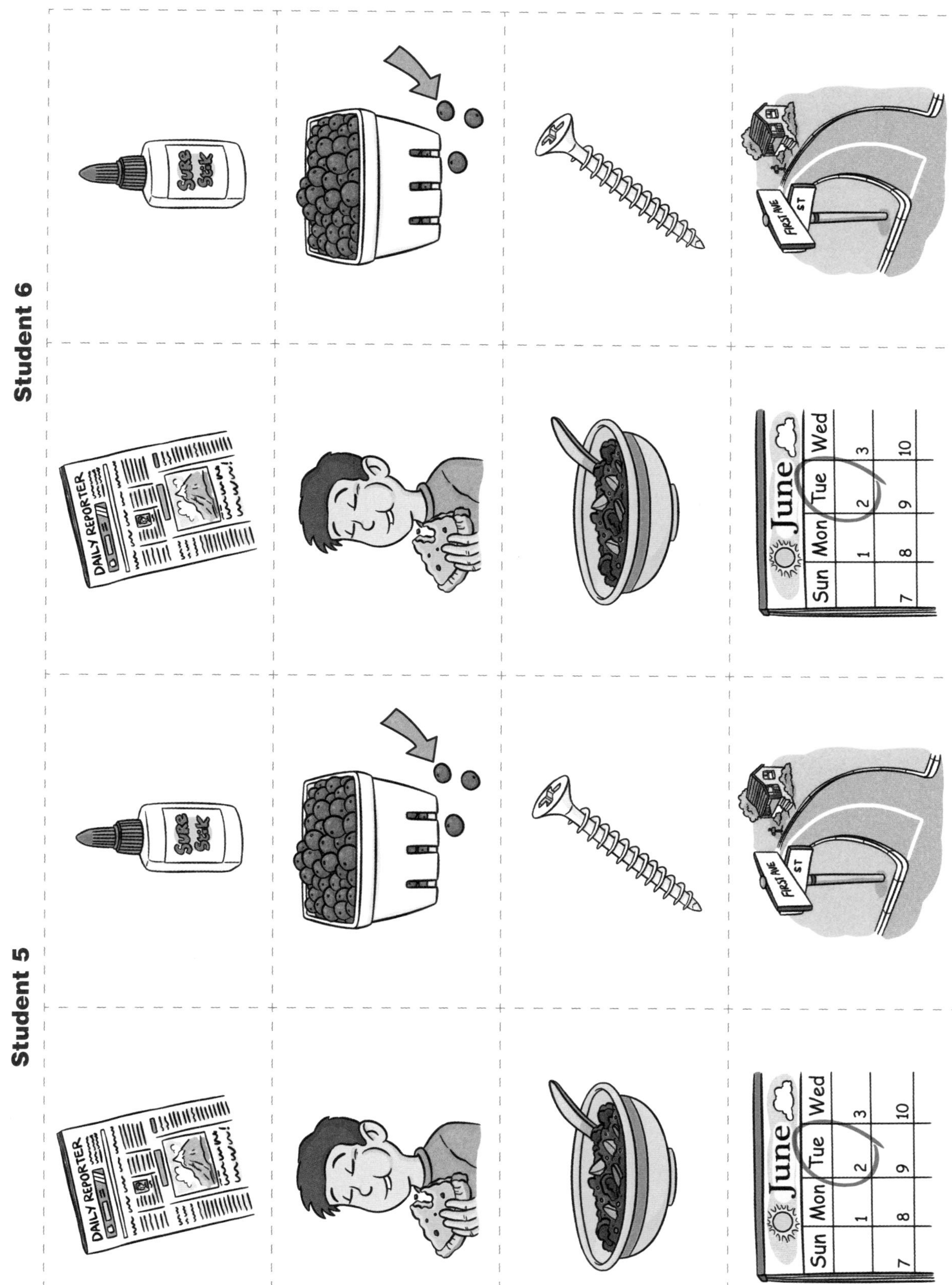
Student 6
Student 5
DAILY REPORTER
June
Sun Mon Tue Wed
1 2 3
7 8 9 10
FIRST AVE
ST

Student 6
EMC 3527 • Center 5 • Mat B

Student 6
EMC 3527 • Center 5 • Mat B

Student 6
EMC 3527 • Center 5 • Mat B

Student 6
EMC 3527 • Center 5 • Mat B

Student 6
EMC 3527 • Center 5 • Mat B

Student 6
EMC 3527 • Center 5 • Mat B

Student 6
EMC 3527 • Center 5 • Mat B

Student 6
EMC 3527 • Center 5 • Mat B

Student 5
EMC 3527 • Center 5 • Mat B

Student 5
EMC 3527 • Center 5 • Mat B

Student 5
EMC 3527 • Center 5 • Mat B

Student 5
EMC 3527 • Center 5 • Mat B

Student 5
EMC 3527 • Center 5 • Mat B

Student 5
EMC 3527 • Center 5 • Mat B

Student 5
EMC 3527 • Center 5 • Mat B

Student 5
EMC 3527 • Center 5 • Mat B

INTERMEDIATE

The oo Digraph

For the Teacher

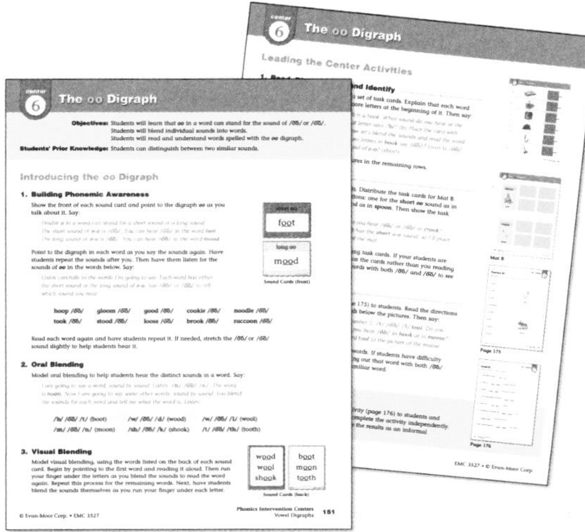

Lesson Plan

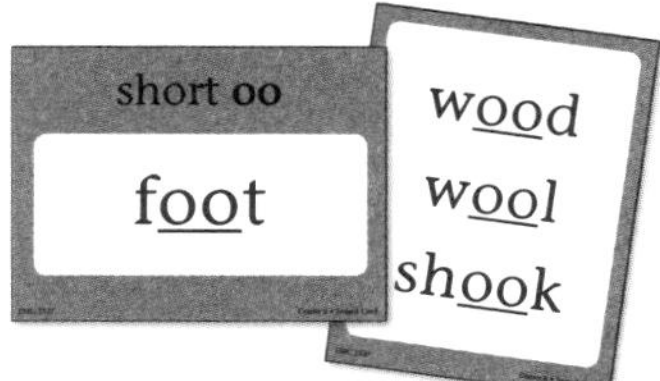

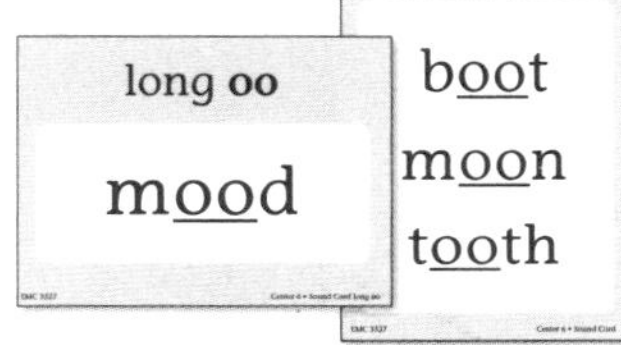

Sound Cards

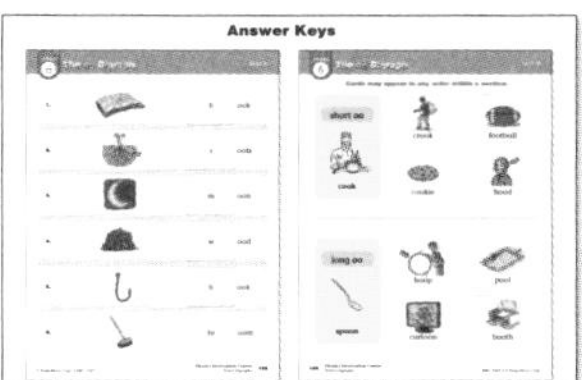

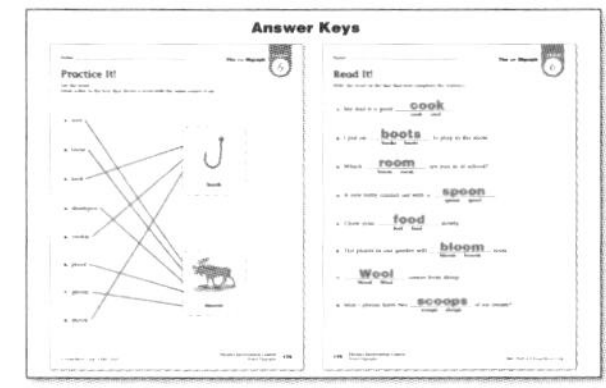

Answer Keys

For the Student

front (Mat A)

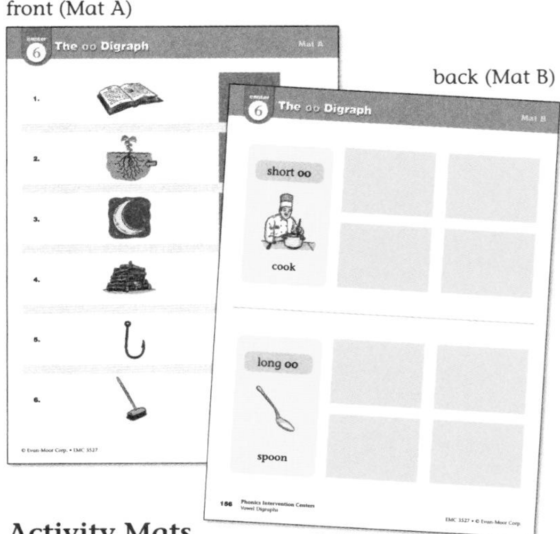

back (Mat B)

Activity Mats

Task Cards

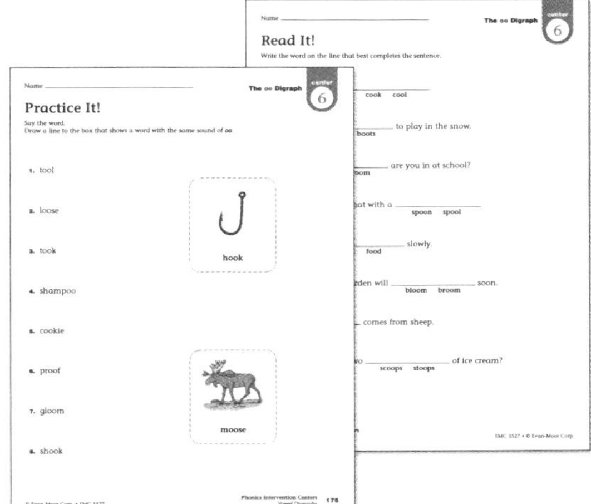

Practice and Assessment Activities

The oo Digraph

Objectives: Students will learn that ***oo*** in a word can stand for the sound of /o͝o/ or /o͞o/.
Students will blend individual sounds into words.
Students will read and understand words spelled with the ***oo*** digraph.

Students' Prior Knowledge: Students can distinguish between two similar sounds.

Introducing the *oo* Digraph

1. Building Phonemic Awareness

Show the front of each sound card and point to the digraph ***oo*** as you talk about it. Say:

*Double **o** in a word can stand for a short sound or a long sound.*
*The short sound of **o-o** is /o͝o/. You can hear /o͝o/ in the word **foot**.*
*The long sound of **o-o** is /o͞o/. You can hear /o͞o/ in the word **mood**.*

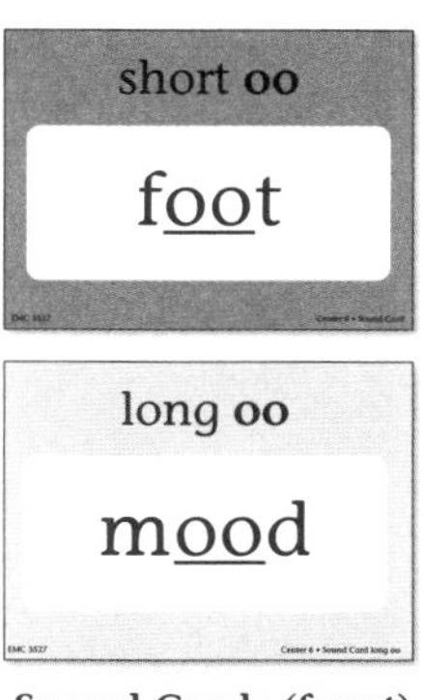

Sound Cards (front)

Point to the digraph in each word as you say the sounds again. Have students repeat the sounds after you. Then have them listen for the sounds of ***oo*** in the words below. Say:

*Listen carefully to the words I'm going to say. Each word has either the short sound or the long sound of **o-o**. Say /o͝o/ or /o͞o/ to tell which sound you hear.*

hoop /o͞o/	**gloom /o͞o/**	**good /o͝o/**	**cookie /o͝o/**	**noodle /o͞o/**
took /o͝o/	**stood /o͝o/**	**loose /o͞o/**	**brook /o͝o/**	**raccoon /o͞o/**

Read each word again and have students repeat it. If needed, stretch the /o͝o/ or /o͞o/ sound slightly to help students hear it.

2. Oral Blending

Model oral blending to help students hear the distinct sounds in a word. Say:

*I am going to say a word, sound by sound. Listen: /**n**/ /**o͞o**/ /**n**/. The word is **noon**. Now I am going to say some other words, sound by sound. You blend the sounds for each word and tell me what the word is. Listen:*

/b/ /o͞o/ /t/ (boot)	**/w/ /o͝o/ /d/** (wood)	**/w/ /o͝o/ /l/** (wool)
/m/ /o͞o/ /n/ (moon)	**/sh/ /o͝o/ /k/** (shook)	**/t/ /o͞o/ /th/** (tooth)

3. Visual Blending

Model visual blending, using the words listed on the back of each sound card. Begin by pointing to the first word and reading it aloud. Then run your finger under the letters as you blend the sounds to read the word again. Repeat this process for the remaining words. Next, have students blend the sounds themselves as you run your finger under each letter.

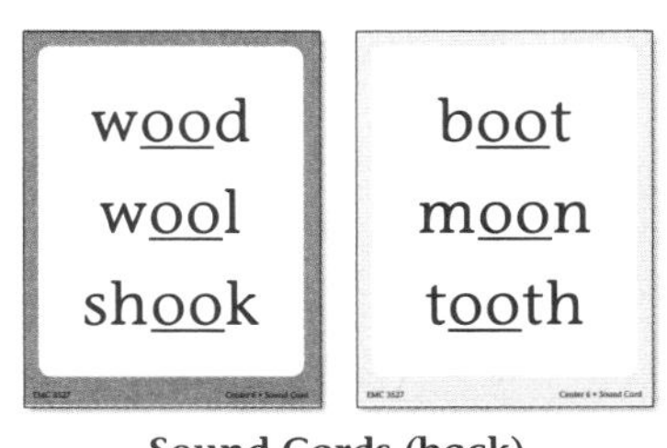

Sound Cards (back)

Leading the Center Activities

1. Read, Discriminate, and Identify

Give each student Mat A and a set of task cards. Explain that each word on the mat is missing one or more letters at the beginning of it. Then say:

> *Look at the picture in row 1. It is a book. What sound do you hear at the beginning of* ***book****?* (/b/) *What letter says* **/b/***?* (b) *Place the card with the letter* ***b*** *on it in the box. Now let's blend the sounds and read the word:* **/b/ /o͝o/ /k/** ***book****. Which two letters in* ***book*** *say* **/o͝o/***?* (o-o) *Is* **/o͝o/** *the short sound or the long sound of* ***o-o****?* (short)

Repeat this process with the pictures in the remaining rows.

2. Read and Understand

Have students turn over their mats. Distribute the task cards for Mat B. Explain that this mat has two sections: one for the **short *oo*** sound as in **cook** and one for the **long *oo*** sound as in **spoon**. Then show the task card for **crook** and say:

> *The word on this card is* ***crook****. Do you hear* **/o͝o/** *or* **/o͞o/** *in* ***crook****?* (/o͝o/) *That's right; the word* ***crook*** *has the* ***short o-o*** *sound, so I'll place this card in the* ***short o-o*** *section of the mat.*

Repeat this process with the remaining task cards. If your students are capable, have them read the words on the cards rather than you reading them. Model how to sound out the words with both **/o͝o/** and **/o͞o/** to see which one makes a familiar word.

3. Practice the Skill

Distribute the Practice It! activity (page 175) to students. Read the directions aloud and have students read the words below the pictures. Then say:

> *Let's blend the sounds to read word number 1:* **/t/ /o͞o/ /l/** ***tool****. Do you hear* **/o͝o/** *or* **/o͞o/** *in* ***tool****?* (/o͞o/) *Do you hear* **/o͞o/** *in* ***hook*** *or in* ***moose****?* (moose) *Now draw a line from the word* ***tool*** *to the picture of the moose.*

Repeat this process with the remaining words. If students have difficulty decoding a word, tell them to try sounding out that word with both **/o͝o/** and **/o͞o/** to see which sound makes a familiar word.

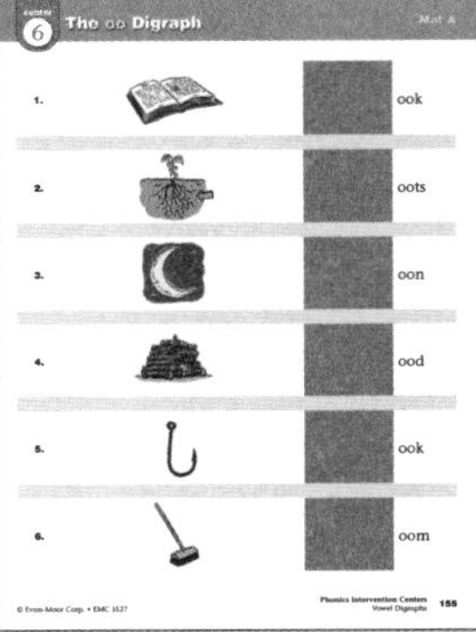

Mat A

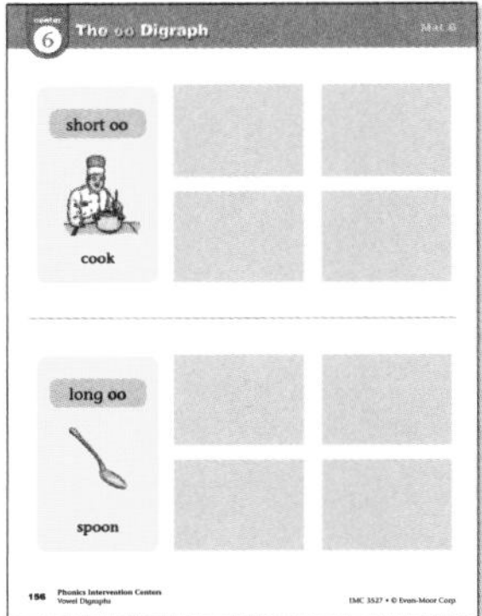

Mat B

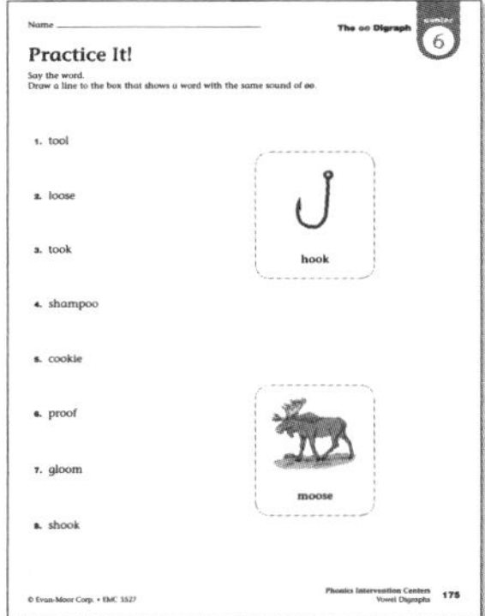

Page 175

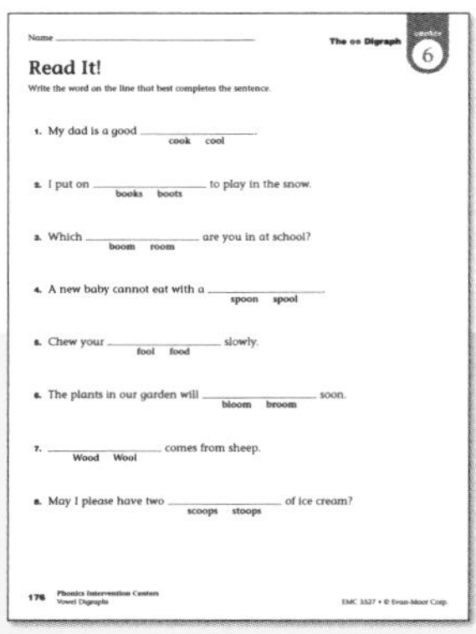

Page 176

Apply and Assess

After the lesson, distribute the Read It! activity (page 176) to students and read the directions aloud. Have students complete the activity independently. Then listen to them read the sentences. Use the results as an informal assessment of students' skill mastery.

short **oo**

f<u>oo</u>t

Center 6 • Sound Card

EMC 3527

long **oo**

m<u>oo</u>d

Center 6 • Sound Card long oo

EMC 3527

Answer Keys

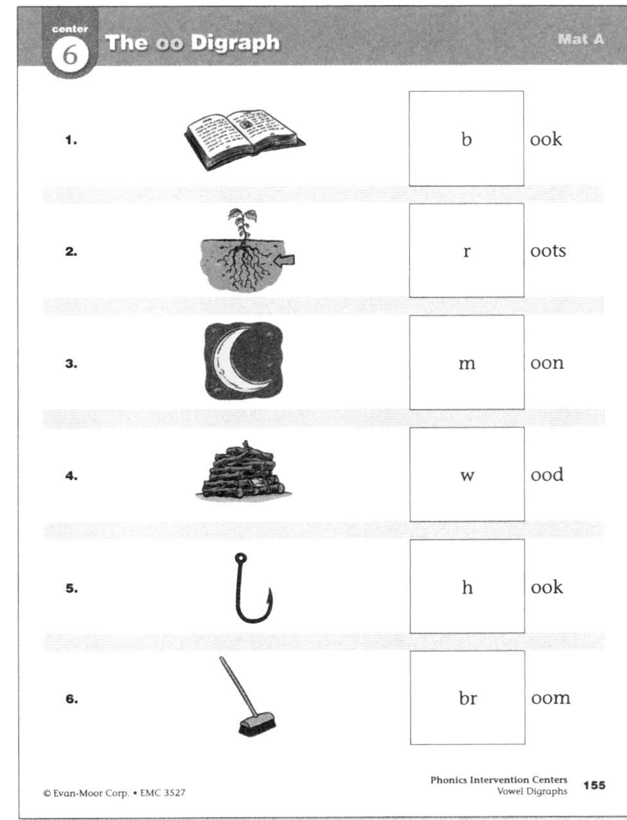

center 6 **The oo Digraph** Mat A

1.		b	ook
2.		r	oots
3.		m	oon
4.		w	ood
5.		h	ook
6.		br	oom

© Evan-Moor Corp. • EMC 3527 Phonics Intervention Centers Vowel Digraphs 155

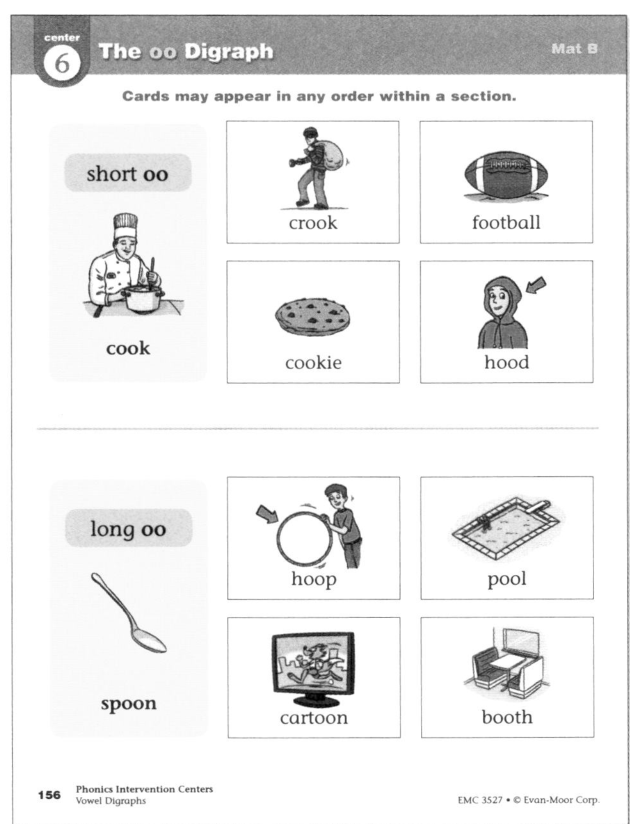

center 6 **The oo Digraph** Mat B

Cards may appear in any order within a section.

short oo		
cook	crook	football
	cookie	hood

long oo		
spoon	hoop	pool
	cartoon	booth

156 Phonics Intervention Centers Vowel Digraphs EMC 3527 • © Evan-Moor Corp.

boot

moon

tooth

EMC 3527 Center 6 • Sound Card

wood

wool

shook

EMC 3527 Center 6 • Sound Card

Answer Keys

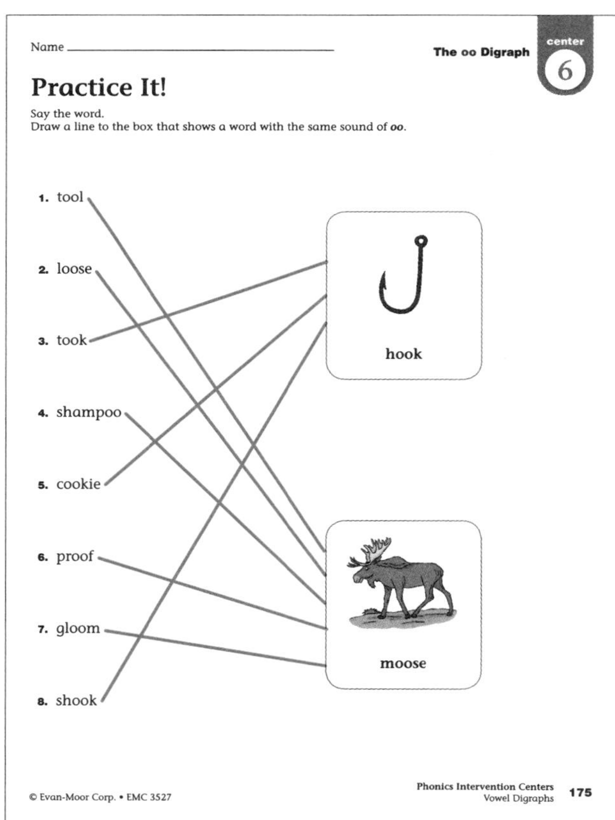
Name ______________________

The oo Digraph center 6

Practice It!

Say the word.
Draw a line to the box that shows a word with the same sound of *oo*.

1. tool
2. loose
3. took
4. shampoo
5. cookie
6. proof
7. gloom
8. shook

© Evan-Moor Corp. • EMC 3527 Phonics Intervention Centers Vowel Digraphs 175

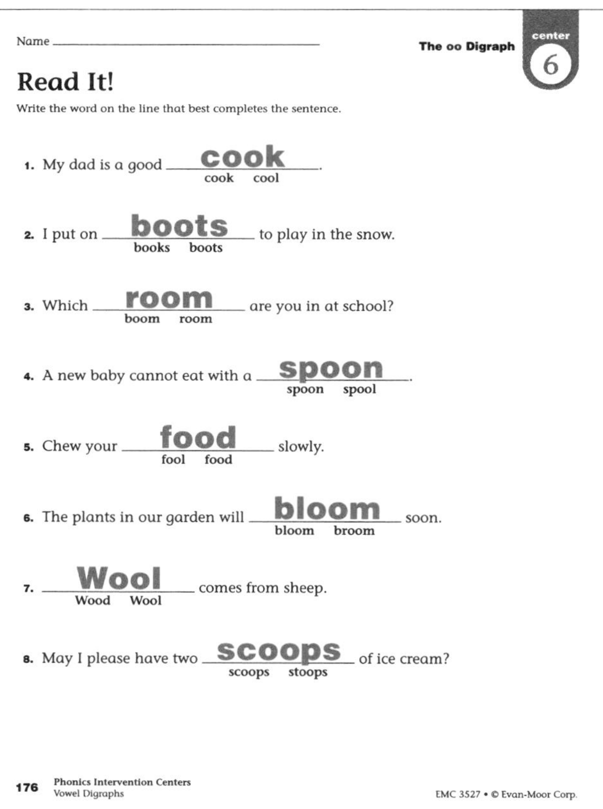
Name ______________________

The oo Digraph center 6

Read It!

Write the word on the line that best completes the sentence.

1. My dad is a good **cook**. (cook cool)
2. I put on **boots** to play in the snow. (books boots)
3. Which **room** are you in at school? (boom room)
4. A new baby cannot eat with a **spoon**. (spoon spool)
5. Chew your **food** slowly. (fool food)
6. The plants in our garden will **bloom** soon. (bloom broom)
7. **Wool** comes from sheep. (Wood Wool)
8. May I please have two **scoops** of ice cream? (scoops stoops)

176 Phonics Intervention Centers Vowel Digraphs EMC 3527 • © Evan-Moor Corp.

The oo Digraph

1.			ook
2.			oots
3.			oon
4.			ood
5.			ook
6.			oom

The oo Digraph

short **oo**

cook

long **oo**

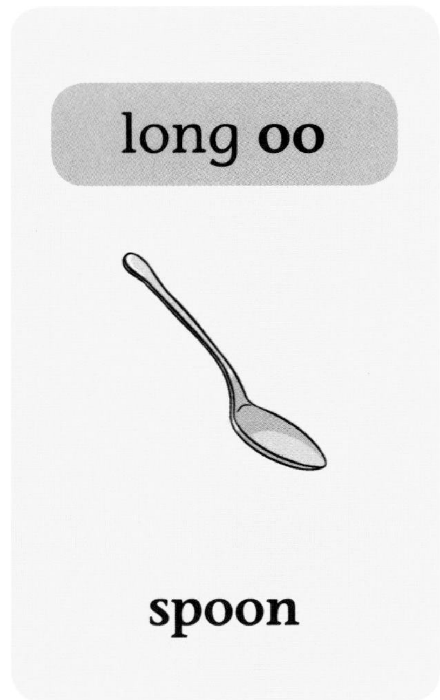

spoon

The oo Digraph

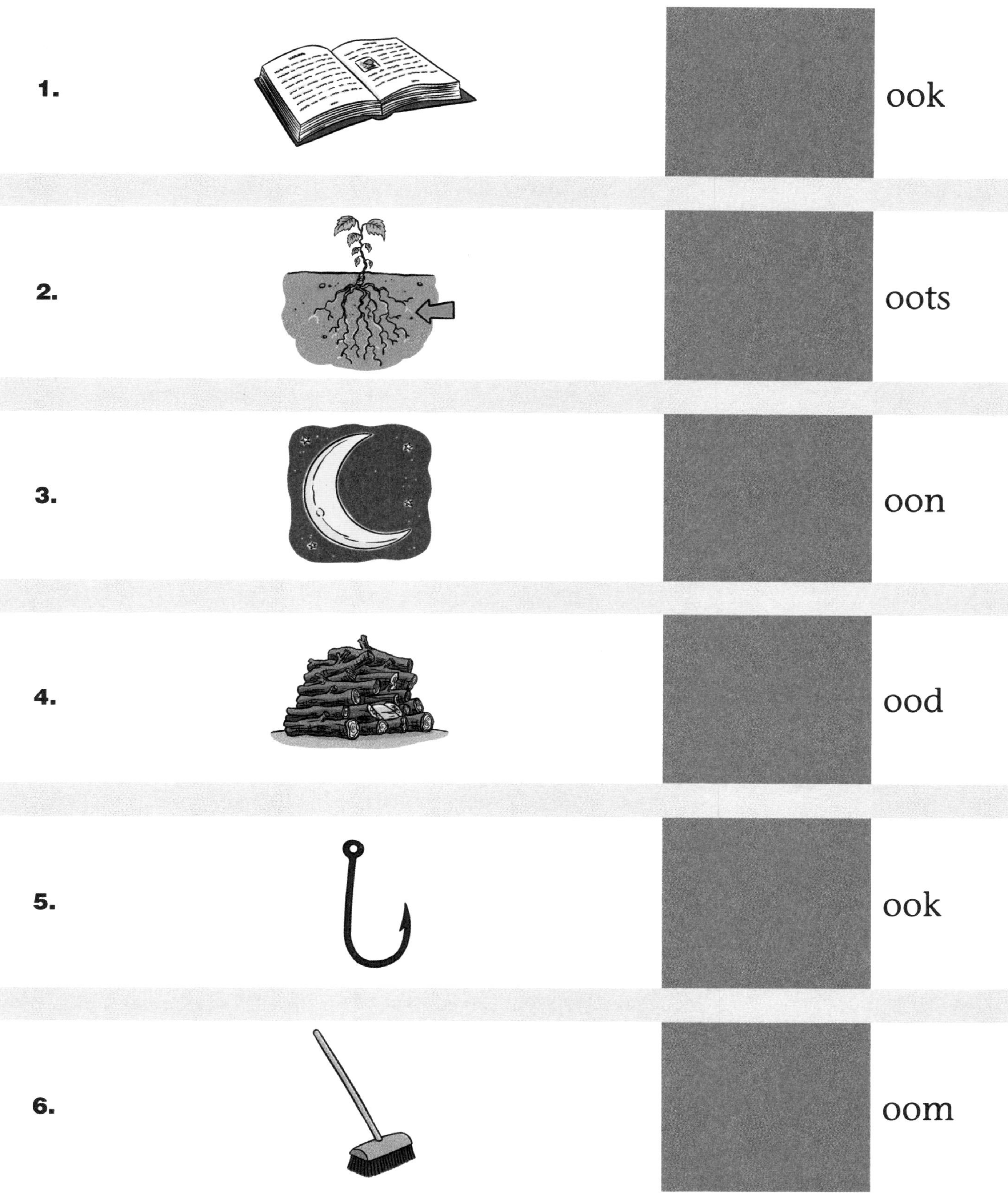

The oo Digraph

Mat B

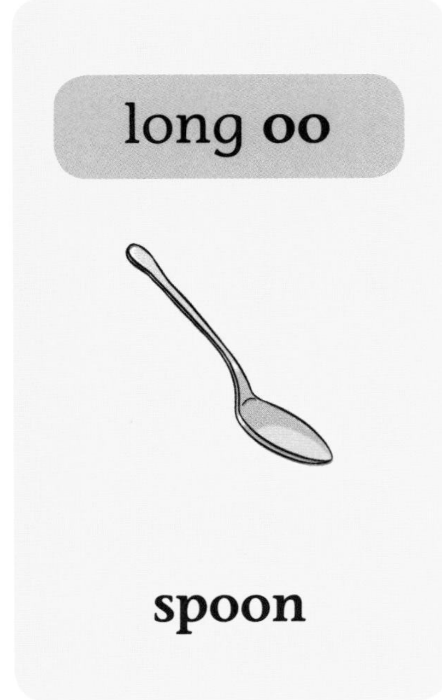

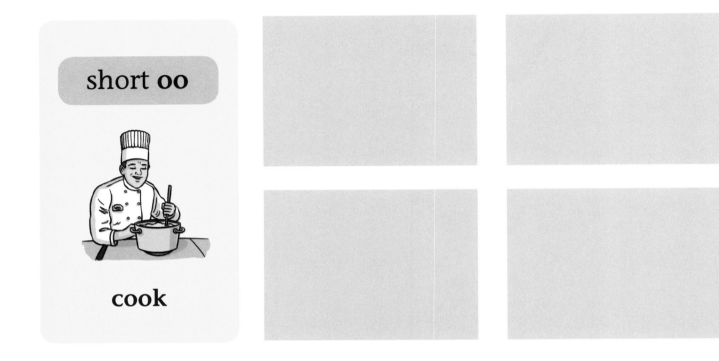

center 6

The oo Digraph

Mat A

1. ook

2. oots

3. oon

4. ood

5. ook

6.  oom

The oo Digraph

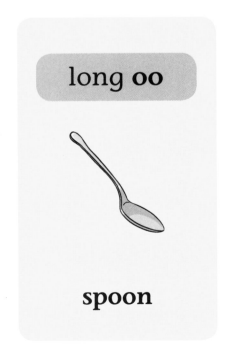

The oo Digraph

Mat A

1.  ook

2. 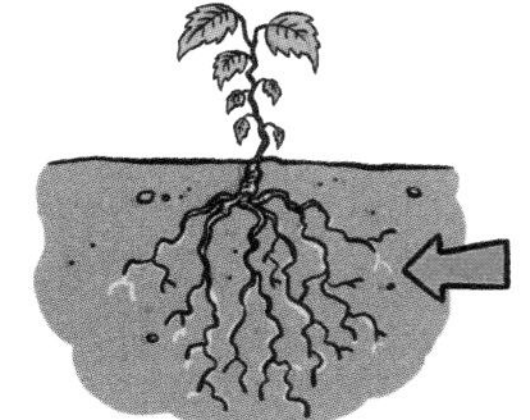 oots

3.  oon

4.  ood

5.  ook

6.  oom

The oo Digraph

short **oo**

cook

long **oo**

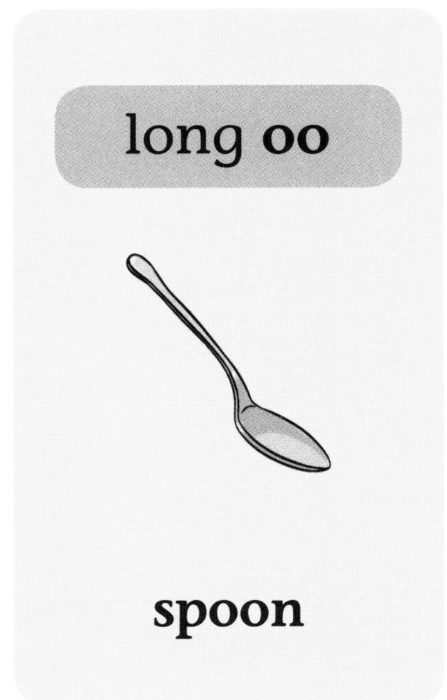

spoon

The oo Digraph

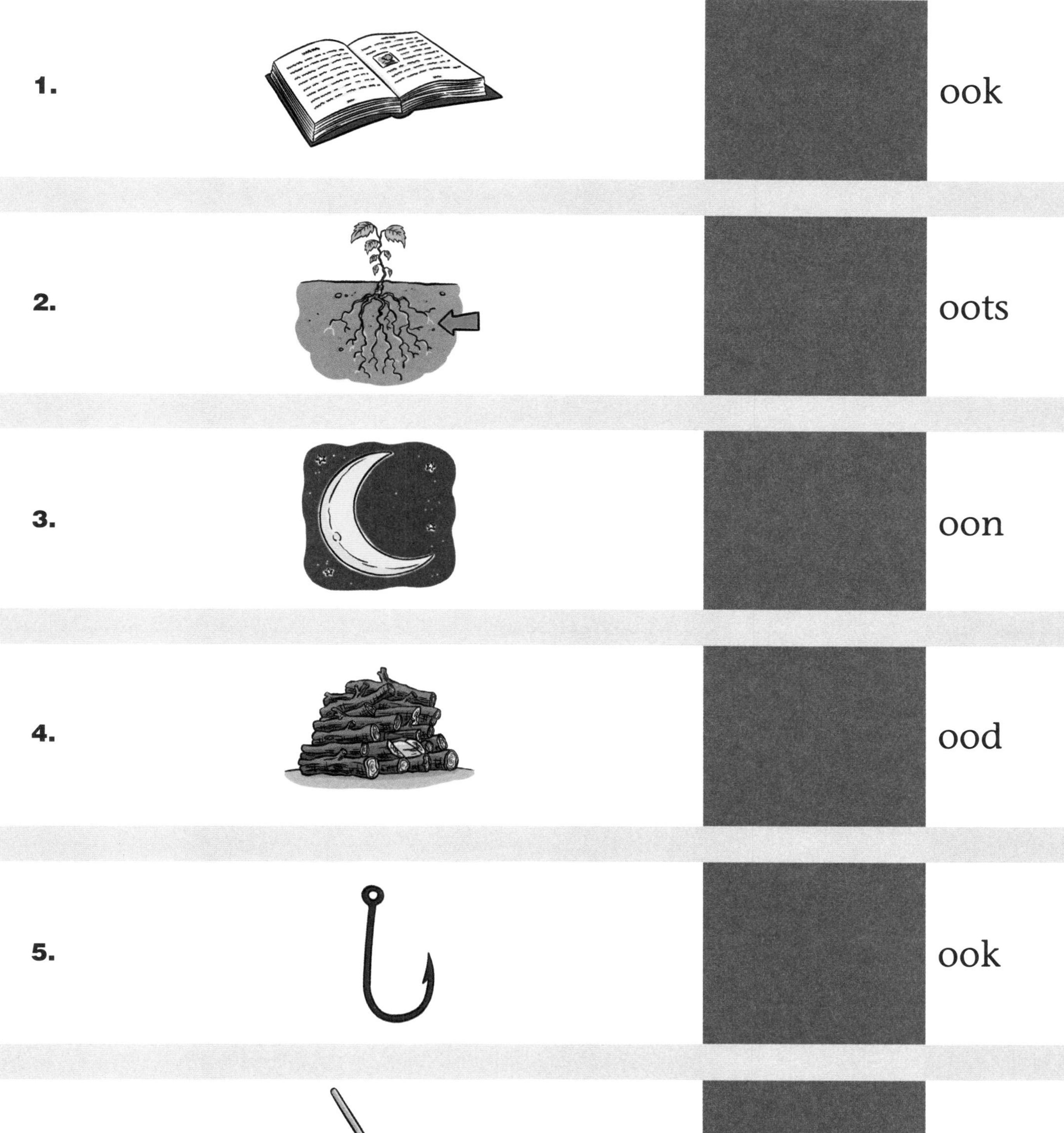

1. ook
2. oots
3. oon
4. ood
5. ook
6. oom

The oo Digraph

short oo

cook

long oo

spoon

The oo Digraph

1.  ook

2. 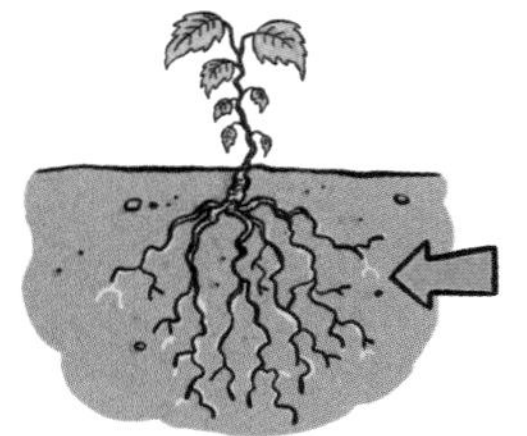 oots

3.  oon

4.  ood

5.  ook

6.  oom

The oo Digraph

short **oo**

cook

long **oo**

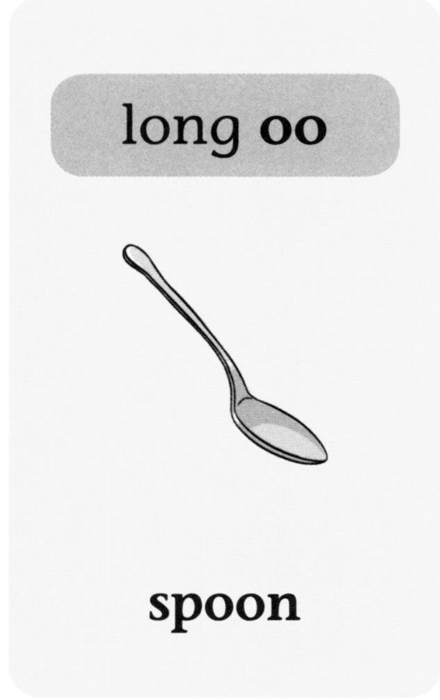

spoon

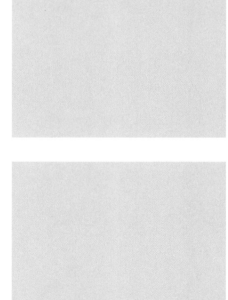

Task Cards

Student 6	b	br	h	m	r	w
Student 5	b	br	h	m	r	w
Student 4	b	br	h	m	r	w
Student 3	b	br	h	m	r	w
Student 2	b	br	h	m	r	w
Student 1	b	br	h	m	r	w

center 6

Task Cards

Mat A

Student 6
EMC 3527
Center 6 • Mat A

Student 6
EMC 3527
Center 6 • Mat A

Student 6
EMC 3527
Center 6 • Mat A

Student 6
EMC 3527
Center 6 • Mat A

Student 6
EMC 3527
Center 6 • Mat A

Student 6
EMC 3527
Center 6 • Mat A

Student 5
EMC 3527
Center 6 • Mat A

Student 5
EMC 3527
Center 6 • Mat A

Student 5
EMC 3527
Center 6 • Mat A

Student 5
EMC 3527
Center 6 • Mat A

Student 5
EMC 3527
Center 6 • Mat A

Student 5
EMC 3527
Center 6 • Mat A

Student 4
EMC 3527
Center 6 • Mat A

Student 4
EMC 3527
Center 6 • Mat A

Student 4
EMC 3527
Center 6 • Mat A

Student 4
EMC 3527
Center 6 • Mat A

Student 4
EMC 3527
Center 6 • Mat A

Student 4
EMC 3527
Center 6 • Mat A

Student 3
EMC 3527
Center 6 • Mat A

Student 3
EMC 3527
Center 6 • Mat A

Student 3
EMC 3527
Center 6 • Mat A

Student 3
EMC 3527
Center 6 • Mat A

Student 3
EMC 3527
Center 6 • Mat A

Student 3
EMC 3527
Center 6 • Mat A

Student 2
EMC 3527
Center 6 • Mat A

Student 2
EMC 3527
Center 6 • Mat A

Student 2
EMC 3527
Center 6 • Mat A

Student 2
EMC 3527
Center 6 • Mat A

Student 2
EMC 3527
Center 6 • Mat A

Student 2
EMC 3527
Center 6 • Mat A

Student 1
EMC 3527
Center 6 • Mat A

Student 1
EMC 3527
Center 6 • Mat A

Student 1
EMC 3527
Center 6 • Mat A

Student 1
EMC 3527
Center 6 • Mat A

Student 1
EMC 3527
Center 6 • Mat A

Student 1
EMC 3527
Center 6 • Mat A

Task Cards

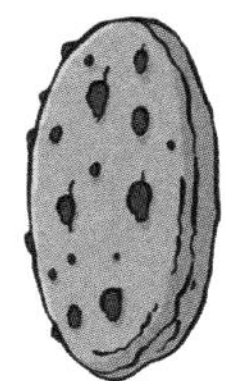
cookie

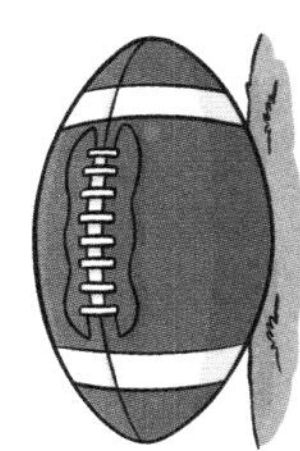
football

hoop

pool

Student 2

crook

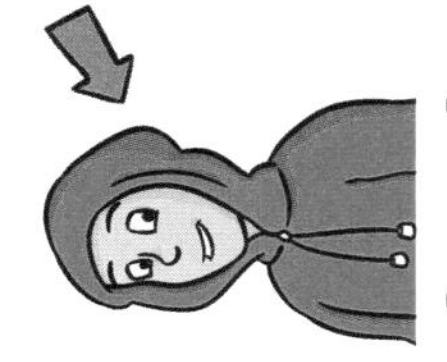
hood

cartoon

booth

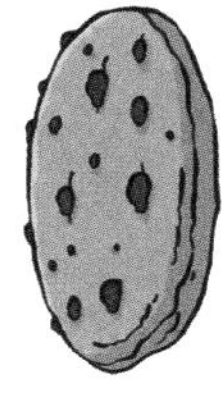
cookie

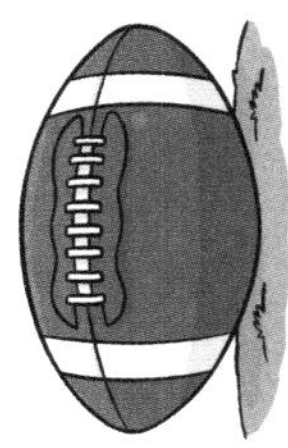
football

hoop

pool

Student 1

crook

hood

cartoon

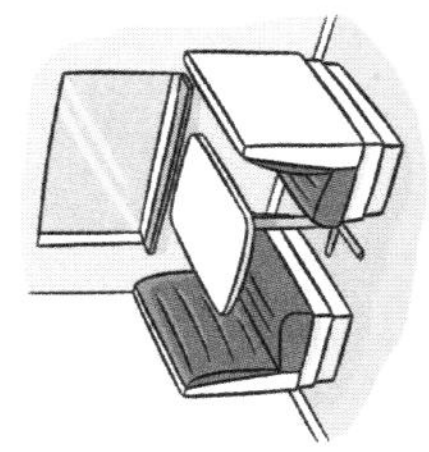
booth

Student 2
EMC 3527 • Center 6 • Mat B

Student 2
EMC 3527 • Center 6 • Mat B

Student 2
EMC 3527 • Center 6 • Mat B

Student 2
EMC 3527 • Center 6 • Mat B

Student 2
EMC 3527 • Center 6 • Mat B

Student 2
EMC 3527 • Center 6 • Mat B

Student 2
EMC 3527 • Center 6 • Mat B

Student 2
EMC 3527 • Center 6 • Mat B

Student 1
EMC 3527 • Center 6 • Mat B

Student 1
EMC 3527 • Center 6 • Mat B

Student 1
EMC 3527 • Center 6 • Mat B

Student 1
EMC 3527 • Center 6 • Mat B

Student 1
EMC 3527 • Center 6 • Mat B

Student 1
EMC 3527 • Center 6 • Mat B

Student 1
EMC 3527 • Center 6 • Mat B

Student 1
EMC 3527 • Center 6 • Mat B

Student 4

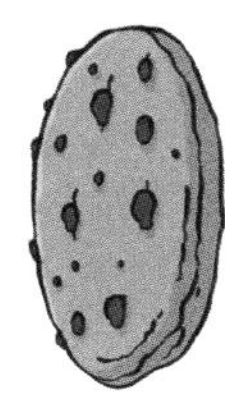
cookie

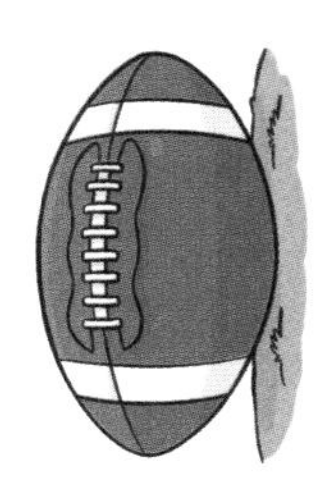
football

hoop

pool

crook

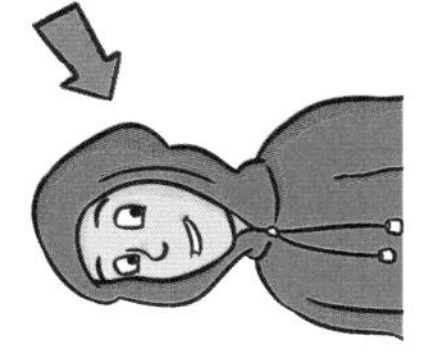
hood

cartoon

booth

Student 3

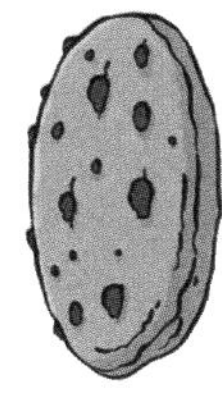
cookie

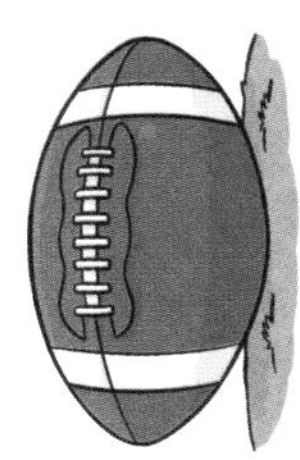
football

hoop

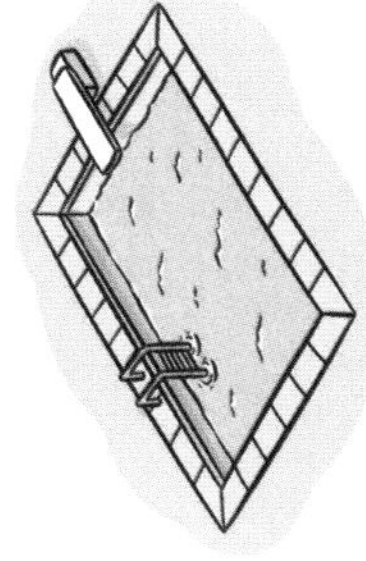
pool

crook

hood

cartoon

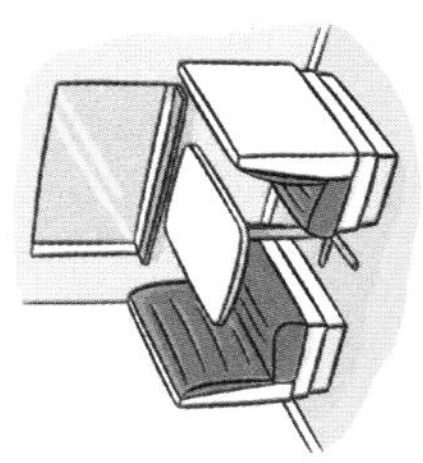
booth

Task Cards

Student 4
EMC 3527 • Center 6 • Mat B

Student 4
EMC 3527 • Center 6 • Mat B

Student 4
EMC 3527 • Center 6 • Mat B

Student 4
EMC 3527 • Center 6 • Mat B

Student 4
EMC 3527 • Center 6 • Mat B

Student 4
EMC 3527 • Center 6 • Mat B

Student 4
EMC 3527 • Center 6 • Mat B

Student 4
EMC 3527 • Center 6 • Mat B

Student 3
EMC 3527 • Center 6 • Mat B

Student 3
EMC 3527 • Center 6 • Mat B

Student 3
EMC 3527 • Center 6 • Mat B

Student 3
EMC 3527 • Center 6 • Mat B

Student 3
EMC 3527 • Center 6 • Mat B

Student 3
EMC 3527 • Center 6 • Mat B

Student 3
EMC 3527 • Center 6 • Mat B

Student 3
EMC 3527 • Center 6 • Mat B

Student 6

cookie

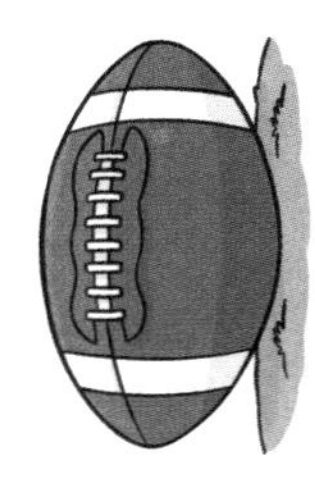
football

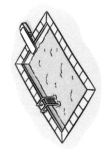

hoop

pool

crook

hood

cartoon

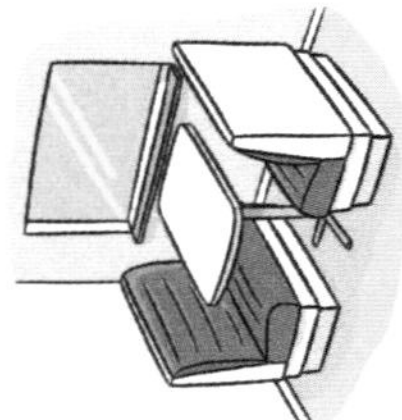
booth

Student 5

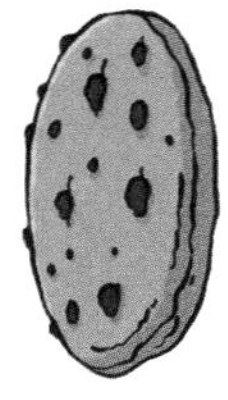
cookie

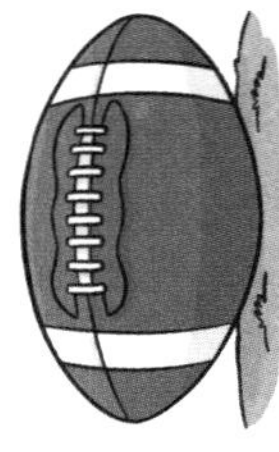
football

hoop

pool

crook

hood

cartoon

booth

Task Cards

Student 6
EMC 3527 • Center 6 • Mat B

Student 6
EMC 3527 • Center 6 • Mat B

Student 6
EMC 3527 • Center 6 • Mat B

Student 6
EMC 3527 • Center 6 • Mat B

Student 6
EMC 3527 • Center 6 • Mat B

Student 6
EMC 3527 • Center 6 • Mat B

Student 6
EMC 3527 • Center 6 • Mat B

Student 6
EMC 3527 • Center 6 • Mat B

Student 5
EMC 3527 • Center 6 • Mat B

Student 5
EMC 3527 • Center 6 • Mat B

Student 5
EMC 3527 • Center 6 • Mat B

Student 5
EMC 3527 • Center 6 • Mat B

Student 5
EMC 3527 • Center 6 • Mat B

Student 5
EMC 3527 • Center 6 • Mat B

Student 5
EMC 3527 • Center 6 • Mat B

Student 5
EMC 3527 • Center 6 • Mat B

Name ______________________________

Practice It!

Say the word.
Draw a line to the box that shows a word with the same sound of ***oo***.

1. tool
2. loose
3. took
4. shampoo
5. cookie
6. proof
7. gloom
8. shook

hook

moose

Name ______________________________

Read It!

Write the word on the line that best completes the sentence.

1. My dad is a good ______________________.
   cook **cool**

2. I put on ______________________ to play in the snow.
   books **boots**

3. Which ______________________ are you in at school?
   boom **room**

4. A new baby cannot eat with a ______________________.
   spoon **spool**

5. Chew your ______________________ slowly.
   fool **food**

6. The plants in our garden will ______________________ soon.
   bloom **broom**

7. ______________________ comes from sheep.
   Wood **Wool**

8. May I please have two ______________________ of ice cream?
   scoops **stoops**

center 7

INTERMEDIATE

The au • aw Digraphs

For the Teacher

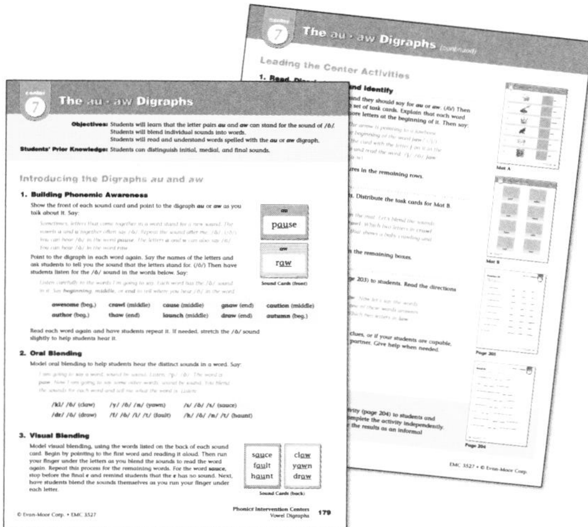

Lesson Plan

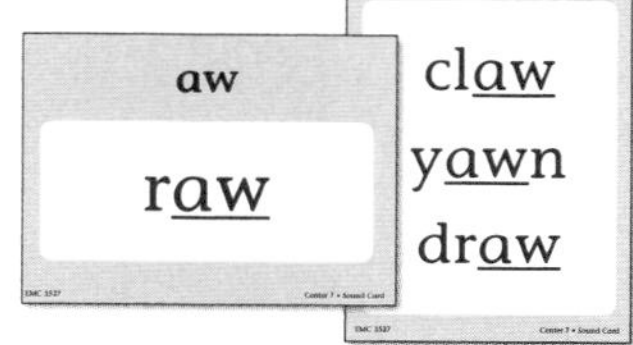

Sound Cards

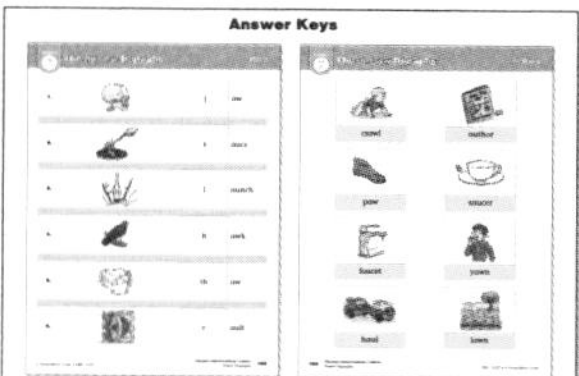

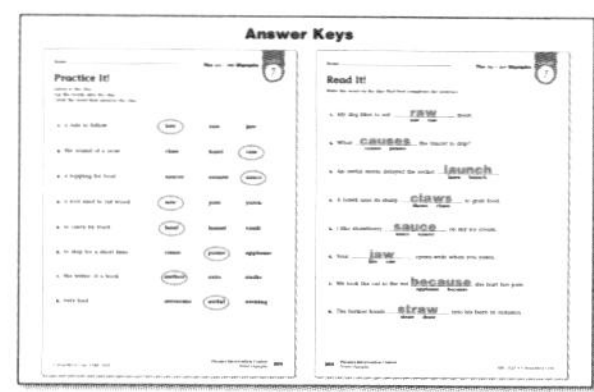

Answer Keys

For the Student

front (Mat A)

back (Mat B)

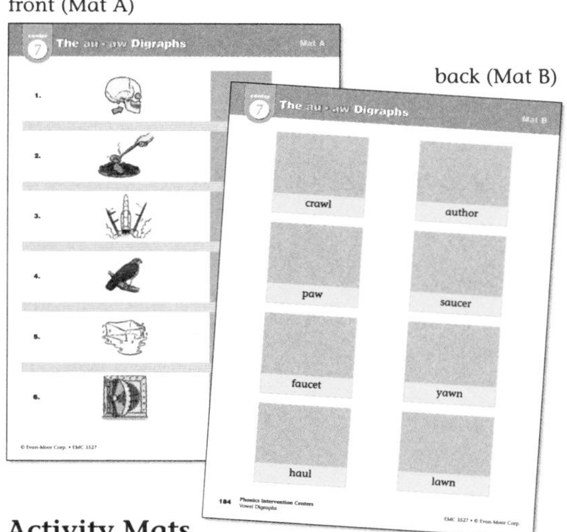

Activity Mats

Task Cards

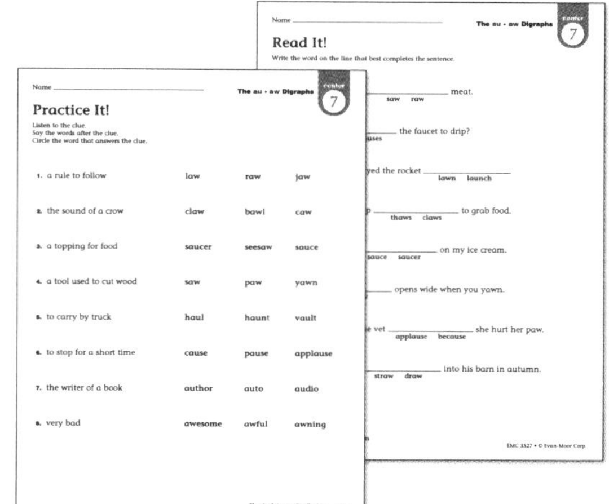

Practice and Assessment Activities

The au • aw Digraphs

Objectives: Students will learn that the letter pairs ***au*** and ***aw*** can stand for the sound of /ô/.
Students will blend individual sounds into words.
Students will read and understand words spelled with the ***au*** or ***aw*** digraph.

Students' Prior Knowledge: Students can distinguish initial, medial, and final sounds.

Introducing the Digraphs *au* and *aw*

1. Building Phonemic Awareness

Show the front of each sound card and point to the digraph ***au*** or ***aw*** as you talk about it. Say:

*Sometimes, letters that come together in a word stand for a new sound. The vowels **a** and **u** together often say /ô/. Repeat the sound after me: /ô/. (/ô/) You can hear /ô/ in the word **pause**. The letters **a** and **w** can also say /ô/. You can hear /ô/ in the word **raw**.*

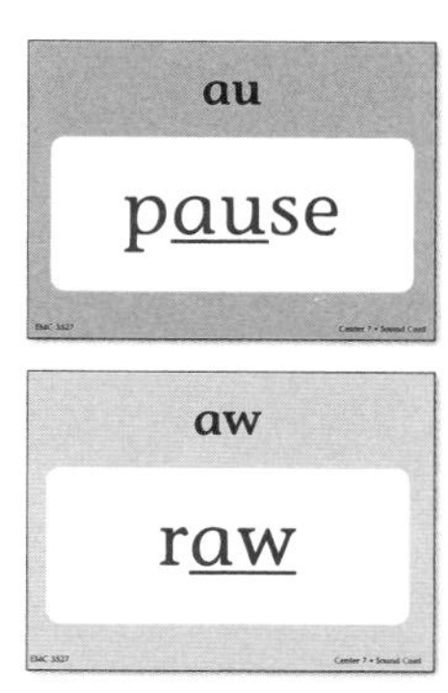

Sound Cards (front)

Point to the digraph in each word again. Say the names of the letters and ask students to tell you the sound that the letters stand for. (/ô/) Then have students listen for the /ô/ sound in the words below. Say:

*Listen carefully to the words I'm going to say. Each word has the /ô/ sound in it. Say **beginning**, **middle**, or **end** to tell where you hear /ô/ in the word.*

awesome (beg.)	**crawl** (middle)	**cause** (middle)	**gnaw** (end)	**caution** (middle)
author (beg.)	**thaw** (end)	**launch** (middle)	**draw** (end)	**autumn** (beg.)

Read each word again and have students repeat it. If needed, stretch the /ô/ sound slightly to help students hear it.

2. Oral Blending

Model oral blending to help students hear the distinct sounds in a word. Say:

*I am going to say a word, sound by sound. Listen: /**p**/ /ô/. The word is **paw**. Now I am going to say some other words, sound by sound. You blend the sounds for each word and tell me what the word is. Listen:*

/**kl**/ /ô/ (claw)	/**y**/ /ô/ /**n**/ (yawn)	/**s**/ /ô/ /**s**/ (sauce)
/**dr**/ /ô/ (draw)	/**f**/ /ô/ /**l**/ /**t**/ (fault)	/**h**/ /ô/ /**n**/ /**t**/ (haunt)

3. Visual Blending

Model visual blending, using the words listed on the back of each sound card. Begin by pointing to the first word and reading it aloud. Then run your finger under the letters as you blend the sounds to read the word again. Repeat this process for the remaining words. For the word **sauce**, stop before the final ***e*** and remind students that the ***e*** has no sound. Next, have students blend the sounds themselves as you run your finger under each letter.

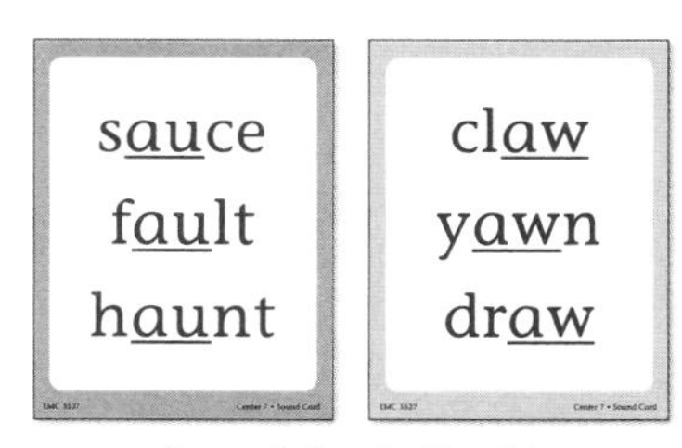

Sound Cards (back)

Leading the Center Activities

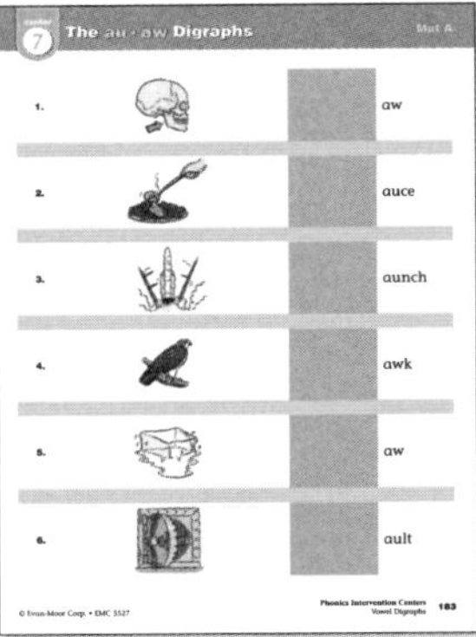

Mat A

1. Read, Discriminate, and Identify

Ask students to tell you the sound they should say for ***au*** or ***aw***. (/ô/) Then give each student Mat A and a set of task cards. Explain that each word on the mat is missing one or more letters at the beginning of it. Then say:

> *Look at the picture in row 1. The arrow is pointing to a jawbone. What sound do you hear at the beginning of the word **jaw**?* (/j/) *What letter says* **/j/**? (j) *Place the card with the letter **j** on it in the box. Now let's blend the sounds and read the word:* **/j/ /ô/ *jaw***. *Which letters in **jaw** say* **/ô/**? (a-w)

Repeat this process with the pictures in the remaining rows.

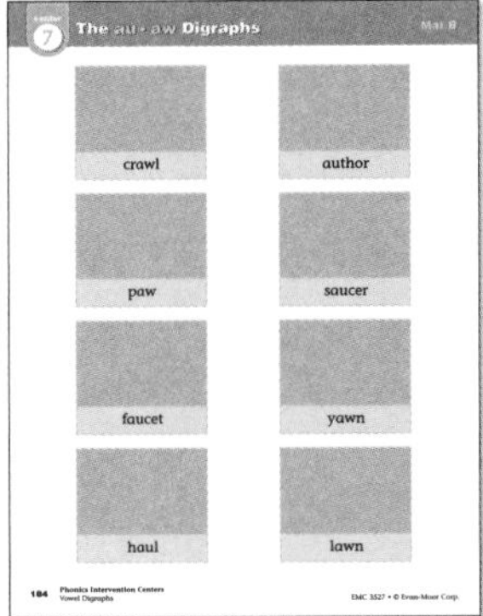

Mat B

2. Read and Understand

Have students turn over their mats. Distribute the task cards for Mat B. Then say:

> *Look at the word in the first box on the mat. Let's blend the sounds to read the word:* **/kr/ /ô/ /l/ *crawl***. *Which two letters in **crawl** say* **/ô/**? (a-w) *Now find the card that shows a baby crawling and place it above the word.*

Repeat this process with the words in the remaining boxes.

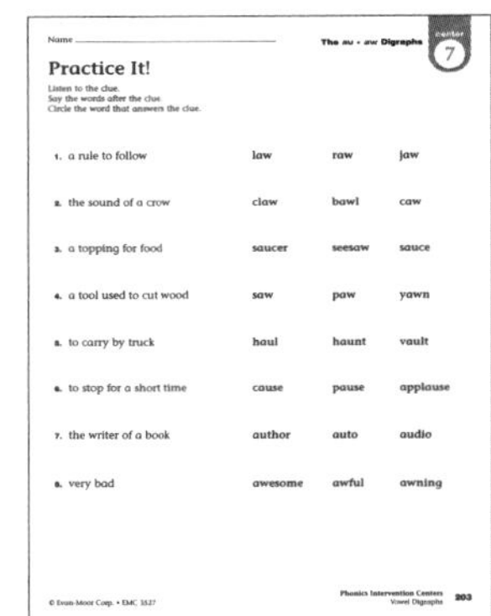
Practice It!

Listen to the clue. Say the words after the clue. Circle the word that answers the clue.

1. a rule to follow	law	raw	jaw
2. the sound of a crow	claw	bawl	caw
3. a topping for food	saucer	seesaw	sauce
4. a tool used to cut wood	saw	paw	yawn
5. to carry by truck	haul	haunt	vault
6. to stop for a short time	cause	pause	applause
7. the writer of a book	author	auto	audio
8. very bad	awesome	awful	awning

Page 203

3. Practice the Skill

Distribute the Practice It! activity (page 203) to students. Read the directions aloud. Then say:

> *Listen to the first clue:* ***a rule to follow***. *Now let's say the words after the clue:* ***law, raw, jaw***. *Which one of these words answers the clue?* (law) *Circle the word **law**. Which two letters in **law** say* **/ô/**? (a-w)

Repeat this process with the remaining clues, or if your students are capable, have them complete the activity with a partner. Give help when needed. Then go over the answers as a group.

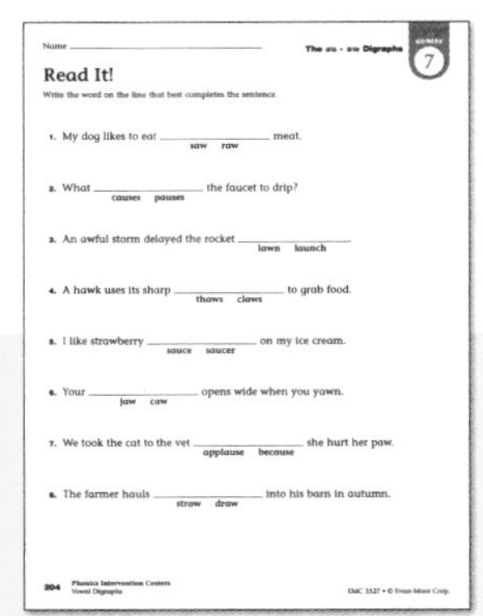
Read It!

Write the word on the line that best completes the sentence.

1. My dog likes to eat ________ meat. (saw raw)
2. What ________ the faucet to drip? (causes pauses)
3. An awful storm delayed the rocket ________. (lawn launch)
4. A hawk uses its sharp ________ to grab food. (thaws claws)
5. I like strawberry ________ on my ice cream. (sauce saucer)
6. Your ________ opens wide when you yawn. (jaw caw)
7. We took the cat to the vet ________ she hurt her paw. (applause because)
8. The farmer hauls ________ into his barn in autumn. (straw draw)

Page 204

Apply and Assess

After the lesson, distribute the Read It! activity (page 204) to students and read the directions aloud. Have students complete the activity independently. Then listen to them read the sentences. Use the results as an informal assessment of students' skill mastery.

au

pause

Center 7 • Sound Card

EMC 3527

aw

raw

Center 7 • Sound Card

EMC 3527

Answer Keys

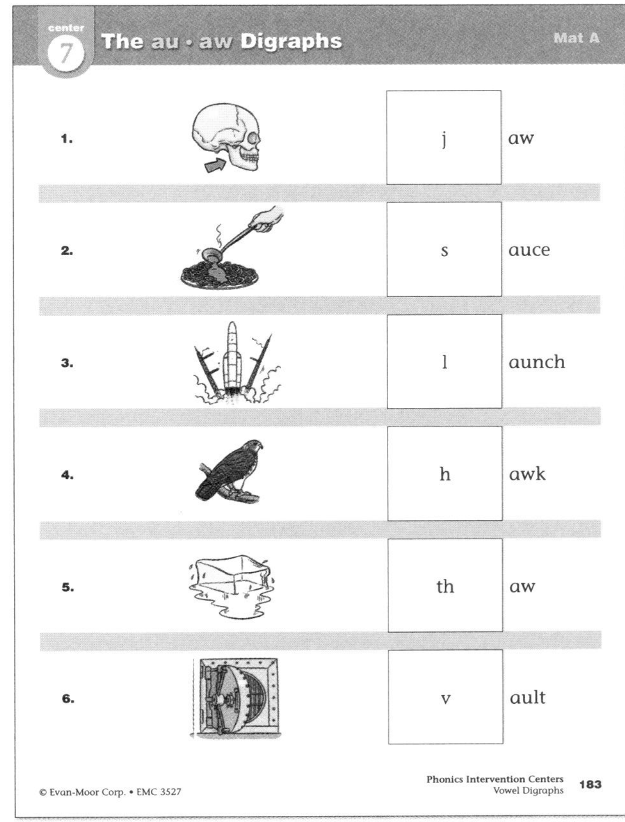

center 7 **The au · aw Digraphs** Mat A

1.	j	aw
2.	s	auce
3.	l	aunch
4.	h	awk
5.	th	aw
6.	v	ault

© Evan-Moor Corp. • EMC 3527 — Phonics Intervention Centers, Vowel Digraphs 183

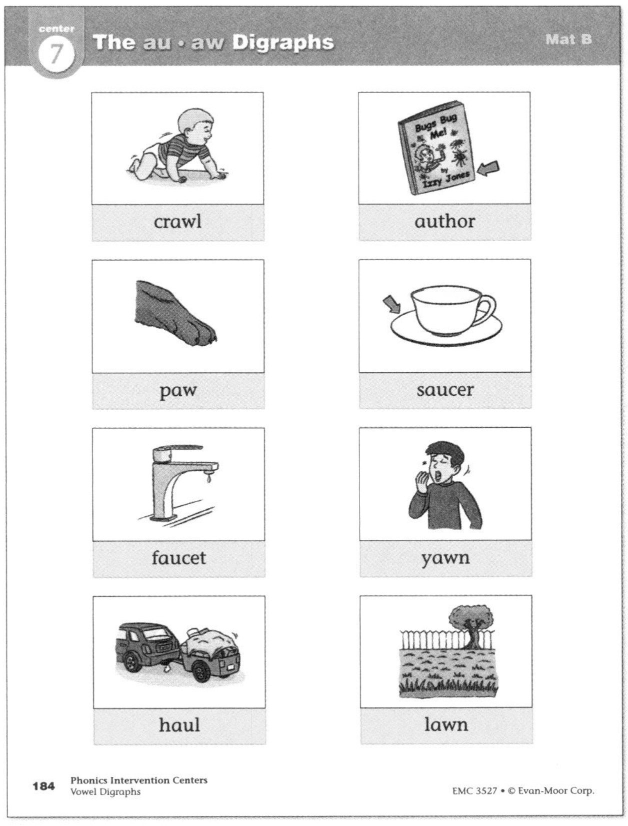

center 7 **The au · aw Digraphs** Mat B

crawl	author
paw	saucer
faucet	yawn
haul	lawn

184 Phonics Intervention Centers, Vowel Digraphs — EMC 3527 • © Evan-Moor Corp.

claw

yawn

draw

EMC 3527 Center 7 • Sound Card

sauce

fault

haunt

EMC 3527 Center 7 • Sound Card

Answer Keys

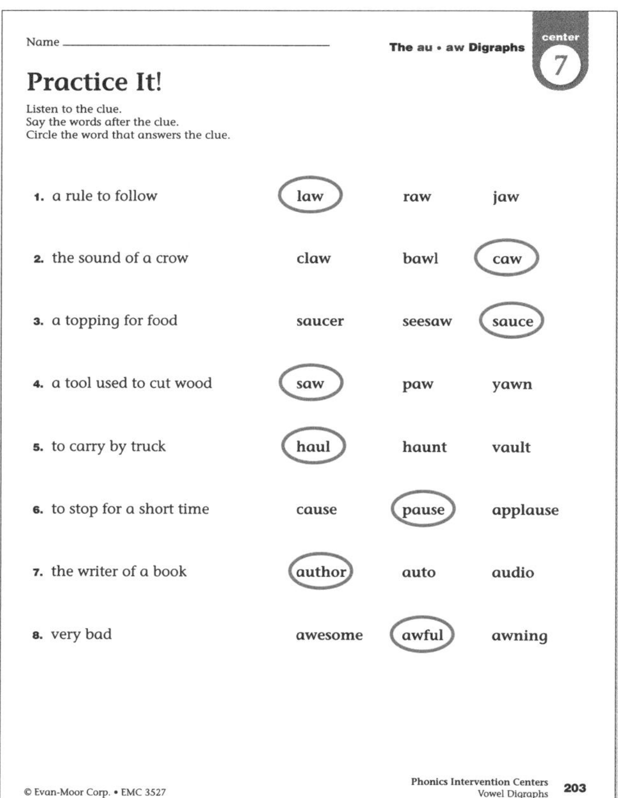

Name ______ The au • aw Digraphs center 7

Practice It!

Listen to the clue.
Say the words after the clue.
Circle the word that answers the clue.

1. a rule to follow — (law) raw jaw
2. the sound of a crow — claw bawl (caw)
3. a topping for food — saucer seesaw (sauce)
4. a tool used to cut wood — (saw) paw yawn
5. to carry by truck — (haul) haunt vault
6. to stop for a short time — cause (pause) applause
7. the writer of a book — (author) auto audio
8. very bad — awesome (awful) awning

© Evan-Moor Corp. • EMC 3527 Phonics Intervention Centers Vowel Digraphs 203

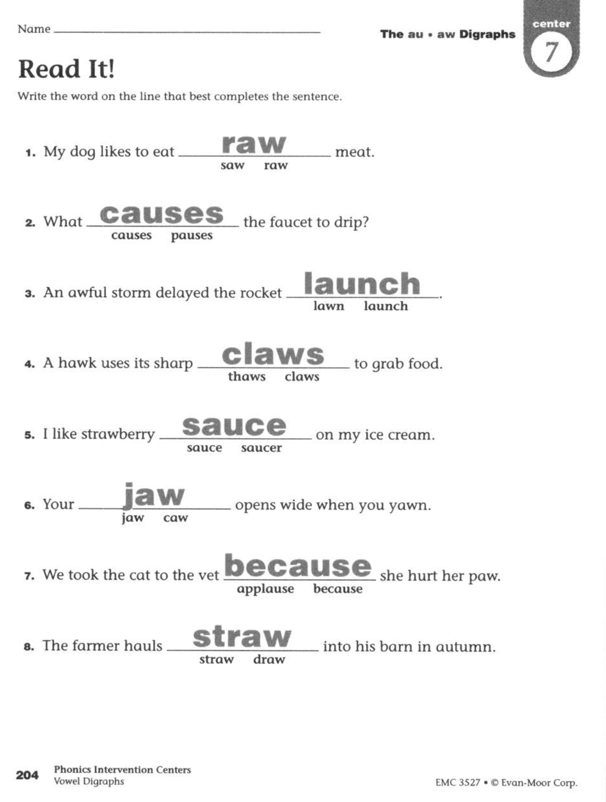

Name ______ The au • aw Digraphs center 7

Read It!

Write the word on the line that best completes the sentence.

1. My dog likes to eat **raw** meat. (saw raw)
2. What **causes** the faucet to drip? (causes pauses)
3. An awful storm delayed the rocket **launch**. (lawn launch)
4. A hawk uses its sharp **claws** to grab food. (thaws claws)
5. I like strawberry **sauce** on my ice cream. (sauce saucer)
6. Your **jaw** opens wide when you yawn. (jaw caw)
7. We took the cat to the vet **because** she hurt her paw. (applause because)
8. The farmer hauls **straw** into his barn in autumn. (straw draw)

204 Phonics Intervention Centers Vowel Digraphs EMC 3527 • © Evan-Moor Corp.

The au • aw Digraphs

1. 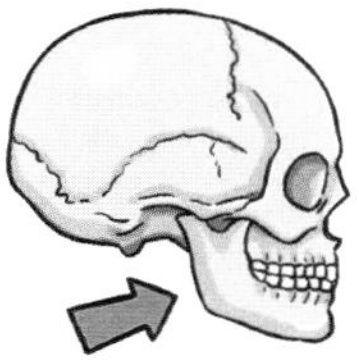 aw

2.  auce

3.  aunch

4.  awk

5.  aw

6.  ault

The au • aw Digraphs

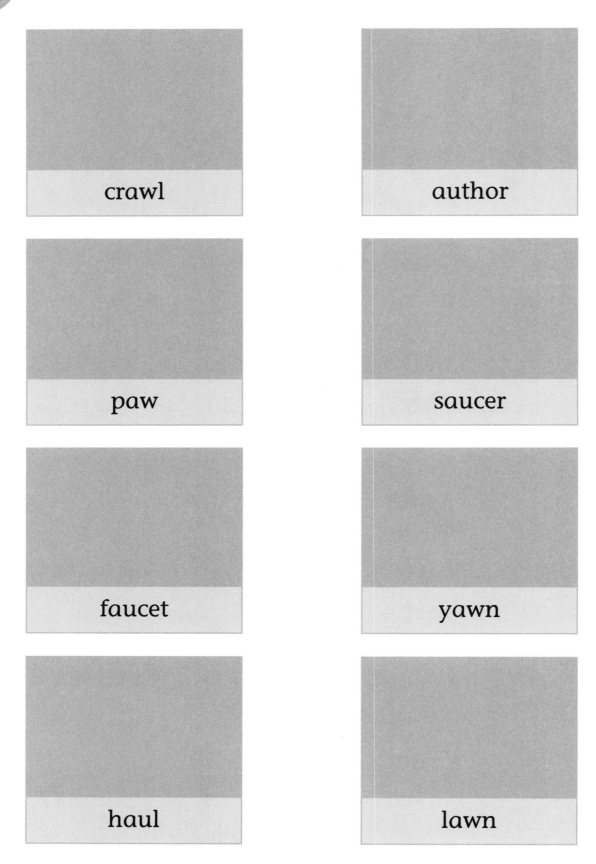

crawl	author
paw	saucer
faucet	yawn
haul	lawn

The au • aw Digraphs

1. 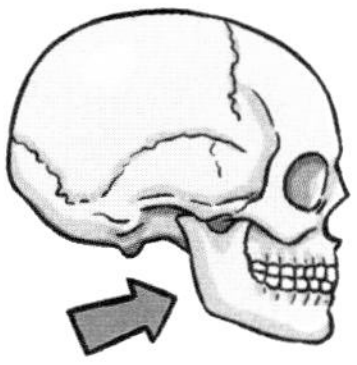 aw

2.  auce

3.  aunch

4.  awk

5.  aw

6.  ault

The au • aw Digraphs

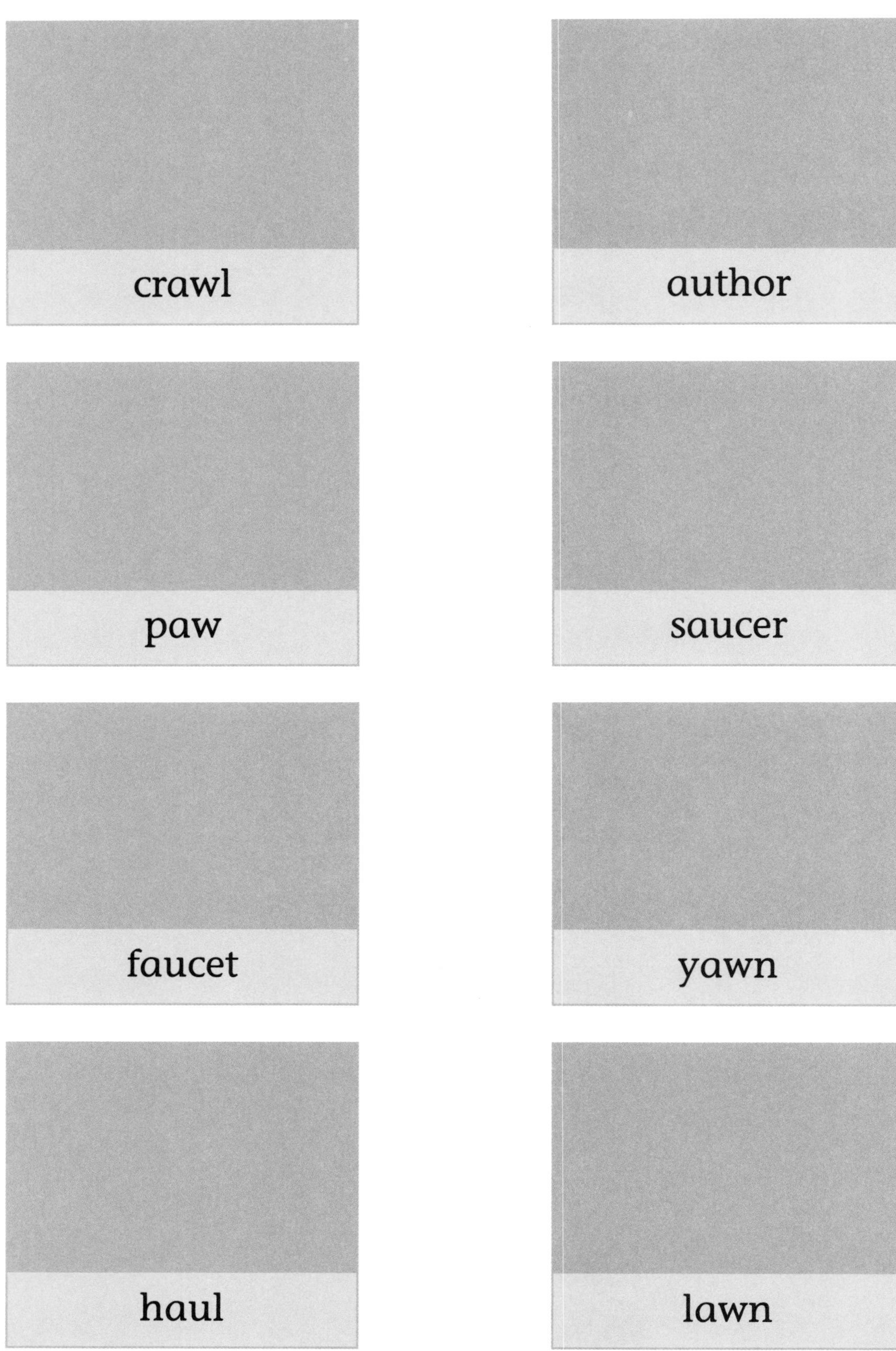

The au • aw Digraphs

1. 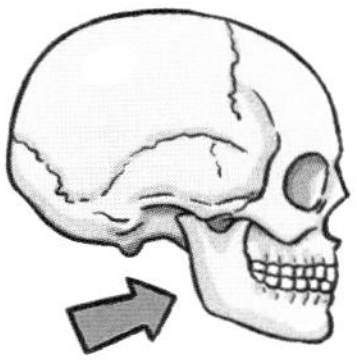 aw

2.  auce

3.  aunch

4.  awk

5.  aw

6.  ault

The au • aw Digraphs

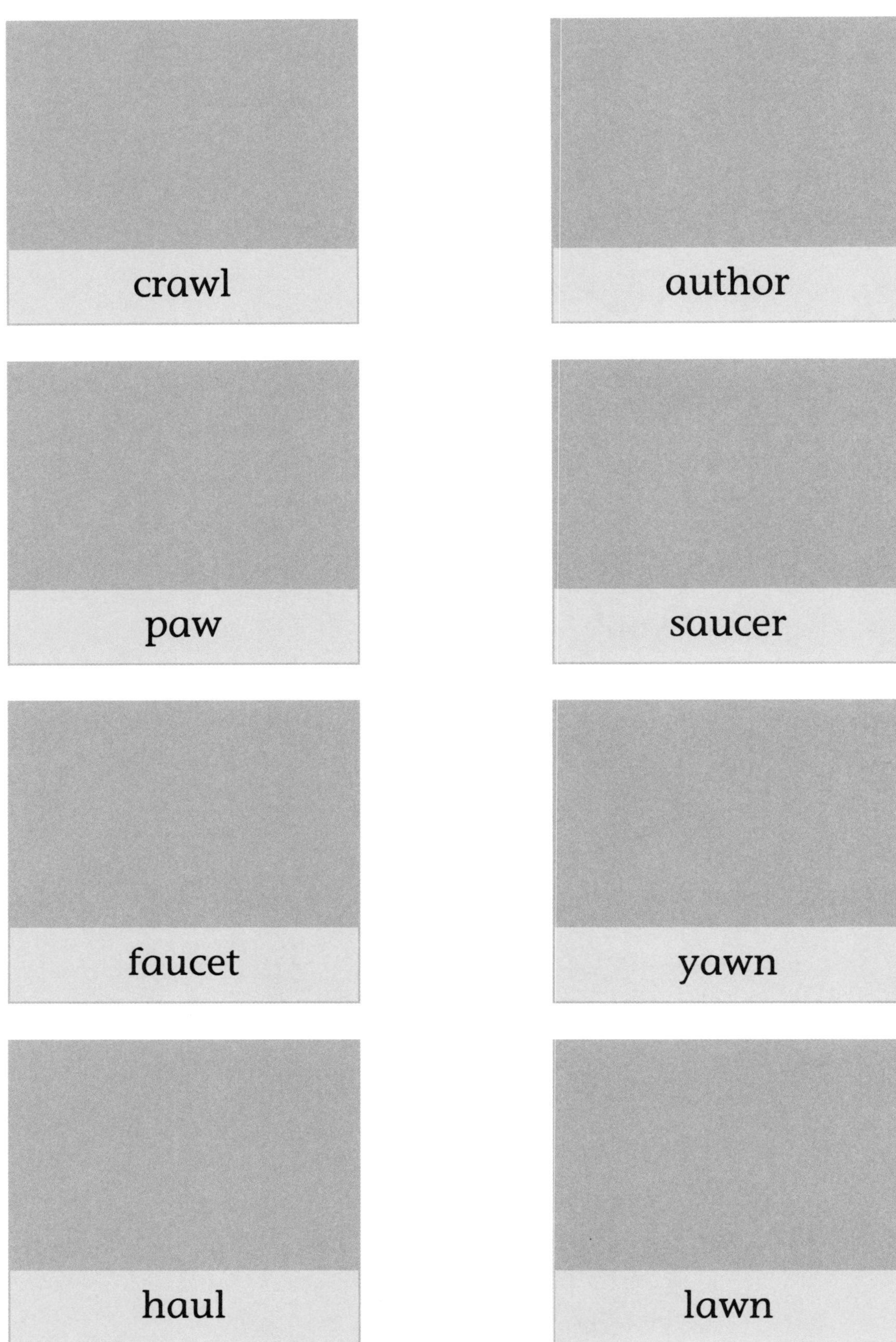

center 7

The au • aw Digraphs

Mat A

1. 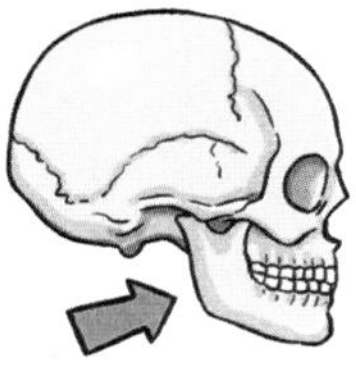 aw

2.  auce

3.  aunch

4.  awk

5.  aw

6.  ault

The au • aw Digraphs

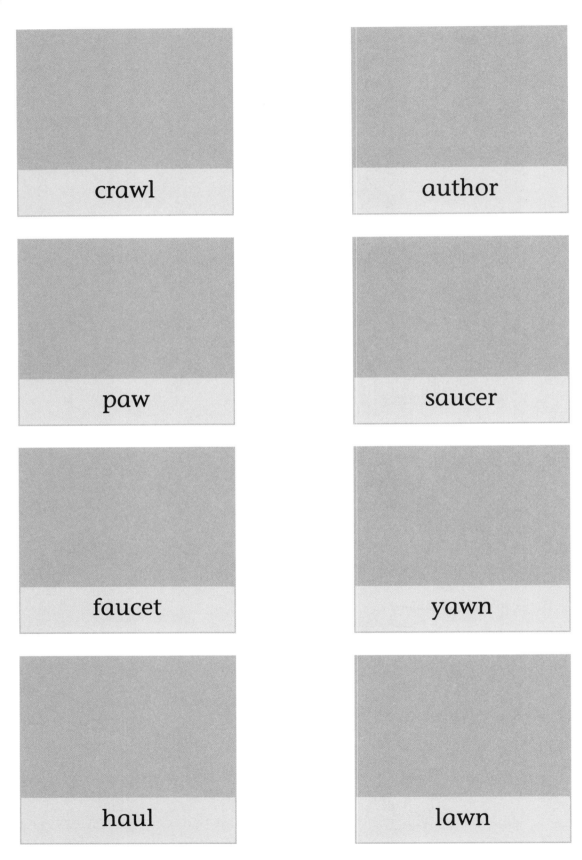

crawl	author
paw	saucer
faucet	yawn
haul	lawn

The au • aw Digraphs

Mat A

1. 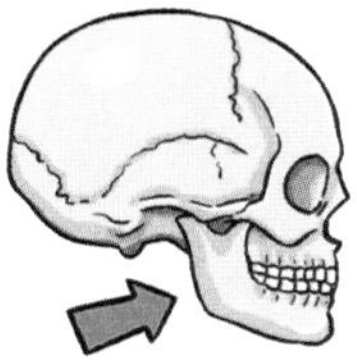 aw

2.  auce

3.  aunch

4.  awk

5.  aw

6.  ault

The au • aw Digraphs

Mat B

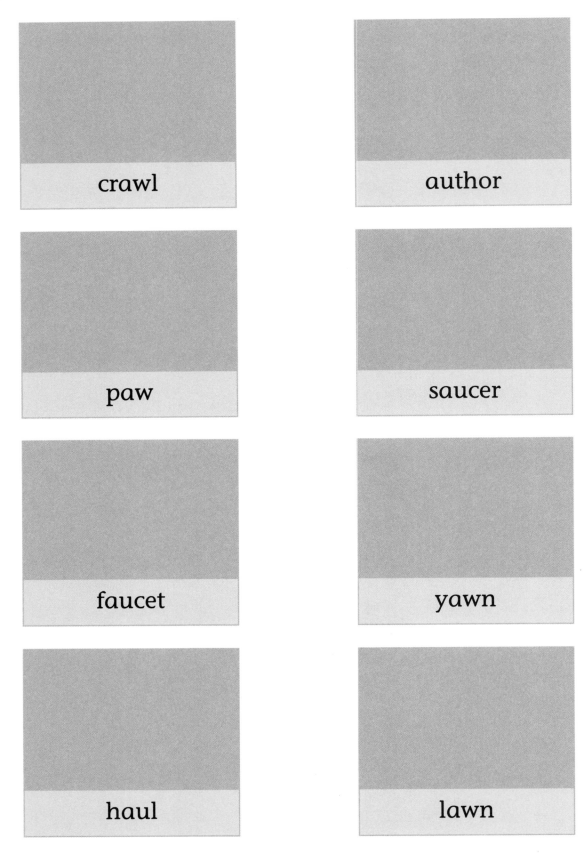

crawl	author
paw	saucer
faucet	yawn
haul	lawn

The au • aw Digraphs

1. 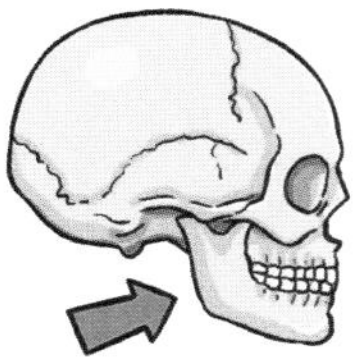 aw

2.  auce

3.  aunch

4.  awk

5.  aw

6.  ault

The au • aw Digraphs

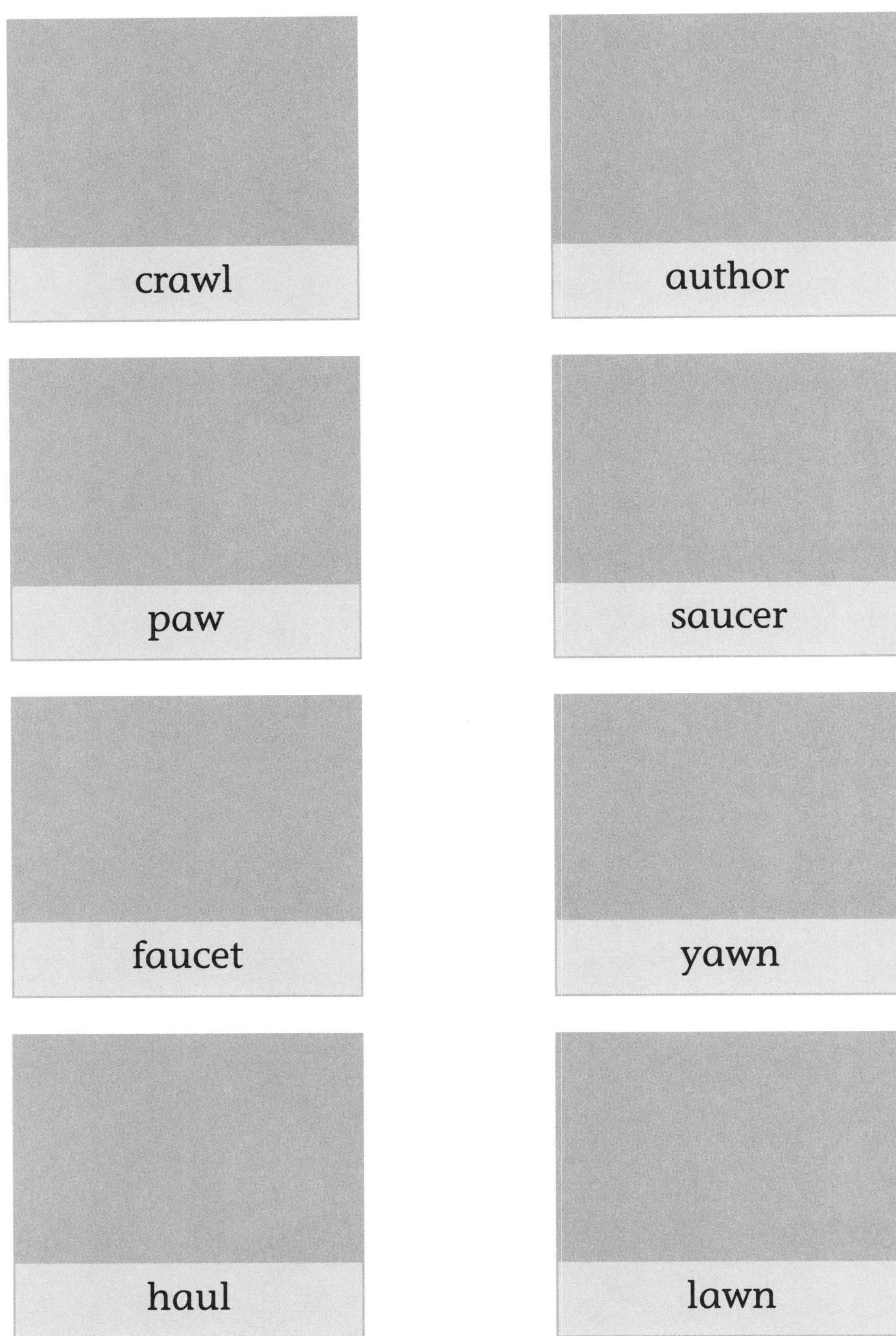

Task Cards

Mat A

Student 6	h	v	j	l	s	th
Student 5	h	v	j	l	s	th
Student 4	h	v	j	l	s	th
Student 3	h	v	j	l	s	th
Student 2	h	v	j	l	s	th
Student 1	h	v	j	l	s	th

Student 6
EMC 3527
Center 7 • Mat A

Student 6
EMC 3527
Center 7 • Mat A

Student 6
EMC 3527
Center 7 • Mat A

Student 6
EMC 3527
Center 7 • Mat A

Student 6
EMC 3527
Center 7 • Mat A

Student 6
EMC 3527
Center 7 • Mat A

Student 5
EMC 3527
Center 7 • Mat A

Student 5
EMC 3527
Center 7 • Mat A

Student 5
EMC 3527
Center 7 • Mat A

Student 5
EMC 3527
Center 7 • Mat A

Student 5
EMC 3527
Center 7 • Mat A

Student 5
EMC 3527
Center 7 • Mat A

Student 4
EMC 3527
Center 7 • Mat A

Student 4
EMC 3527
Center 7 • Mat A

Student 4
EMC 3527
Center 7 • Mat A

Student 4
EMC 3527
Center 7 • Mat A

Student 4
EMC 3527
Center 7 • Mat A

Student 4
EMC 3527
Center 7 • Mat A

Student 3
EMC 3527
Center 7 • Mat A

Student 3
EMC 3527
Center 7 • Mat A

Student 3
EMC 3527
Center 7 • Mat A

Student 3
EMC 3527
Center 7 • Mat A

Student 3
EMC 3527
Center 7 • Mat A

Student 3
EMC 3527
Center 7 • Mat A

Student 2
EMC 3527
Center 7 • Mat A

Student 2
EMC 3527
Center 7 • Mat A

Student 2
EMC 3527
Center 7 • Mat A

Student 2
EMC 3527
Center 7 • Mat A

Student 2
EMC 3527
Center 7 • Mat A

Student 2
EMC 3527
Center 7 • Mat A

Student 1
EMC 3527
Center 7 • Mat A

Student 1
EMC 3527
Center 7 • Mat A

Student 1
EMC 3527
Center 7 • Mat A

Student 1
EMC 3527
Center 7 • Mat A

Student 1
EMC 3527
Center 7 • Mat A

Student 1
EMC 3527
Center 7 • Mat A

Task Cards

Mat B

Student 2

Student 1

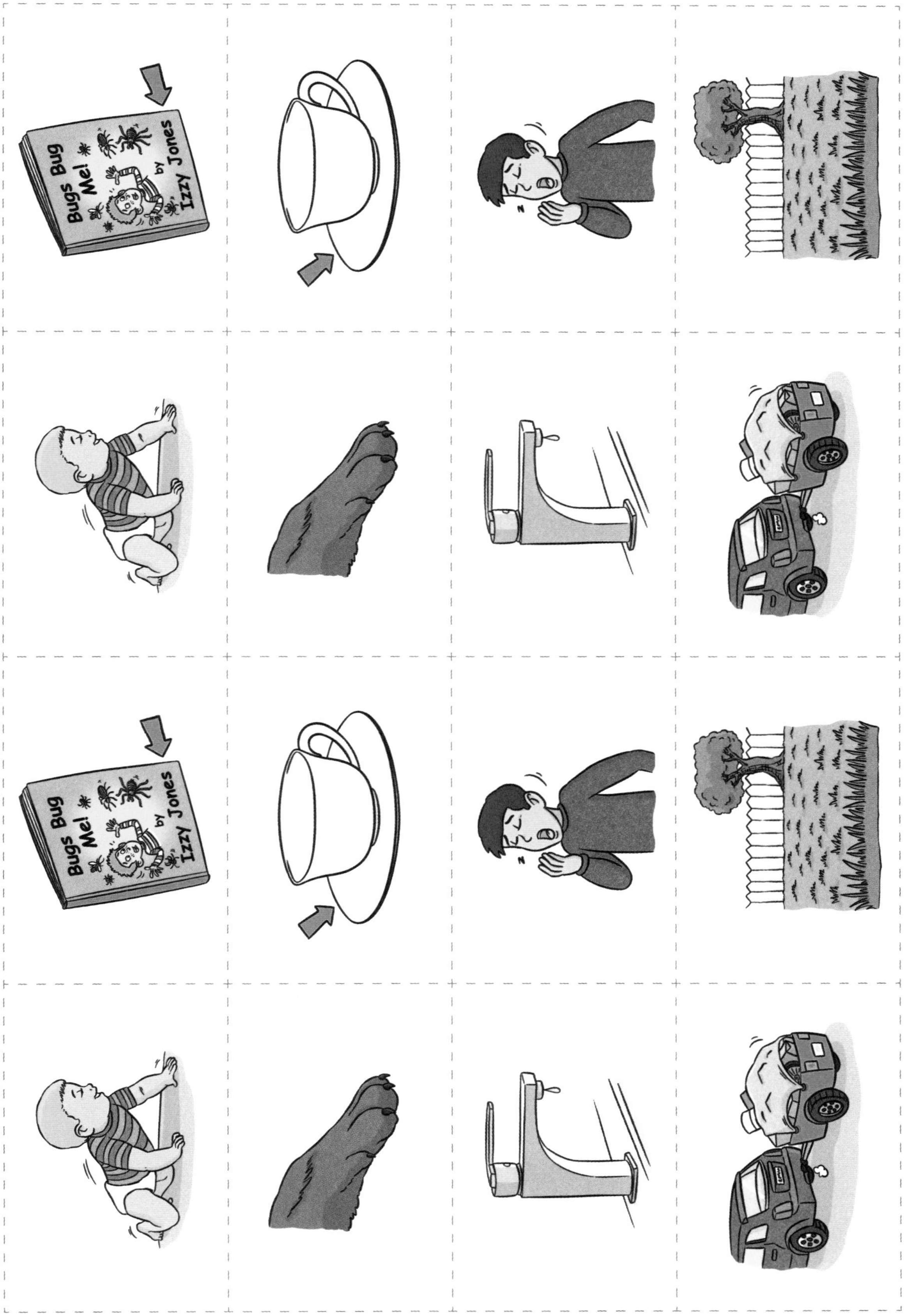

Task Cards

Student 2
EMC 3527 • Center 7 • Mat B

Student 2
EMC 3527 • Center 7 • Mat B

Student 2
EMC 3527 • Center 7 • Mat B

Student 2
EMC 3527 • Center 7 • Mat B

Student 2
EMC 3527 • Center 7 • Mat B

Student 2
EMC 3527 • Center 7 • Mat B

Student 2
EMC 3527 • Center 7 • Mat B

Student 2
EMC 3527 • Center 7 • Mat B

Student 1
EMC 3527 • Center 7 • Mat B

Student 1
EMC 3527 • Center 7 • Mat B

Student 1
EMC 3527 • Center 7 • Mat B

Student 1
EMC 3527 • Center 7 • Mat B

Student 1
EMC 3527 • Center 7 • Mat B

Student 1
EMC 3527 • Center 7 • Mat B

Student 1
EMC 3527 • Center 7 • Mat B

Student 1
EMC 3527 • Center 7 • Mat B

Task Cards

Student 4

Student 3

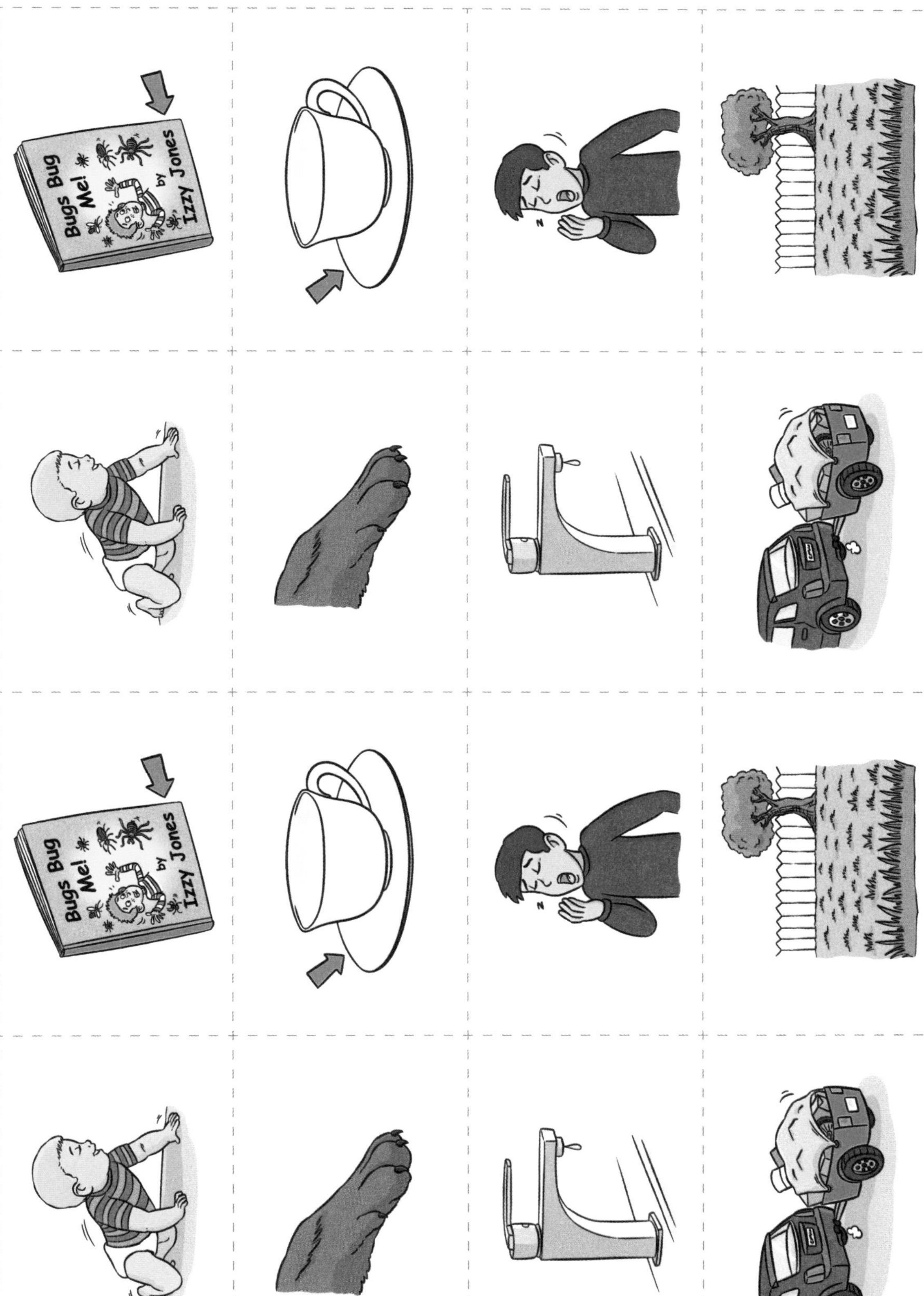

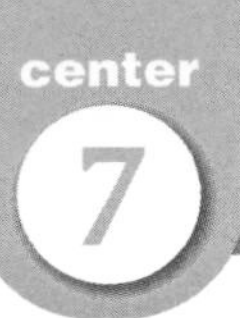

Task Cards

Student 4
EMC 3527 • Center 7 • Mat B

Student 4
EMC 3527 • Center 7 • Mat B

Student 4
EMC 3527 • Center 7 • Mat B

Student 4
EMC 3527 • Center 7 • Mat B

Student 4
EMC 3527 • Center 7 • Mat B

Student 4
EMC 3527 • Center 7 • Mat B

Student 4
EMC 3527 • Center 7 • Mat B

Student 4
EMC 3527 • Center 7 • Mat B

Student 3
EMC 3527 • Center 7 • Mat B

Student 3
EMC 3527 • Center 7 • Mat B

Student 3
EMC 3527 • Center 7 • Mat B

Student 3
EMC 3527 • Center 7 • Mat B

Student 3
EMC 3527 • Center 7 • Mat B

Student 3
EMC 3527 • Center 7 • Mat B

Student 3
EMC 3527 • Center 7 • Mat B

Student 3
EMC 3527 • Center 7 • Mat B

Task Cards

Student 6

Student 5

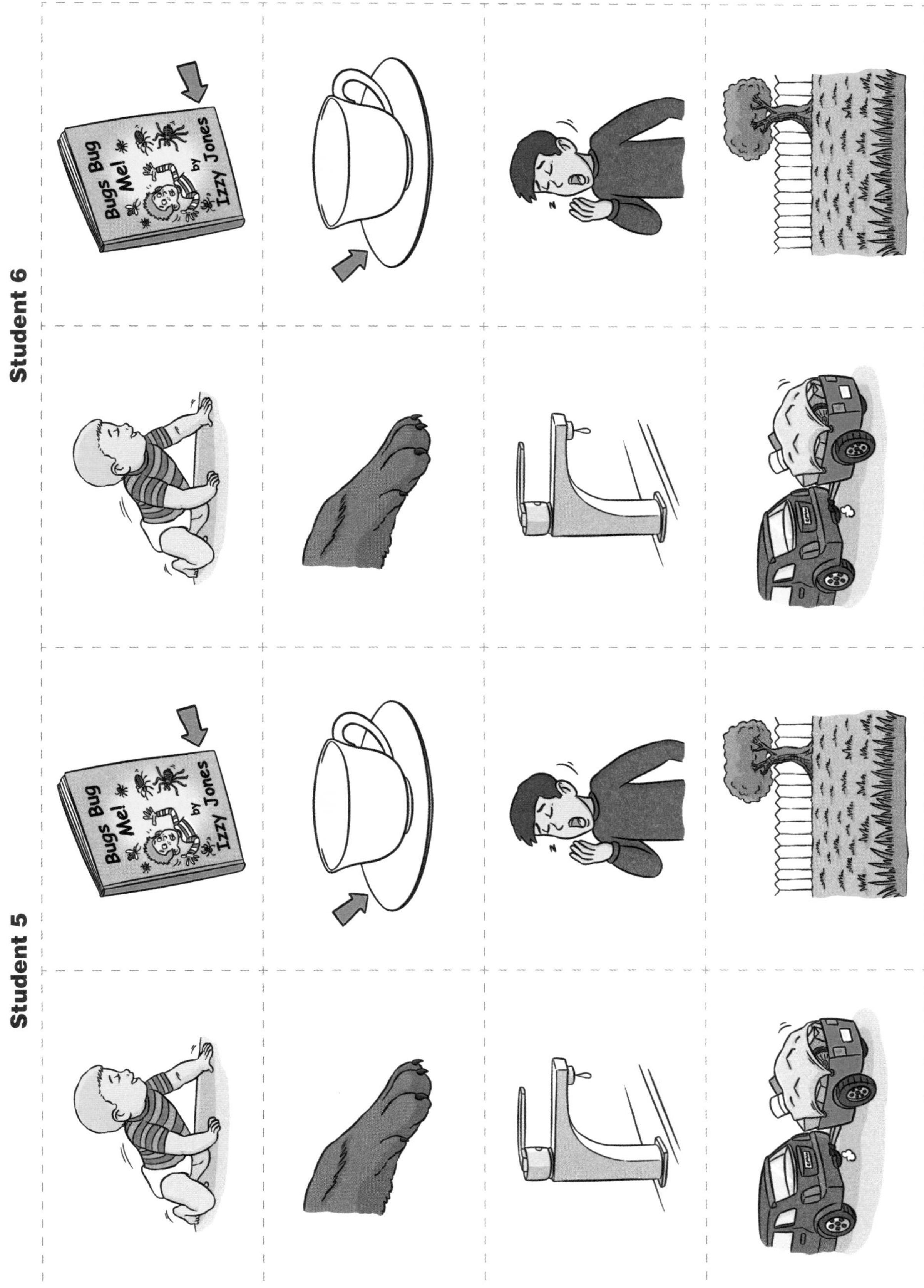

Student 6
EMC 3527 • Center 7 • Mat B

Student 6
EMC 3527 • Center 7 • Mat B

Student 6
EMC 3527 • Center 7 • Mat B

Student 6
EMC 3527 • Center 7 • Mat B

Student 6
EMC 3527 • Center 7 • Mat B

Student 6
EMC 3527 • Center 7 • Mat B

Student 6
EMC 3527 • Center 7 • Mat B

Student 6
EMC 3527 • Center 7 • Mat B

Student 5
EMC 3527 • Center 7 • Mat B

Student 5
EMC 3527 • Center 7 • Mat B

Student 5
EMC 3527 • Center 7 • Mat B

Student 5
EMC 3527 • Center 7 • Mat B

Student 5
EMC 3527 • Center 7 • Mat B

Student 5
EMC 3527 • Center 7 • Mat B

Student 5
EMC 3527 • Center 7 • Mat B

Student 5
EMC 3527 • Center 7 • Mat B

Name ______________________________

Practice It!

Listen to the clue.
Say the words after the clue.
Circle the word that answers the clue.

1. a rule to follow	**law**	**raw**	**jaw**
2. the sound of a crow	**claw**	**bawl**	**caw**
3. a topping for food	**saucer**	**seesaw**	**sauce**
4. a tool used to cut wood	**saw**	**paw**	**yawn**
5. to carry by truck	**haul**	**haunt**	**vault**
6. to stop for a short time	**cause**	**pause**	**applause**
7. the writer of a book	**author**	**auto**	**audio**
8. very bad	**awesome**	**awful**	**awning**

Name ______________________________

Read It!

Write the word on the line that best completes the sentence.

1. My dog likes to eat ______________ meat.
   saw raw

2. What ______________ the faucet to drip?
   causes pauses

3. An awful storm delayed the rocket ______________.
   lawn launch

4. A hawk uses its sharp ______________ to grab food.
   thaws claws

5. I like strawberry ______________ on my ice cream.
   sauce saucer

6. Your ______________ opens wide when you yawn.
   jaw caw

7. We took the cat to the vet ______________ she hurt her paw.
   applause because

8. The farmer hauls ______________ into his barn in autumn.
   straw draw

center **8**

INTERMEDIATE

Vowel Digraphs Review

For the Teacher

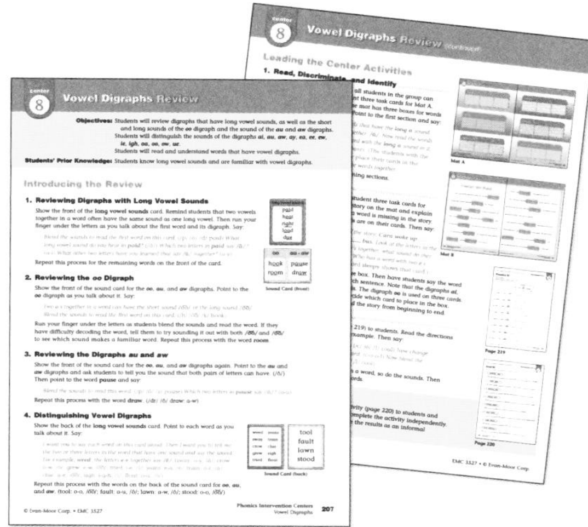

Lesson Plan

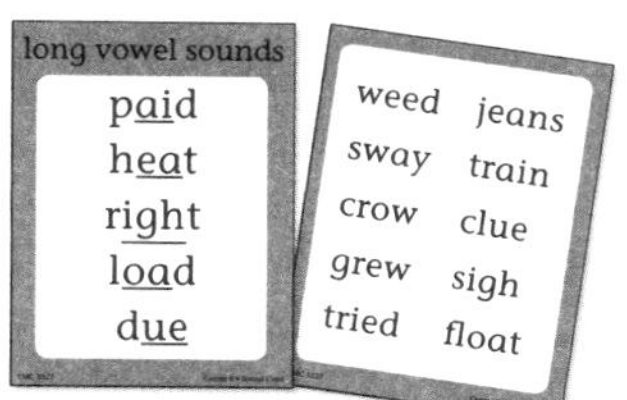

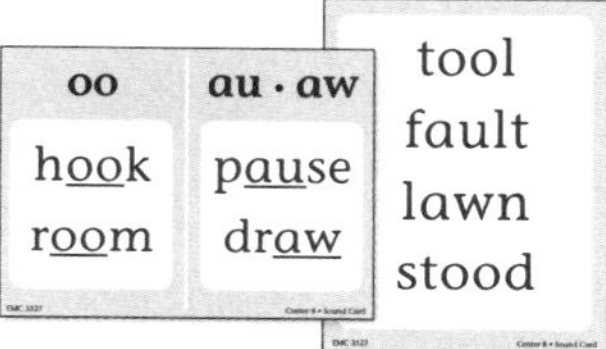

Sound Cards

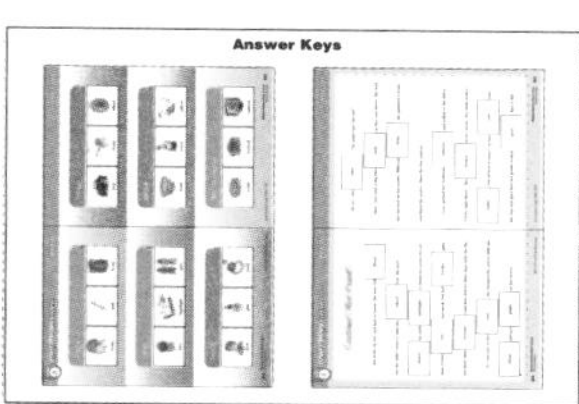

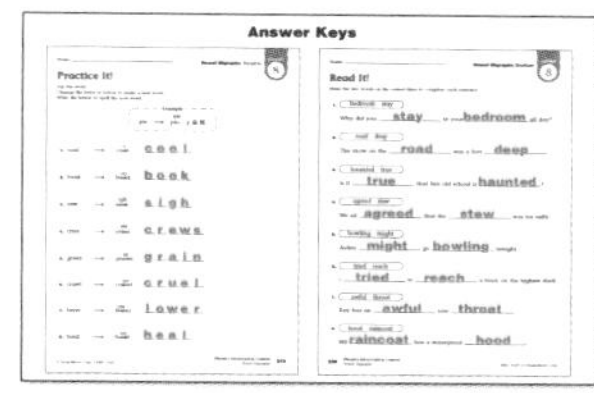

Answer Keys

For the Student

front (Mat A)

To make Mat A, place pages 212 and 213 side by side and laminate. (Turn over for Mat B.)

back (Mat B)

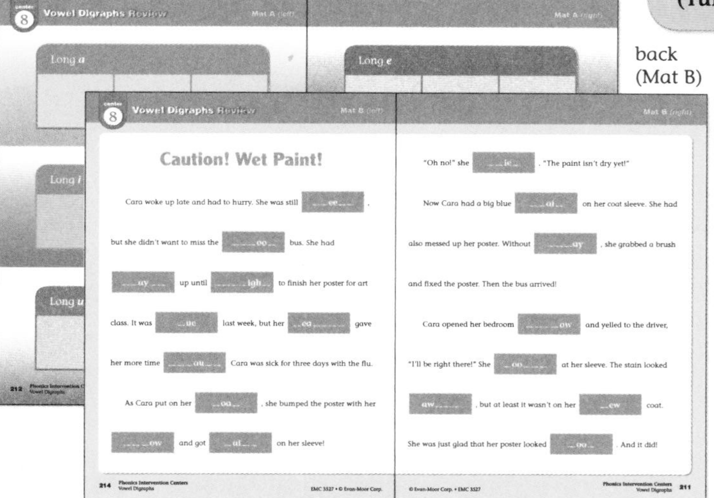

Activity Mats

Task Cards

Read It!

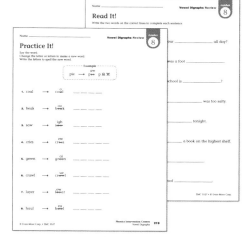

Practice It!

Practice and Assessment Activities

Vowel Digraphs Review

Objectives: Students will review digraphs that have long vowel sounds, as well as the short and long sounds of the ***oo*** digraph and the sound of the ***au*** and ***aw*** digraphs.
Students will distinguish the sounds of the digraphs ***ai***, ***au***, ***aw***, ***ay***, ***ea***, ***ee***, ***ew***, ***ie***, ***igh***, ***oa***, ***oo***, ***ow***, ***ue***.
Students will read and understand words that have vowel digraphs.

Students' Prior Knowledge: Students know long vowel sounds and are familiar with vowel digraphs.

Introducing the Review

1. Reviewing Digraphs with Long Vowel Sounds

Show the front of the **long vowel sounds** card. Remind students that two vowels together in a word often have the same sound as one long vowel. Then run your finger under the letters as you talk about the first word and its digraph. Say:

Blend the sounds to read the first word on this card. (/p/ /ā/ /d/ paid) *What long vowel sound do you hear in **paid**?* (/ā/) *Which two letters in **paid** say /ā/?* (a-i) *What other two letters have you learned that say /ā/ together?* (a-y)

Repeat this process for the remaining words on the front of the card.

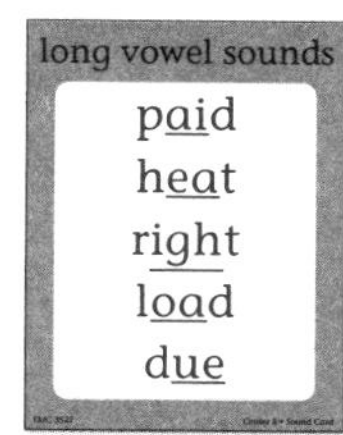

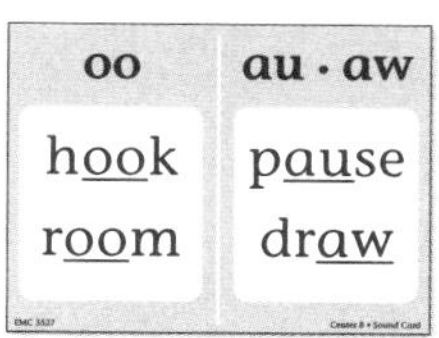

Sound Card (front)

2. Reviewing the *oo* Digraph

Show the front of the sound card for the ***oo***, ***au***, and ***aw*** digraphs. Point to the ***oo*** digraph as you talk about it. Say:

*Two **o**'s together in a word can have the short sound /o͝o/ or the long sound /o͞o/. Blend the sounds to read the first word on this card.* (/h/ /o͝o/ /k/ hook)

Run your finger under the letters as students blend the sounds and read the word. If they have difficulty decoding the word, tell them to try sounding it out with both **/o͝o/** and **/o͞o/** to see which sound makes a familiar word. Repeat this process with the word **room**.

3. Reviewing the Digraphs *au* and *aw*

Show the front of the sound card for the ***oo***, ***au***, and ***aw*** digraphs again. Point to the ***au*** and ***aw*** digraphs and ask students to tell you the sound that both pairs of letters can have. (/ô/) Then point to the word **pause** and say:

Blend the sounds to read this word. (/p/ /ô/ /z/ pause) *Which two letters in **pause** say /ô/?* (a-u)

Repeat this process with the word **draw**. (/dr/ /ô/ draw; a-w)

4. Distinguishing Vowel Digraphs

Show the back of the **long vowel sounds** card. Point to each word as you talk about it. Say:

*I want you to say each word on this card aloud. Then I want you to tell me the two or three letters in the word that have one sound and say the sound. For example, **weed**: the letters **e-e** together say /ē/.* (sway: a-y, /ā/; crow: o-w, /ō/; grew: e-w, /o͞o/; tried: i-e, /ī/; jeans: e-a, /ē/; train: a-i, /ā/; clue: u-e, /o͞o/; sigh: i-g-h, /ī/; float: o-a, /ō/)

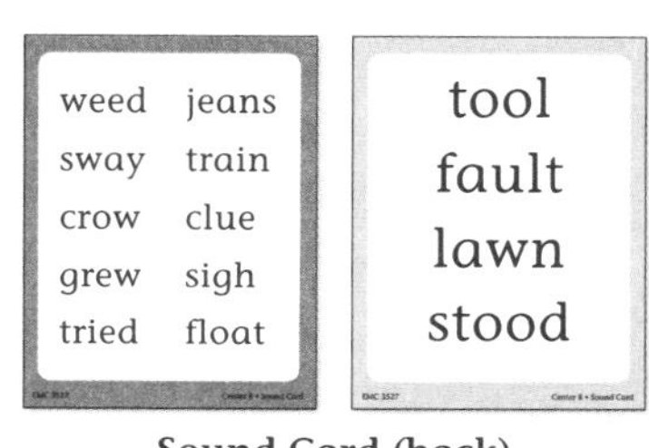

Sound Card (back)

Repeat this process with the words on the back of the sound card for ***oo***, ***au***, and ***aw***. (tool: o-o, /o͞o/; fault: a-u, /ô/; lawn: a-w, /ô/; stood: o-o, /o͝o/)

Leading the Center Activities

1. Read, Discriminate, and Identify

Place Mat A on a table where all students in the group can reach it. Then give each student three task cards for Mat A. Explain that each section of the mat has three boxes for words that have a particular sound. Point to the first section and say:

> *These green boxes are for words that have the* ***long a*** *sound. Let's say the* ***long a*** *sound together: /ā/. Now read the words on your cards. If you have a word with the* ***long a*** *sound in it, place the card in one of these boxes.* (The students with the words **brain**, **nail**, and **X-ray** place their cards in the green boxes.) *Now let's read the words together.*

Repeat this process for the remaining sections.

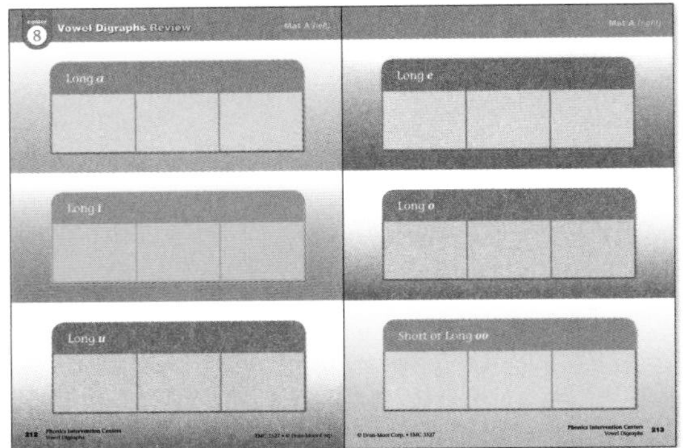

Mat A

2. Read and Understand

Turn over the mat and give each student three task cards for Mat B. Read aloud the title of the story on the mat and explain that each green box shows where a word is missing in the story. Tell students that the missing words are on their cards. Then say:

> *Listen to me read the beginning of the story:* ***Cara woke up .... She was still _____, but ... the _____ bus.*** *Look at the letters in the first green box. When you see two* ***e's*** *together, what sound do they have? (/ē/) Now look at your cards. Who has a word with two* ***e's*** *together?* (The student with the word **sleepy** shows that card.)

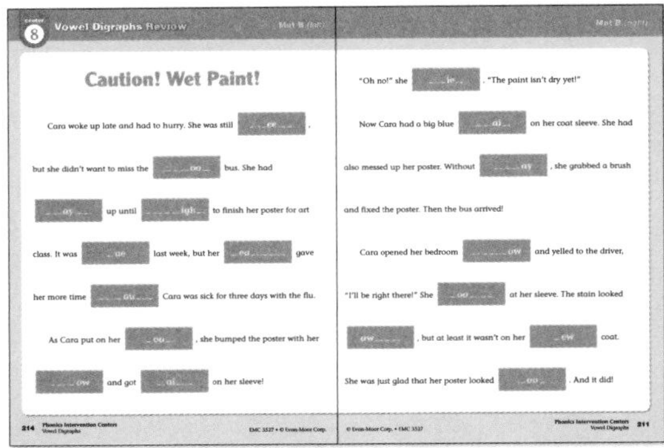

Mat B

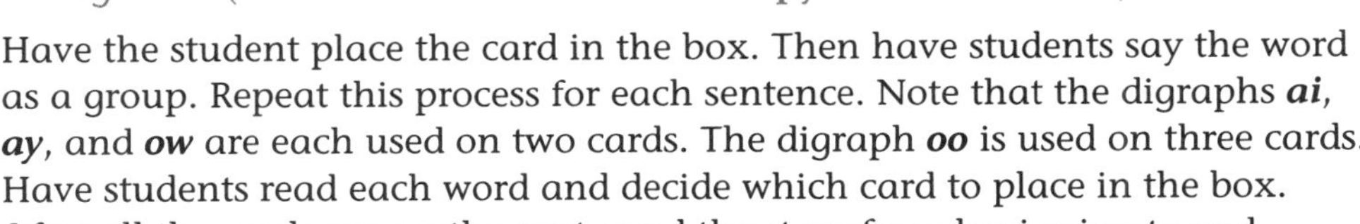

Have the student place the card in the box. Then have students say the word as a group. Repeat this process for each sentence. Note that the digraphs ***ai***, ***ay***, and ***ow*** are each used on two cards. The digraph ***oo*** is used on three cards. Have students read each word and decide which card to place in the box. After all the cards are on the mat, read the story from beginning to end.

3. Practice the Skill

Distribute the Practice It! activity (page 219) to students. Read the directions aloud and guide students through the example. Then say:

> *Blend the sounds to read the first word.* (/c/ /ō/ /l/ coal) *Now change the letter* ***a*** *to an* ***o*** *and write the new word.* (c-o-o-l) *Now blend the sounds and read the new word.* (/c/ /o͞o/ /l/ cool)

Remind students that as letters change in a word, so do the sounds. Then repeat this process with the remaining words.

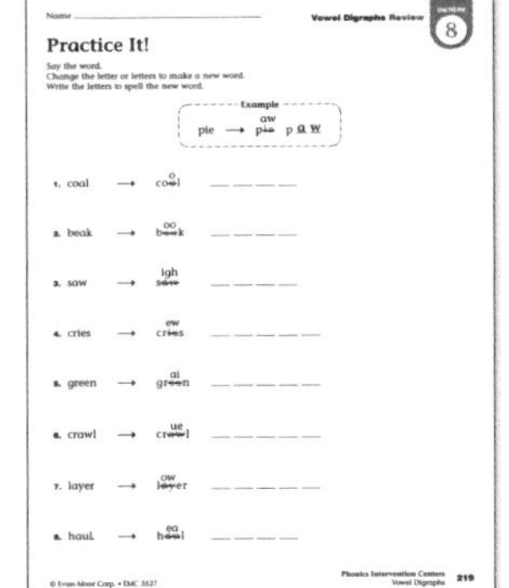

Page 219

Page 220

Apply and Assess

After the lesson, distribute the Read It! activity (page 220) to students and read the directions aloud. Have students complete the activity independently. Then listen to them read the sentences. Use the results as an informal assessment of students' skill mastery.

long vowel sounds

paid
heat
right
load
due

EMC 3527 Center 8 • Sound Card

au • aw

pause
draw

oo

hook
room

Center 8 • Sound Card EMC 3527

Answer Keys

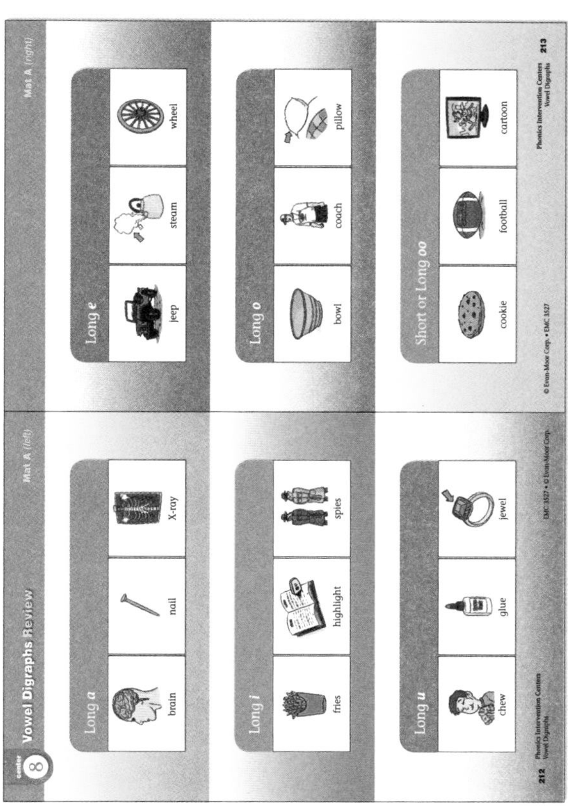
Center 8 Vowel Digraphs Review — Mat A (left)

Long a: brain, nail, X-ray

Long i: fries, highlight, spies

Long u: chew, glue, jewel

212 Phonics Intervention Centers Vowel Digraphs EMC 3527 • © Evan-Moor Corp.

Mat A (right)

Long e: jeep, steam, wheel

Long o: bowl, coach, pillow

Short or Long oo: cookie, football, cartoon

© Evan-Moor Corp. • EMC 3527 Phonics Intervention Centers Vowel Digraphs 213

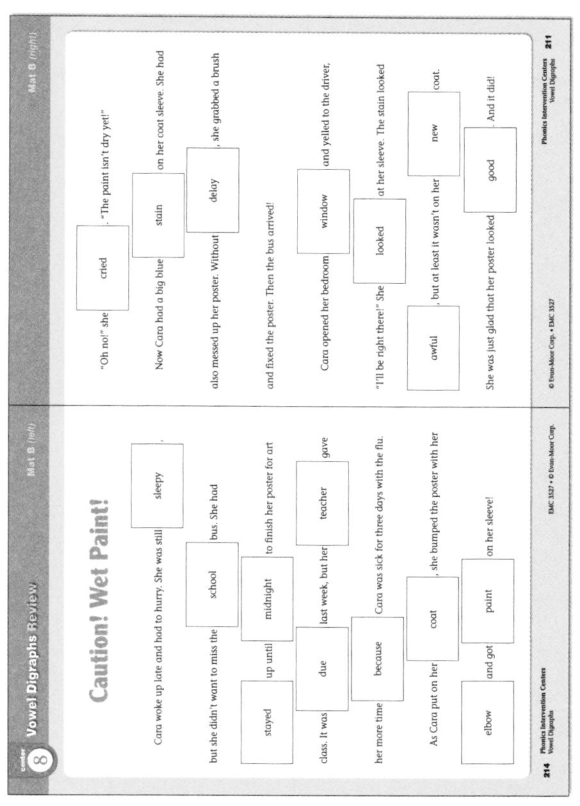
Center 8 Vowel Digraphs Review — Mat B (left)

Caution! Wet Paint!

Cara woke up late and had to hurry. She was still [sleepy]. but she didn't want to miss the [school] bus. She had [stayed] up until [midnight] to finish her poster for art class. It was [due] last week, but her [teacher] gave her more time [because] Cara was sick for three days with the flu. As Cara put on her [coat], she bumped the poster with her [elbow] and got [paint] on her sleeve!

214 Phonics Intervention Centers Vowel Digraphs EMC 3527 • © Evan-Moor Corp.

Mat B (right)

"Oh no!" she [cried]. "The paint isn't dry yet!" Now Cara had a big blue [stain] on her coat sleeve. She had also messed up her poster. Without [delay], she grabbed a brush and fixed the poster. Then the bus arrived! Cara opened her bedroom [window] and yelled to the driver, "I'll be right there!" She [looked] at her sleeve. The stain looked [awful], but at least it wasn't on her [new] coat. She was just glad that her poster looked [good]. And it did!

© Evan-Moor Corp. • EMC 3527 Phonics Intervention Centers Vowel Digraphs 211

tool

fault

lawn

stood

EMC 3527 Center 8 • Sound Card

weed jeans

sway train

crow clue

grew sigh

tried float

EMC 3527 Center 8 • Sound Card

Answer Keys

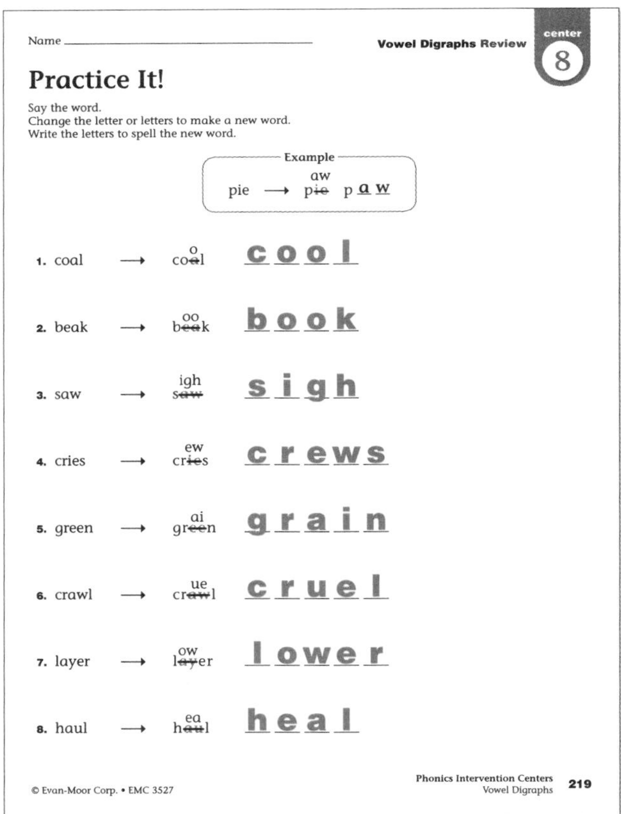

Name ____________ Vowel Digraphs Review center 8

Practice It!

Say the word.
Change the letter or letters to make a new word.
Write the letters to spell the new word.

Example: pie → p~~ie~~ (aw) → p a w

1. coal → co~~a~~l (o) → c o o l
2. beak → b~~ea~~k (oo) → b o o k
3. saw → ~~saw~~ (igh) → s i g h
4. cries → cr~~ie~~s (ew) → c r e w s
5. green → gr~~ee~~n (ai) → g r a i n
6. crawl → cr~~aw~~l (ue) → c r u e l
7. layer → l~~ay~~er (ow) → l o w e r
8. haul → h~~au~~l (ea) → h e a l

© Evan-Moor Corp. • EMC 3527 Phonics Intervention Centers Vowel Digraphs 219

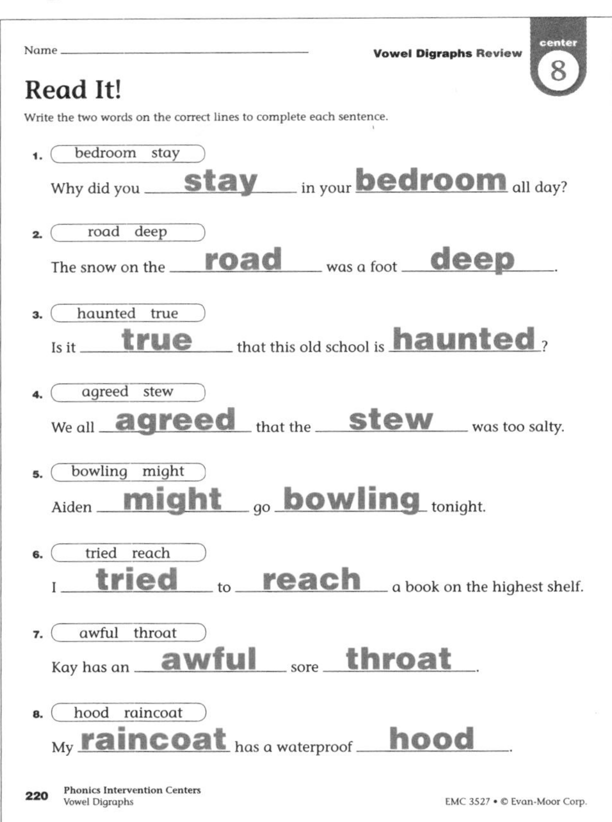

Name ____________ Vowel Digraphs Review center 8

Read It!

Write the two words on the correct lines to complete each sentence.

1. (bedroom stay) Why did you **stay** in your **bedroom** all day?
2. (road deep) The snow on the **road** was a foot **deep**.
3. (haunted true) Is it **true** that this old school is **haunted**?
4. (agreed stew) We all **agreed** that the **stew** was too salty.
5. (bowling might) Aiden **might** go **bowling** tonight.
6. (tried reach) I **tried** to **reach** a book on the highest shelf.
7. (awful throat) Kay has an **awful** sore **throat**.
8. (hood raincoat) My **raincoat** has a waterproof **hood**.

220 Phonics Intervention Centers Vowel Digraphs EMC 3527 • © Evan-Moor Corp.

"Oh no!" she ___ie_ . "The paint isn't dry yet!"

Now Cara had a big blue __ai_ on her coat sleeve. She had also messed up her poster. Without ____ay , she grabbed a brush and fixed the poster. Then the bus arrived!

Cara opened her bedroom _____ow and yelled to the driver, "I'll be right there!" She _oo___ at her sleeve. The stain looked aw___ , but at least it wasn't on her _ew coat. She was just glad that her poster looked _oo_ . And it did!

Long *a*

Long *i*

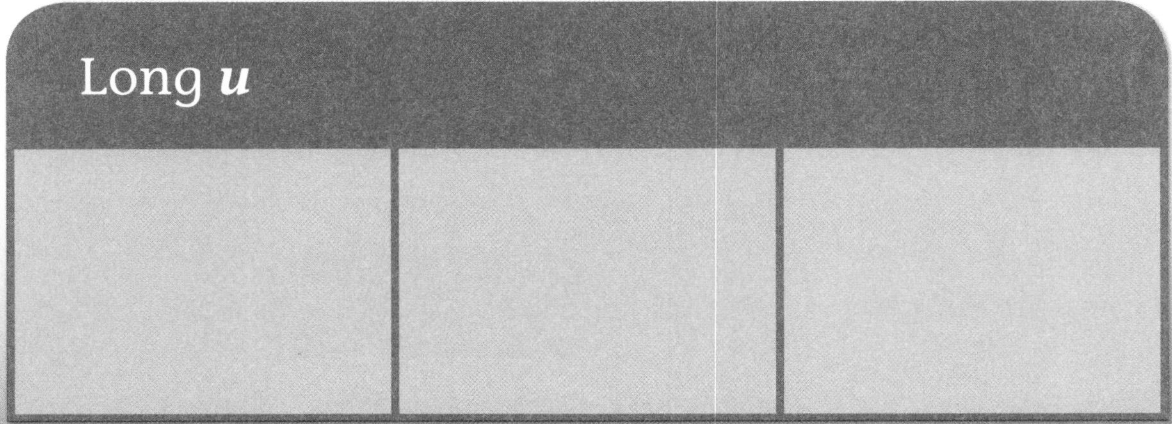
Long *u*

Long *e*

Long *o*

Short or Long *oo*

Caution! Wet Paint!

Cara woke up late and had to hurry. She was still __ __ee__ __ , but she didn't want to miss the __ __ __oo__ bus. She had __ __ay__ __ up until __ __ __ __igh__ to finish her poster for art class. It was __ue last week, but her __ea__ __ __ __ __ gave her more time __ __ __au__ __ Cara was sick for three days with the flu.

As Cara put on her __oa__ , she bumped the poster with her __ __ __ow and got __ai__ __ on her sleeve!

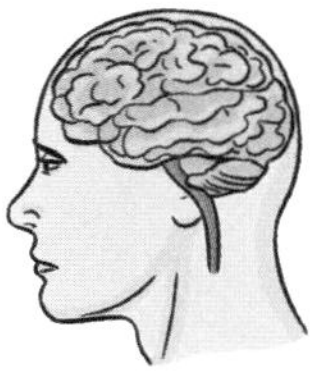

brain	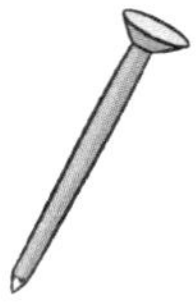 nail	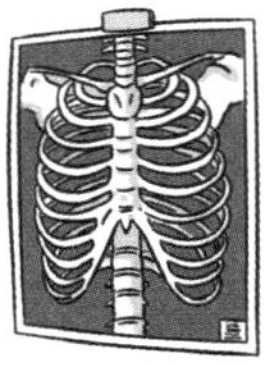 X-ray
 jeep	 steam	 wheel
 fries	 highlight	 spies
 bowl	coach	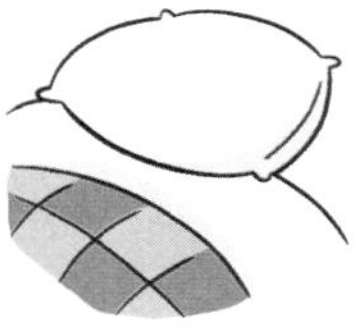 pillow
 chew	glue	 jewel
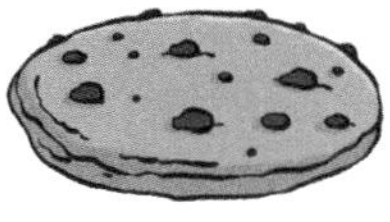 cookie	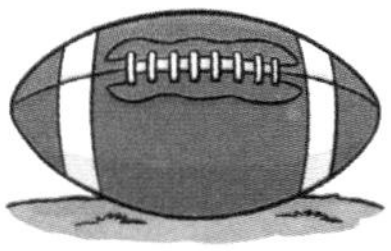 football	 cartoon

Task Cards

EMC 3527 • Center 8 • Mat A
EMC 3527 • Center 8 • Mat A
EMC 3527 • Center 8 • Mat A

EMC 3527 • Center 8 • Mat A
EMC 3527 • Center 8 • Mat A
EMC 3527 • Center 8 • Mat A

EMC 3527 • Center 8 • Mat A
EMC 3527 • Center 8 • Mat A
EMC 3527 • Center 8 • Mat A

EMC 3527 • Center 8 • Mat A
EMC 3527 • Center 8 • Mat A
EMC 3527 • Center 8 • Mat A

EMC 3527 • Center 8 • Mat A
EMC 3527 • Center 8 • Mat A
EMC 3527 • Center 8 • Mat A

EMC 3527 • Center 8 • Mat A
EMC 3527 • Center 8 • Mat A
EMC 3527 • Center 8 • Mat A

Task Cards

awful	because	coat
delay	cried	due
elbow	good	looked
midnight	new	paint
school	sleepy	stain
stayed	teacher	window

EMC 3527 Center 8 • Mat B	EMC 3527 Center 8 • Mat B	EMC 3527 Center 8 • Mat B
EMC 3527 Center 8 • Mat B	EMC 3527 Center 8 • Mat B	EMC 3527 Center 8 • Mat B
EMC 3527 Center 8 • Mat B	EMC 3527 Center 8 • Mat B	EMC 3527 Center 8 • Mat B
EMC 3527 Center 8 • Mat B	EMC 3527 Center 8 • Mat B	EMC 3527 Center 8 • Mat B
EMC 3527 Center 8 • Mat B	EMC 3527 Center 8 • Mat B	EMC 3527 Center 8 • Mat B
EMC 3527 Center 8 • Mat B	EMC 3527 Center 8 • Mat B	EMC 3527 Center 8 • Mat B

Name ______________________________

Practice It!

Say the word.
Change the letter or letters to make a new word.
Write the letters to spell the new word.

Example

pie → p~~ie~~ (aw) p **a** **w**

1. coal → co~~a~~l (o) ___ ___ ___ ___

2. beak → b~~ea~~k (oo) ___ ___ ___ ___

3. saw → s~~aw~~ (igh) ___ ___ ___ ___

4. cries → cr~~ie~~s (ew) ___ ___ ___ ___ ___

5. green → gr~~ee~~n (ai) ___ ___ ___ ___ ___

6. crawl → cr~~aw~~l (ue) ___ ___ ___ ___ ___

7. layer → l~~ay~~er (ow) ___ ___ ___ ___ ___

8. haul → h~~au~~l (ea) ___ ___ ___ ___

Read It!

Write the two words on the correct lines to complete each sentence.

1. bedroom stay

Why did you ____________ in your ____________ all day?

2. road deep

The snow on the ____________ was a foot ____________.

3. haunted true

Is it ____________ that this old school is ____________?

4. agreed stew

We all ____________ that the ____________ was too salty.

5. bowling might

Aiden ____________ go ____________ tonight.

6. tried reach

I ____________ to ____________ a book on the highest shelf.

7. awful throat

Kay has an ____________ sore ____________.

8. hood raincoat

My ____________ has a waterproof ____________.

Provide students with important reading and language arts skill practice!

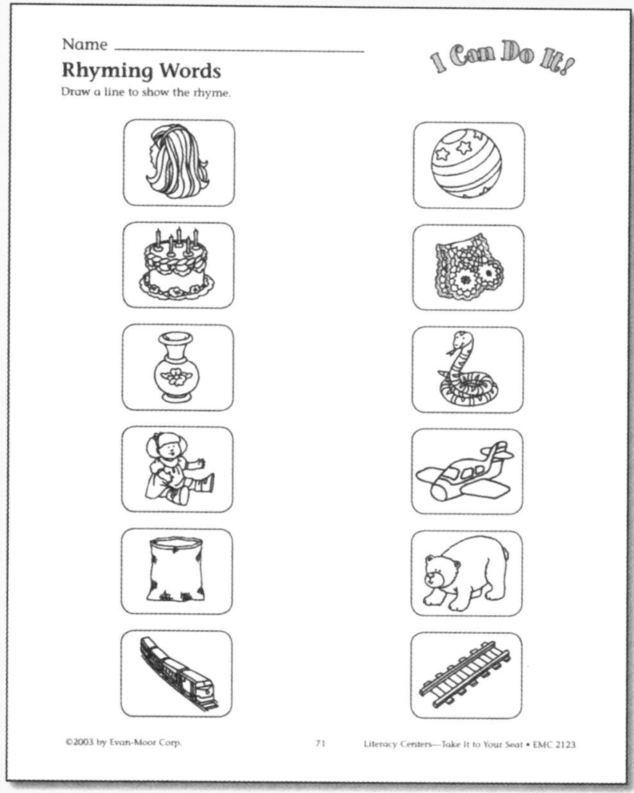

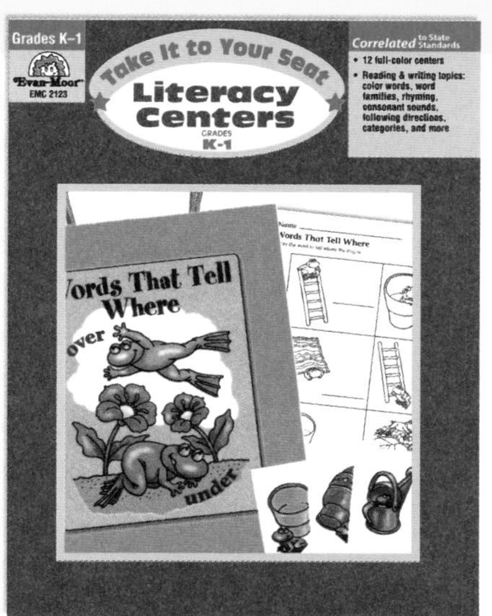

Take It to Your Seat
Literacy Centers

Grade	
PreK–K	EMC 2401
K–1	EMC 2123
1–3	EMC 788
2–3	EMC 2723
3–4	EMC 2124
4–5	EMC 2724
4–6	EMC 2719

Features:

- Provide students with important reading and language arts skill practice that feels more like fun than work!
- Each book comes with up to 18 self-contained centers that students can pick up and take anywhere.
- They're a perfect way to provide students with the extra practice they need to strengthen language skills.

Grades 3–4
Evan-Moor
EMC 3022
Take It to Your Seat
Math Centers
Grades 3-4
Correlated to State Standards
Read a Graph

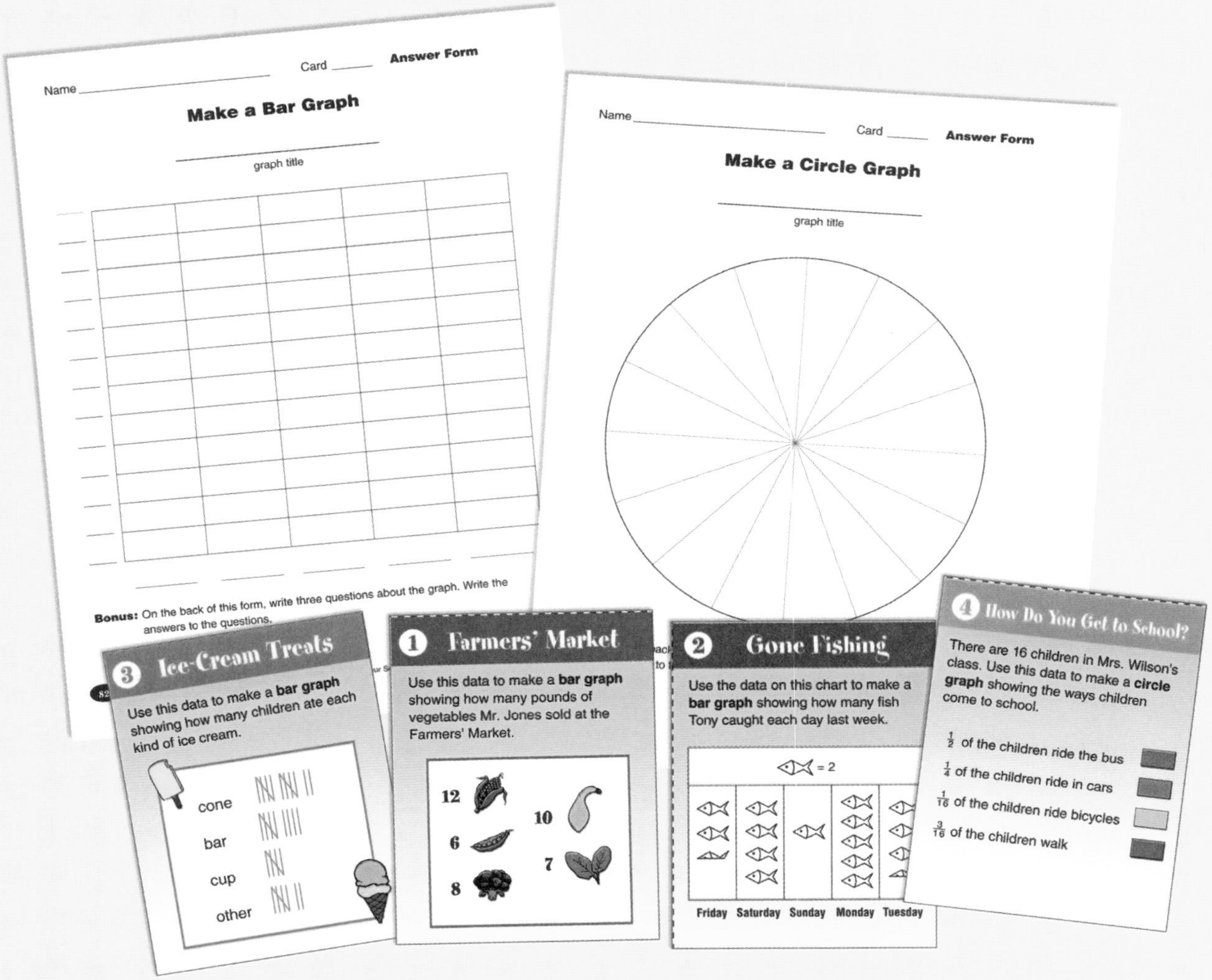

Enrich any core writing or language arts program!

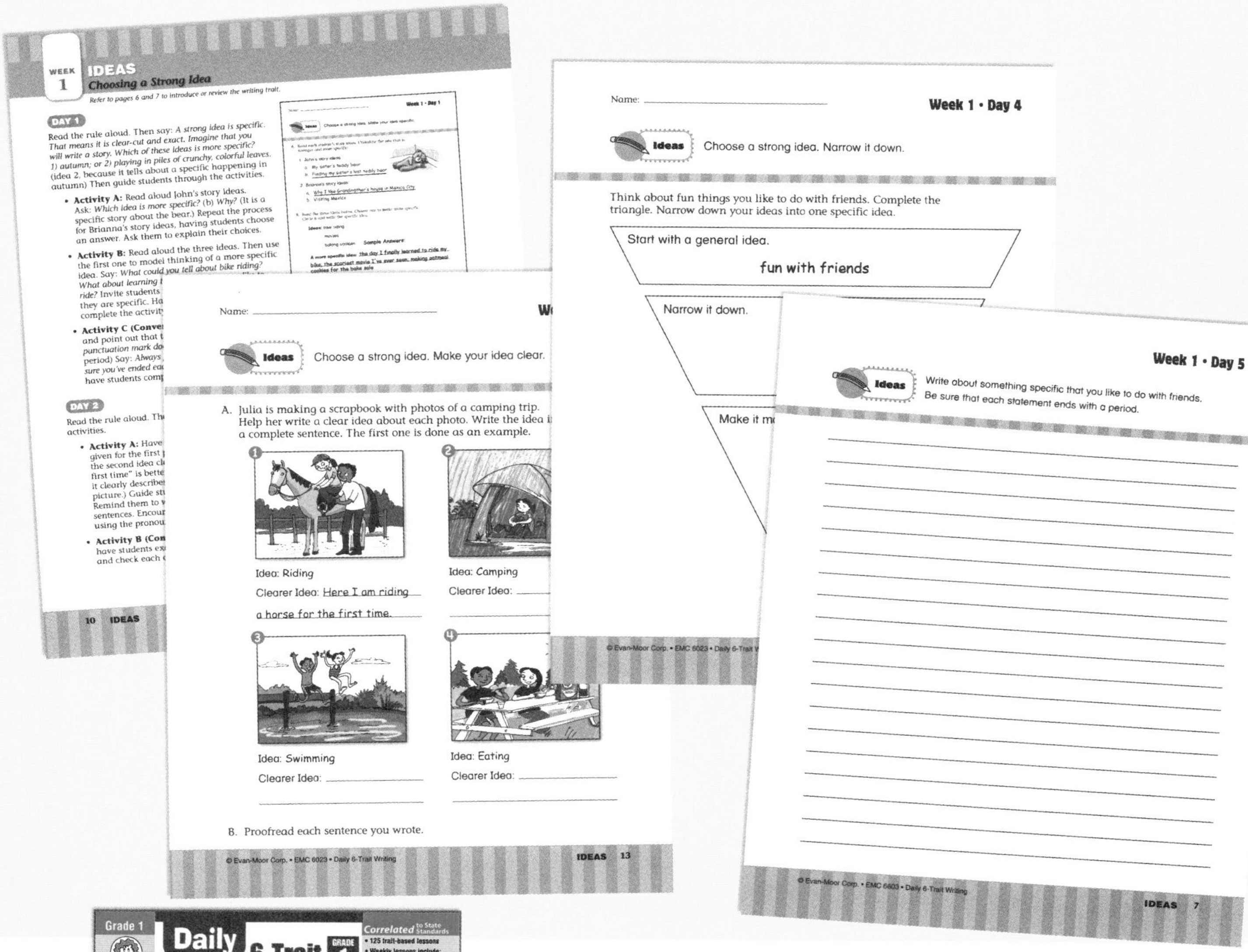

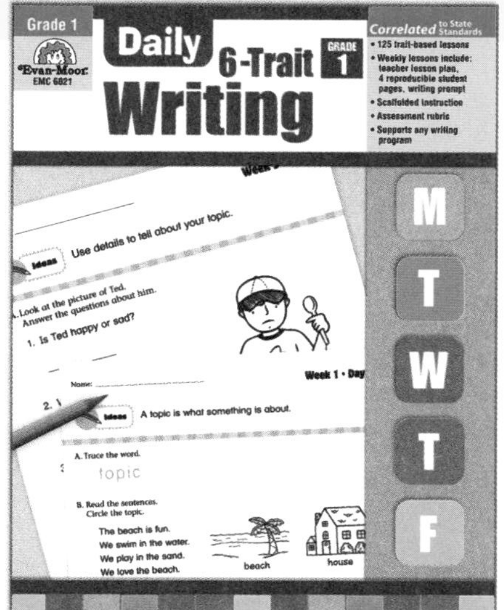

Daily 6-Trait Writing

Grade

1	EMC 6021
2	EMC 6022
3	EMC 6023
4	EMC 6024
5	EMC 6025
6+	EMC 6026

Features:

- 125 scaffolded, trait-based writing lessons
- A trait-based writing rubric
- Teacher pages that include an easy-to-follow teaching path and ideas for modeling and eliciting student responses
- Activities that cover narrative, expository, descriptive, and persuasive writing

Help build your child's language skills!

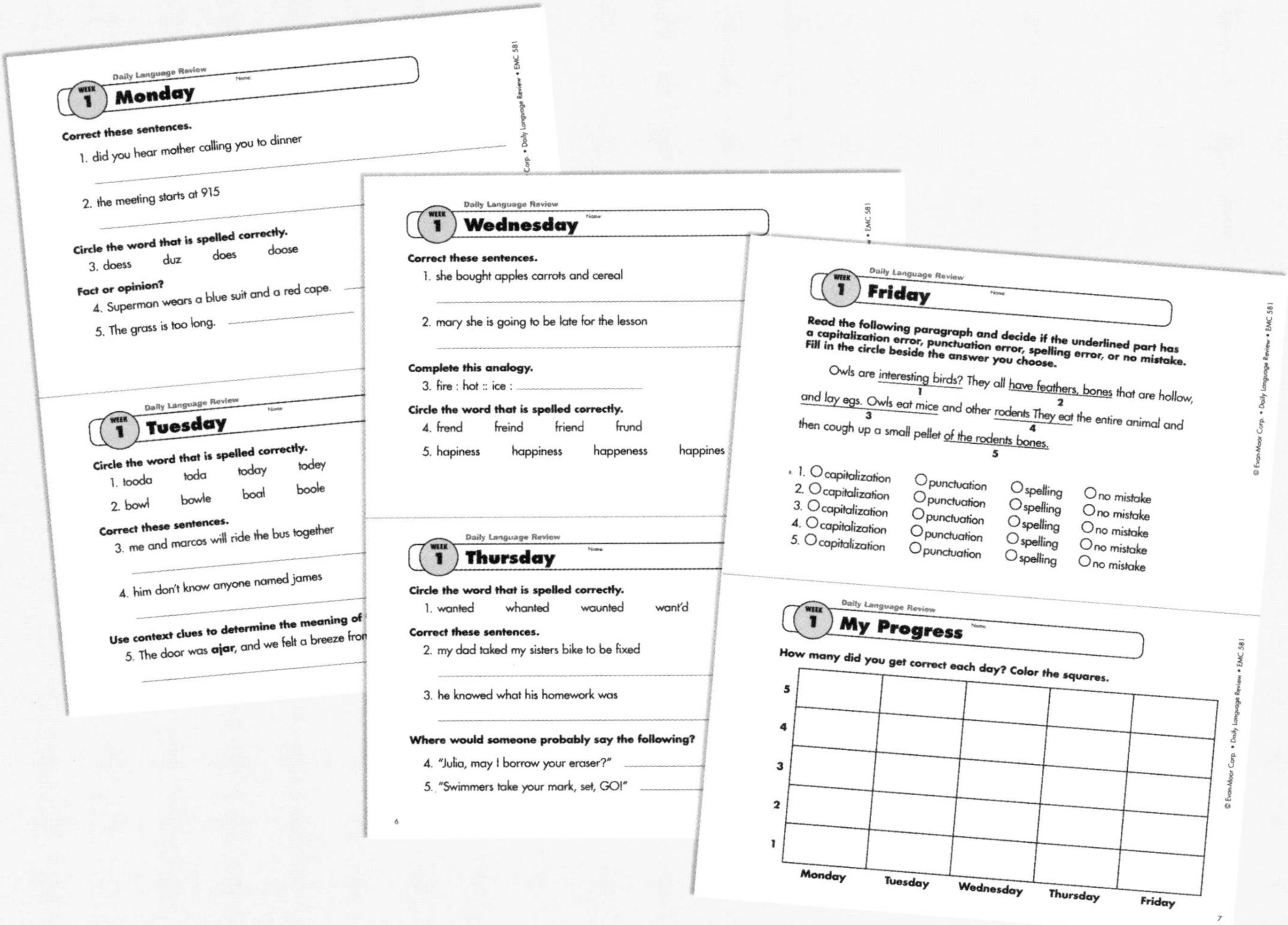

Repeated, focused practice in:

- sentence editing
- corrections in punctuation, capitalization, spelling, grammar, and vocabulary
- additional activities that cover a wide range of language and reading skills

Daily Language Review

Grade	
1	EMC 579
2	EMC 580
3	EMC 581
4	EMC 582
5	EMC 583
6	EMC 576
7	EMC 2797
8	EMC 2798

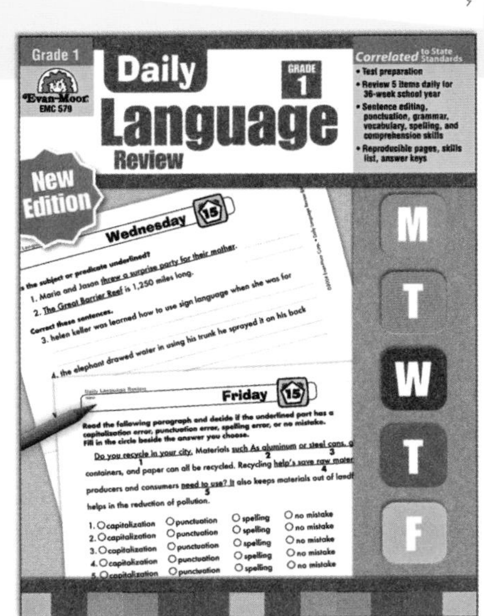